THE HOMEOWNER'S GUIDE TO
PAINT AND PAINTING

THE HOMEOWNER'S GUIDE TO

PAINT AND PAINTING

J.T. Adams

ARCO PUBLISHING, INC.
NEW YORK

Published by Arco Publishing, Inc.
215 Park Avenue South, New York, N.Y. 10003

Library of Congress Cataloging in Publication Data

Adams, Jeannette T.
  The homeowner's guide to paint and painting.

  Includes index
  1. House painting.   I. Title.
TT320.A33   698'.1   81-19149
ISBN 0-668-05124-8   AACR2

Printed in the United States of America

Contents

Acknowledgments

The Author desires to acknowledge with thanks the assistance of the following firms, national organizations, and branches of the government that have cooperated in the production of this book:

American Concrete Institute
American Society for Testing Materials
American Water Works Association
American Wood Preservers Association
Devoe & Reynolds Company
Federal Aviation Agency
Forest Products Laboratory
General Services Administration
National Association of Corrosion Engineers
National Lumber Manufacturers Association
National Paint and Coatings Association
National Paint, Varnish and Lacquer Association
Portland Cement Association
Science and Education Administration—U.S. Department of
    Agriculture
Sherwin–Williams Company
Steel Structures Painting Council
Texas Education Agency
Union Carbide Corporation
U.S. Department of Interior—Bureau of Reclamation
Western Pine Association

Preface

The purpose of this book is to insure that you get the right paint, the best paint for each job, and that you start the job with all the accessories required to accomplish the work. Interior and exterior painting is easy when you have the proper tools and accessories. A little preplanning helps you paint more easily, and even improves the look of the final job. Furthermore, by painting and doing it right you can add to your home's value. In a nationwide survey, real estate experts agreed that a good paint job increases the value of a house at least twelve percent.

The *Guide to Paint and Painting* has been produced for the professional as well as the nonprofessional painter. It will provide you with the basic information you need about suitable materials, tools, and equipment; color and how to use it; painting of woodwork, metalwork, concrete, masonry, or miscellaneous surfaces; whitewashing; paint failures; and painting safety. Or, if you prefer to have all or part of your painting done by a professional painter, it will teach you enough to judge the quality and cost of the work.

The author hopes this book makes your painting job easier, more enjoyable, and more attractive.

J.T.A.

THE HOMEOWNER'S GUIDE TO

PAINT AND PAINTING

SECTION 1

PAINT AND PAINT MATERIALS

The term "paint" commonly applies to only a few coating materials used to protect and decorate structures and equipment, but other materials which cannot technically be designated as paint are also discussed in this section. These include varnishes, lacquers, plastics, hot-applied bituminous products, and cement mortars. The words *paint* and *painting* are frequently used in a broad sense for simplicity.

1

Selecting Coatings

This chapter differentiates various kinds of paints and other coating materials and provides general information concerning their composition and properties. Information concerning specific paints and painting applications is presented in subsequent chapters.

When you plan to paint, selection of the coating should be based on careful analysis of both what is desired and possible. First, note whether the item to be painted is wood, ferrous or nonferrous metal, or concrete or masonry. Second, determine the environment or exposure conditions. Do they fall within the broad categories of indoor or outdoor atmospheric, freshwater submergence, or a combination referred to as an alternate or intermittent submergence exposure? Buried pipelines, for example, are essentially subject to submergence exposure with an added need for abrasion, soil stress, and puncture resistance. The deteriorative factors present in these environments include light, heat, oxygen, and water. However, a particular exposure may require additional resistance to erosion, abrasion, cavitation, high water velocity, bacteria or fungi attack, or especially deleterious chemical conditions.

The substrate and the exposure substantially limit the selection of suitable paints, and further restrictions may also apply. For instance, meeting the surface preparation requirements for a desirable coating may not be feasible under the job conditions. Similarly, temperature, humidity, ventilation, access, and the requirement of unusual specialized skills often further restrict the choice. Coatings should be chosen that are easy to live with. Can the coating be applied easily? Does it exhibit the greatest tolerance for deviations from ideal conditions at all stages of the application? Such characteristics contribute to a higher average level of coating quality. A coating choice may also take into consideration attributes such as appearance, subordinating the protective function to decorative qualities.

Obviously, cost is a primary consideration. Properly, cost should be calculated on an annual basis and not judged solely on the material or initial application price. Durability clearly exerts enormous influence on the real cost of coatings. For coatings such as coal–tar enamel or cement mortar, with an estimated service life of 50 to 100 years, the initial cost becomes almost unimportant. Moreover, the indirect benefits of high durability may far overshadow more readily calculable savings. For example, coating water pipes or sealing electrical conduit will avoid costly power and water outages over the years. Reducing the cost and nuisance of performing annual maintenance may justify a much higher initial cost. Thus, very durable coatings can be worth the high initial expenditures and effort entailed in their application.

The fully evaluated job circumstances and requirements must then be matched with appropriate coating characteristics and potentialities. This book attempts to furnish the necessary basic coating information.

PIGMENTED COATINGS

Pigmented paints are formulated from a wide variety of materials and have a broad range of usage. Each, however, consists essentially of pigment and a vehicle, and these components determine the characteristics and function of the paint. (*See* the following sections on Pigments and Vehicles.) Pigmented coatings include common house paints, machinery paints, red lead paints, aluminum paints, colored lacquers, and water paints, as well as certain specialized products such as vinyl resin paint.

The use of suitable raw materials does not guarantee good quality pigmented paints without effective processing. Only factory machinery can adequately grind and disperse pigment throughout the vehicle. Mixing dry pigments and a vehicle by hand generally produces paint lacking in smoothness and good application properties. Almost all paints are marketed ready-mixed for immediate use except for stirring, and, in some cases, thinning. Exceptions to this—paints that require mixing the components just before use—include aluminum paints, paints utilizing heavy metallic pigments such as zinc, and catalyst-cured materials. The latter two are marketed as component materials that deter the excessive separation and caking of heavy metallic pigments and delay the curing reaction in catalyzed materials. For example, the pigment in aluminum paints is not mixed into the vehicle until just before use, because a reaction between the vehicle and the pigment begins almost immediately. In a relatively short time, the bright shine of the flake aluminum is gone, and a dull gray paint film takes its place.

A wide variety of pigmented paints has been formulated to suit specific purposes. The vehicle most suitable for an outside wood paint may not be desirable for an interior paint. Fade-resistant pigments are used in finish paints for machinery; rust-inhibiting pigments are used in priming paints. Washable semigloss paint is needed for walls and woodwork in kitchens, but a flat finish is usually considered desirable for living room walls.

Pigments

Pigments are natural and synthetic, organic and inorganic. There are hundreds of different kinds and makes. Some of the more common ones will be described.

Lead and zinc are terms frequently applied to paint pigments. In this usage, they do not necessarily denote pulverized metals, but they do indicate the chemical compounds of the metals, such as lead carbonate, lead sulfate, and zinc oxide. White lead is either basic lead carbonate or basic lead sulfate, or a combination of the two. Red lead, which is commonly used in metal priming paint, is one of the lead oxides. Lithopone contains zinc sulfide, and titanium indicates a pigment containing titanium dioxide. These are all inorganic pigments, as are Prussian blue, chrome green, zinc yellow, and the siennas, umbers, and ochres. Synthetic organic pigments include the toluidines in reds and yellows and the phthalocyanines in blues and greens. Originally, pigments were employed solely to impart color. They are now recognized for their influence on many other paint properties as well, and are seldom used singly. Selecting and proportioning pigments for different colors are specialized arts, but effective combinations must also be judged on the basis of their effects on hiding power, settling, workability, stability after exposure, and ability to protect organic vehicle binders from damaging sunlight.

Hiding power, or the paint's ability to obscure underlying color, varies markedly in different pigments. Generally, the more opaque dark pigments are more effective than light pigments in this respect. The difference between the vehicle's index of refraction and that of the pigment largely determines the hiding power.

White lead has a refractive index of 1.95, zinc oxide 2.00, and titanium dioxide 2.70. Most nonvolatile vehicles have an index of from 1.47 to 1.52. Thus, titanium dioxide has the greatest hiding power while white lead is the least effective of the commonly used white pigments. Pigments with good hiding power also effectively minimize damage by sunlight since deflection of the sun's rays depends on the ability of the pigment to refract light.

Another factor affecting the hiding power of paint is the particle size of the pigment. Within limits, the finer the pigment is ground, the greater the hiding power of the resulting paint. Fine grinding also is necessary to provide smoothness in the paint film, which is especially desirable in enamels and machinery paints. The particle size for most commercial paint pigments ranges in average diameter from 0.0001 to 0.006 millimeter.

Fading and color change in paint result largely from instability of the pigmentation. Pigment stability is particularly important in paints designed for exposure to sunlight and industrial fumes. With the exception of lead pigments subjected to sulfide fumes, white pigments show little color change on exposure. The iron oxide pigments in reds and browns and most blacks are also relatively stable. Blue and green pigments generally are most susceptible to fading in sunlight, although some varieties, including the improved fadeproof pigments, are more stable. For example, chromic oxide green is more stable when compared with pure chrome green, and phthalocyanine blue is more stable than Prussian blue. Excessive chalking (disintegration at the exposed surface of the paint film) also causes color change, but this can be controlled by appropriately selecting pigments and properly proportioning the total pigment to vehicle solids. Moderate chalking, though, is purposely induced in some paints to impart self-cleaning properties.

Some pigments improve paints through their ability to form stable reaction products with vehicle ingredients. Certain lead and zinc pigments, for example, are combined with drying oils to make a stronger, more stable paint. Zinc oxide generally contributes hardness to the paint film; white lead and titanium dioxide impart chalking or self-cleaning properties. Certain metallic chromates and red lead pigments are especially suitable for metal priming paints because they inhibit rusting. Flaked aluminum pigment is highly effective in deflecting sunlight and is thus very effective as a top coat for outside exposure. Zinc dust pigment has been found especially suitable for use in paint for galvanized metal. Thus, it is apparent that the paint formulator, in selecting pigments, faces not only the problem of producing desired colors but of obtaining effective all-around performance.

Most pigmented paints contain mineral fillers known as extenders. These may be thought of as low-opacity white or colorless pigments. They contribute very little to hiding power because of their low refractive indexes, but are beneficial in other respects. Extenders high in oil absorption properties minimize settling of the pigments. They are helpful in controlling gloss and in adjusting consistency and workability, and add to durability if properly incorporated into a paint formula. Commonly used extenders are magnesium silicate (talc and asbestine), natural barium sulfate (barytes), synthetic barium sulfate (blanc fixe), barium carbonate, kaolin (china clay), calcium carbonate (whiting), diatomaceous silica, and mica.

The amount of pigment in paint varies from 10 percent by weight in some vinyl resin paints to 80 percent in some red-lead-in-oil paints. House paints contain from 60 to 70 percent pigment. The pigment content influences the gloss or shine of a dried paint film. Generally, the lower the pigment content, the higher the gloss. Proper balance in the relative amounts of vehicle and pigment, rather than a large percentage of either, is a key to good quality in paint.

Vehicles

The liquid portion of pigmented paint is called the vehicle, a term deriving from its role as a carrier for the pigments. The vehicle usually contains both volatile and nonvolatile constituents and is the actual film-forming part of the paint. The volatile portion of the vehicle—the solvents and thinners—facilitates application and contributes, through evaporation, to paint drying, but has no permanent part in the dried paint film. The nonvolatile portion is frequently referred to as the binder since it is an integral part of the dried paint film, binding the pigment particles together. Adhesion of the film to the surface is a function of the nonvolatile vehicle, as are the protective qualities and durability of the paint.

Most vehicles consist basically of drying oils or resins or blends of these (from which the term oleoresinous is derived) and solvent. Linseed oil is the nonvolatile vehicle for most exterior wood paints; varnish, an oil and resin blend, because of its faster drying and better leveling qualities, is used as the vehicle in most interior house paints. When more severe exposure is anticipated, greater use is made of synthetic resin formulations. Thus, vinyl resin, chlorinated rubber, and phenolic resin vehicles are frequently used when the paint film is subjected to chemical solutions or to prolonged exposure under water. Alkyd solutions are principally used as vehicles for enamels. They are especially desirable in white or light tints because they exhibit very little yellowing with age. Where very rapid drying is needed, as in highway striping paint and in production line painting, nitrocellulose lacquer is often used as a vehicle. In recent years, resins and drying oils, emulsified with water, have been used as the vehicle in some decorative paints, and for some time portland cement and lime have been used with water to form the vehicles of cement paint and whitewash, respectively. The possible variations in vehicle composition are innumerable, and many formulations have become quite complex because of the tendency to produce coatings for specific purposes.

Many newer synthetic resins—the epoxies, acrylics, polyurethanes, and others—are being used in paint formulations. Often, two or more resins in the same paint produce results superior to the effects of the individual resins. Generally, they are used to impart specific chemical resistance or other properties to the dried paint film. These are somewhat specialized coatings, not often widely used because of their higher cost and more exacting application procedures. These paints are, however, gaining wider acceptance through recognition of their unique capabilities, greater serviceability, and improved characteristics. Thus, coal–tar epoxy paint became a standard coating a few years ago.

Drying Oils. The word "drying," when used in connection with paints, refers not only to evaporation of volatile material, but also denotes the setting or hardening process that occurs when certain oils, called drying oils, are exposed to the atmosphere in thin films. The drying results solely from absorption of oxygen from the air (oxidation) or the combination of molecules within the oil (polymerization) or both. Linseed oil is the best known of the drying oils. Lubricating oil made from petroleum is an example of a nondrying oil. There also are oils referred to as "semidrying," such as raw fish oil and castor oil, which are affected to a lesser degree by oxidation and polymerization and set slowly to a tacky state rather than to a firm, elastic solid.

The principal drying oils used by the paint and varnish industry are linseed oil, tung (china wood) oil, dehydrated castor oil, perilla oil, oiticica oil, soybean oil, and refined fish oils. Of these, linseed oil, which is derived from flaxseed, is used in larger quantities than all other oils combined. It is commonly prepared in three grades—raw oil, boiled oil, and heat-bodied oil. Raw oil is an alkali- or acid-refined product, but is not processed to accelerate its drying properties. This oil is used when slow drying is unobjectionable and wetting ability is important, as in some priming paints for exterior wood surfaces. Boiled oil is a heat-treated oil to which driers have been added. Processing does not entail actual boiling. This oil is heavier bodied and has a much faster drying rate than raw oil. Organic salts, such as naphthenates, resinates, and linoleates, or heavy metals, such as lead, cobalt, and manganese, are commonly used as driers. (*See* the section on Paint Drier in this chapter.) They are used not only in boiled linseed oil but as required in any drying oil or paint or varnish containing drying oil. Heat-bodied oil, which is often called bodied oil, is a high-viscosity oil prepared from raw oil solely by heat processing.

Tung oil, which is extracted from the nuts of a tree native to China, is used principally in varnishes, where it is invaluable for imparting fast-drying and moisture-resisting properties. Oiticica oil, obtained from a nut tree in Brazil, is similar to tung oil in several respects and is also used in varnish formulations. Perilla oil is obtained from the seeds of a plant cultivated in Asia and is used to some extent as a substitute for linseed oil. As a rule, soybean oil and fish oils have relatively inferior drying properties, although careful processing can produce certain fish oil fractions that have very good drying properties. Dehydrated castor oil is a development in drying oils that has shown versatility and is being used successfully in a variety of paints and varnishes. It is made from castor oil, itself a semidrying oil, and acquires its drying properties through a change in its chemical structure resulting from the removal of water molecules—thus the term *dehydrated*. Importation facilities, crop conditions in various parts of the world, and other factors affecting supply and prices largely influence the extent to which various drying oils are used in the paint industry.

Resins. The resins used in paint vehicles may be either natural resins, such as copals and dammars, which are exudations from trees, or synthetic (manufactured) resins. Natural resins were in use for making varnish many years before the first synthetic resin was produced, and certain varieties were largely responsible for the beautiful finishes applied to furniture and stringed instruments centuries ago. Synthetic resins have steadily grown in favor, however, because close control during their manufacture results in uniform resin products with fairly constant properties. This constancy allows the paint manufacturer to produce consistent paint properties, which in turn allow the paint manufacturer to produce paint materials and paints with uniform and generally superior properties. Durability, waterproofness, toughness, resistance to chemicals, and the dielectric strength of coatings have been greatly improved by the use of synthetics. There are many synthetic resins available; a few of the most common include phenolic, epoxy, alkyd, vinyl, chlorinated rubber, and various hydrocarbon polymers, such as polystyrene. Some are used singly, some in combination with others, and some in combination with drying oils and other vehicle ingredients, to produce effective coatings for specific purposes.

Solvents. The term solvent is used here to indicate the volatile portion of the vehicle. As such, it includes not only liquids that actually dissolve nonvolatile vehicle ingredients but also liquids that act more as suspending agents and might be classed as diluents or thinners. (*See* the section on Thinners later in this chapter.) The foremost reason for incorporating solvents in paint is to reduce viscosity to facilitate application by brushing, spraying, or dipping. Solvents affect consistency, leveling, drying, and even adhesion and durability. They must be carefully selected and blended as required for use with different resins and drying oils.

Mineral spirits, a product of petroleum distillation, and turpentine, which is distilled from the resinous exudations of pine trees, are commonly used as solvents in ordinary oil and varnish vehicle paints. Some synthetic resin formulations require the higher solvent power of the chlorinated hydrocarbons, hydrogenated naphtha, and the coal–tar distillates, toluene and xylene. Special solvents incorporating ketones, esters, or alcohols—for example, methyl, ethyl ketone, amyl acetate, and butyl alcohol—are used in lacquers. Water may be considered the solvent in emulsion paints, whitewash, and portland cement paints. Paint serviceability can be impaired seriously by adding improper thinners.

CLEAR COATINGS

Types and Uses

Varnish, unpigmented lacquer, shellac, and wax polish are the best-known clear coatings. Others are clear sealers and water-repellent compounds. Drying oil, especially linseed oil, also may be considered a clear coating, for which purpose it is sometimes used by itself. Clear coatings generally do not have the durability of pigmented coatings in outside exposure because they lack the protection against sunlight afforded by pigmentation. They are used primarily to beautify and protect surfaces without obscuring natural appearance.

Varnish

Varnish is essentially a homogeneous mixture of resin, drying oil, drier, and solvent. It is manufactured by heat polymerization of the oils in combination with the resins, followed by the addition of solvent and drier after the cooked ingredients have partially cooled. Varnish dries through evaporation of the solvent, followed by oxidation and polymerization of the drying oils and resins. As mentioned previously in the section on Vehicles, varnish is commonly used as the vehicle in quick-drying, smooth-leveling pigmented paints.

The kinds of oils and resins used and the ratio of oil to resin are the principal factors governing varnish properties. Selection depends on the compatibility of different oils and resins and on the intended use of the varnish. It is generally considered that the oils in the finished coating contribute to elasticity, while the resins influence hardness. The ratio of oil to resin in varnish is expressed as the number of gallons of oil that are combined with 100 pounds of resin and is commonly referred to as the length of the varnish. Thus, 50 gallons of oil used with 100 pounds of resin results in a varnish with a 50-gallon length. Varnish containing less than 20 gallons of oil per 100 pounds of resin is usually classed as short-oil varnish. A medium-oil varnish contains from 20 to 30 gallons of oil, and a long-oil varnish uses 30 gallons or more. Short-oil varnishes are used primarily when hardness, a high degree of impermeability, or resistance to alcohols, alkalis, or acids is desirable and film elasticity is relatively unimportant. Varnishes for furniture and interior trim are short or medium in oil length. Short-oil varnishes are especially suitable for creating a rubbed finish, but they are too brittle for floors, for which a medium-oil varnish is most suitable. Varnishes for exterior exposure are usually of long-oil formulation, given the beneficial effect of drying oil in providing elasticity and resistance to weathering. Spar varnish, a high-grade exterior varnish formulated primarily for use on the wooden parts of ships, is a long-oil varnish. With the use of phenolic resins, medium-oil varnishes have been formulated to provide increased moisture resistance without sacrificing sunlight resistance. Recently, clear urethane base varnishes have been giving good results.

Mixing varnishes for aluminum paints and other bronzed paints are special low-viscosity blends, usually of medium- or long-oil length, specially formulated for this use. Some spar varnishes, however, may be used as mixing varnishes if properly thinned.

For the sake of clarifying the terms, shellac varnish and dispersion resin varnish should be mentioned here. These are not varnishes as defined in the preceding, because they dry solely through evaporation of the solvent. (*See* the section on Shellac in this chapter.) Dispersion resin varnish is prepared from a drying oil and phenolic resin that have completely reacted in the manufacturing process, with only solvent evaporation remaining to complete its drying. In this respect, these coatings are more like lacquer than varnish.

Lacquer

Although the term lacquer is frequently applied to nearly any coating that dries quickly and solely by solvent evaporation, this discussion will be limited to coatings having nitrocellulose as the basic nonvolatile constituent. Lacquer is characterized by its very rapid drying and distinctive odor. Both result from the use of low-boiling solvents of high solvency power, such as certain acetates, ketones, and alcohols. Although nitrocellulose is the basic ingredient, manufacturers now incorporate resins, plasticizers, and reacted drying oils to improve adhesion and elasticity.

Lacquers dry tack-free in 5 to 15 minutes and to a firm film in 30 minutes to four hours. They are usually applied by spraying, because of their very rapid drying properties, although special brushing varieties are available for use when spraying is not practicable. Pigmented lacquers are predominately used; clear lacquers are used where thin, colorless, tough films are desired. Clear lacquers are not generally considered as durable as high-grade varnishes for exposure to sunlight and moisture. Their greatest use is in furniture finishing.

Shellac

Shellac, as the term is commonly employed and as it is used here, is a solution of refined lac resin in denatured alcohol. Technically, shellac is a solid in the flaked form of refined lac, and the solution is termed shellac varnish. Lac is formed as a secretion from certain insects abounding in India and the Malayan Peninsula.

Shellac behaves more like lacquer than varnish because it dries quickly by evaporation of the alcohol solvent. The resin is supplied in orange and bleached grades, and the finished product's color depends on the degree of resin refinement. Although white (bleached) shellac is considerably lighter in color than orange shellac, it is not so nearly colorless as might be expected from the name.

Shellac is furnished in various "cuts," which indicate the amount of resin in pounds added to one gallon of solvent. Four-, 4.5-, and 5-pound cuts, which cover the range of light-, medium-, and heavy-bodied materials, are most commonly used. Shellac is often used as a clear finish for woodwork. It is also used to seal knots and pitch streaks before painting, to prime certain kinds of walls to prepare for the application of ceramic, metal, or plastic wall tile, and to seal bituminous coatings preparatory to the application of decorative paints.

Sealers

There are a number of products called clear sealers and water-repellent compounds that are marketed as dampproofing and moisture stabilization treatments for masonry. Composition varies widely, but for the most part these sealers consist of water-insoluble and water-repellent substances dissolved in a solvent such as petroleum naphtha. Waxes, resins, and drying oils, used singly and in combination, together with a water-repellent material such as aluminum stearate, are commonly used as the nonvolatile portion. These compounds are effective in varying degrees by creating a surface that will shed moisture such as rainfall. They are, however, of questionable value for resisting water under appreciable head.

Special clear silicone compounds are also being used successfully in water repellents and damp-proofers on masonry surfaces. Basically there are two kinds—silicone resins that dissolve in volatile solvents, and a compound, sodium methyl siliconate, which is water soluble as a liquid, but is not when dried. Dilute silicone resin solutions are applied in flood coats for maximum penetration, mainly to above-grade masonry structures. The solution, being hydrophobic or water resistant, prevents moisture droplets from entering the treated surface. Other advantages found with silicones are (1) "breathing" properties are not seriously affected since no film is formed; (2) little, if any, discoloration occurs; and (3) efflorescence formation is substantially halted. The silicones may provide acceptable sealing of fairly nonporous surfaces; however, they have proved ineffective against wind-driven water impinging on split-face masonry blocks having macroscopic pores and interconnecting voids.

These materials should not be confused with floor sealer, which, in effect, is a special varnish or lacquer used in finishing wood floors. The lacquer floor sealer is used primarily for sealing oil-treated floors before varnish and waxing. Varnish floor sealer is in the nature of a spar varnish but contains a higher percentage of solvent to provide greater penetrating properties. Floor sealer is now generally preferred to regular varnish as a floor finish.

Another sealer was developed by the Western Pine Association for use in sealing knots and pitch streaks in wood to prevent subsequent staining and peeling of the finish coating. Essentially, this material is composed of phenolic and vinyl resins in an alcohol solvent.

Wax Polish

Polishing wax is seldom used as a coating by itself but is widely used to beautify and protect other finishes, such as those on floors and furniture. Two general kinds are available—one in which mineral spirits or a similar organic solvent is employed, the other in which the wax is emulsified with water to gain fluidity. Carnauba wax, beeswax, and ceresin wax are commonly used in wax polishes. Frequently, they are modified with resins or oils. For example, shellac resin is often added to floor wax to impart nonslip properties. Emulsion wax has an advantage when used on asphalt- and rubber-tile floors because, unlike organic solvents, water doesn't adversely affect these materials. Both water and organic solvents are used over other finishes.

BITUMINOUS COATINGS

Types and Uses

Coal–tar and asphalt coatings are used extensively to protect submerged or buried ferrous metalwork and for waterproofing and roofing purposes. They are specially suited for this purpose because they create a substantial barrier to corrosive environments and can be applied at reasonable cost in thicker coats than most paint films. Similar but generally less resistant asphalt coatings find wider use as dampproofers for below-grade concrete and masonry. In general, asphalt and coal–tar paints are not well suited to atmospheric exposure because relatively thin coats of these materials become brittle from the effects of air, heat, and sunlight.

Coal–Tar Pitch

Coal–tar pitch is a refined, common pitch obtained as a distillation residue from coal tar. Coal tar itself is a black, viscous liquid recovered as a byproduct from coal gas manufacture and coke production. Several grades of coal–tar pitch are marketed, differing principally in hardness and softening point. Coal–tar pitch contains no added mineral filler or solvent and must be melted to fluid consistency for application.

Coal–tar pitch has limited service as a protective coating for metalwork and is used mostly as a waterproofing and roofing material. It can be applied by dipping, which makes it well suited for coating items such as trashracks that are difficult and time-consuming to paint. Its serviceability is nevertheless still limited because its relatively low-temperature softening point, 125°F–155°F causes the pitch to sag when exposed to the sun in warm weather. It also becomes brittle at temperatures below freezing and consequently is susceptible to cracking and disbonding. In addition, water flow tends to produce rippling in the coating, with resultant thin spots that reduce its effectiveness as a protective coating. In instances of high water velocity, the coating is considered unsuitable.

Coal–Tar Enamel

Coal–tar pitch is converted to coal–tar enamel by incorporating a mineral filler. The development of coal–tar enamel was a large step forward in coal–tar protective coatings. While retaining the impervious properties of the common pitch, the enamel has less susceptibility to temperature extremes, both hot and cold, and greater stability in flowing water. This is especially true of the grade called "waterworks" enamel because, in addition to the incorporation of a filler, the pitch is processed (plasticized) to make it more plastic or rubbery. "Pipeline" enamel is made from common pitch; its use is largely confined to the exterior surfaces of buried pipes, where it is subjected only to moderate, constant temperatures.

Coal–tar enamel, including its early forms, has been used successfully for over half a century for protecting buried and submerged steel pipe. It is now recognized as a standard of the waterworks and pipeline industries. Nevertheless, it has limitations. Much enamel is shop-applied, but the specially skilled personnel needed for quality field applications are becoming increasingly rare. Moreover, the obnoxious fumes that accompany its application tend to disrupt other nearby work. Although considerable care is still required, the use of a synthetic resin base primer to replace the old coal–tar primer has largely eliminated the severe bonding problems that once occurred. Coal–tar enamel will not sag at high temperatures (up to 160°F), but it may crack and disbond at temperatures below –20°F.

Enamel-coated pipe requires a great deal of care in handling and back-filling operations to prevent damage to the enamel. In below freezing weather, much care must be taken because of the coating's increased brittleness. However, once the pipe is installed, where it will never be subjected to extreme cold, a properly applied coal–tar enamel interior coating may be considered virtually permanent and is therefore one of the most economical coatings.

Cold-Applied Coal–Tar Paints

Cold-applied coal–tar paints are made by liquefying coal–tar pitch by heat and then combining it with solvents, fillers, and other constituents. The solvent must be a coal–tar distillation product, such as xylene or coal–tar naphtha, or the equivalent in solvency characteristics, to ensure homogeneity of the paint.

Cold-applied coal–tar paints have a distinct advantage in ease of use because they may be applied at ordinary temperatures with a brush or spray. Even so, if hot-applied pitch or enamel coatings can be used, they are preferable because they will outlast the less durable cold-applied finishes by many years.

Coal–tar pitch materials may be combined with synthetic resins, such as epoxy, polyurethane, and polyvinyl chloride, to produce coating materials that provide better protection for metalwork submerged in freshwater than do some paints based on a single resin. However, some of these materials are not suitable for use inside of pipelines and tanks that will contain or carry potable water.

In particular, coal tar has been combined with epoxy resin to form a two-component paint which shows promise of service, far surpassing that possible before. Currently, the industry is marketing quite a number of coal–tar epoxy paints with some variations in their properties.

Coal–Tar Emulsion

The principal difference in composition between coal–tar emulsion and cold-applied coal–tar paint is that water, rather than a coal–tar distillate, is used as the dispersing medium in coal–tar emulsion. Coal–tar pitch, common or processed, is the basic nonvolatile ingredient.

Emulsions have certain advantages over organic solvent paints. They adhere satisfactorily to damp surfaces and are practically odorless. Also, some coal–tar emulsions show better resistance to sunlight.

Asphalt

Asphalt coatings derived from petroleum are available as enamels, cold-applied paints, and emulsions. They are generally considered to be more resistant to weathering and less resistant to moisture penetration than the comparable coal–tar products. As a rule, they are less susceptible to temperature extremes.

Asphalt is used extensively in waterproofing and roofing materials, and as a hot-dip coating for metal pipe. As a hot-dip material, it is better adapted for factory application than is coal tar because it does not deteriorate as fast in heating kettles and is less critical in application characteristics. Asphalt emulsion, in paste form, has special application as a heavy coating for the metalwork stops installed in joints of concrete work.

OTHER TYPES OF COATINGS

Cement–Mortar Coatings

Like coal–tar enamel coatings, cement–mortar coatings have a long record of successful service in the protection of steel pipe. A mixture, basically of portland cement, sand, and water, is applied in a coating normally having a thickness of from $5/16$ to $\frac{1}{2}$ inch for interior linings and one-half to three-fourths inch for exterior coatings. Some users may require different thicknesses. The coating owes its ability to mitigate corrosion largely to the fact that as the portland cement hydrates, calcium hydroxide is liberated which, being a strongly basic compound, stifles rusting.

Lining mortar initially bonds to the metal, but it may subsequently shrink away from the surface as drying and differential expansion and contraction occur. Nonetheless, the mortar is held in position by "arch action" and expands into tight contact upon rewetting. Hairline cracks, up to $\frac{1}{32}$ inch, need be of little concern as they usually close upon wetting. Even if such cracks remain open after wetting, or if a tiny gap persists between the lining and the metal surface, the inhibitive effect of alkalinity prevents significant corrosion. Water-saturated mortar thus protects as well or better than dry mortar.

Cement–mortar coatings are commonly applied by pneumatic and centrifugal methods. They also have been used in rehabilitation work by in-place application on waterlines over four inches in diameter by means of special pipe-cleaning and mortar-application machines. Cement–mortar linings are best adapted to pipe that is continuously filled with water; they may not serve well for linings that will dry out, as in exposed steel siphons. Pneumatically placed, steel-reinforced mortar has been used for some time as an exterior coating for buried steel pipe, and cement–mortar is in wide use on the interior surfaces of steel pipe.

Zinc Coatings

Zinc coatings may be divided into several distinct kinds. The most widely used and best-known zinc coating is that produced by the hot-dip galvanizing process. Structural metalwork (angle iron I-beams, and the like), corrugated and flat sheet stock, and fencing are frequently protected in this manner.

In a discussion of zinc coatings, zinc-pigmented paints should be included. There are several kinds, chief among which are the zinc dust–zinc oxide priming paints for galvanized metalwork. The name itself defines the pigment mixture, which is blended into one of several vehicles—linseed oil, alkyd, or phenolic varnishes—depending on the requirement for anticipated exposure. These paints may be used as primers or they will serve well as top coats if additional finish painting is not desired. Generally, the zinc dust is added to the zinc oxide pigmented vehicle just before use.

Other zinc paints are mainly of the zinc-rich kind; that is, they contain a high percentage of zinc dust with minor additives.

These zinc-rich paints may be further classified as organic or inorganic, referring to the vehicle used. The organic kinds may be air-drying or baking and will have vehicles containing common resins, such as alkyd, phenolic, or chlorinated rubber. The inorganic zinc paints are formulated with various silicate compounds, which act as the binder in the dry paint film which may be quite hard and abrasion resistant. One kind requires baking to cure, another requires application of an acid-curing solution, and a third requires only air-drying. In each of these, the binder changes chemically to form an insoluble matrix in the applied film.

At this time, shop-applied, zinc-filled primers appear to be gaining wide acceptance for structural steel. Formulated to be compatible with top coat paints, such primers are rapidly applied to surfaces that have been thoroughly cleaned by grit-blasting in an assembly line process. The zinc-filled primers reportedly do not interfere with fabrication operations and resist atmospheric corrosion prior to top coating much better than common organic primers.

Plastic Coatings

Plastic, as applied to paints, is an abused term. The appearance of this word or some variation thereof in a trade name does not necessarily mean that the product has extraordinary properties. Any of the synthetic resin paints might be called plastic paints because the phenolic, vinyl, and other synthetic resins commonly used in paints are varieties of plastics, compounded with special grades of solution resins. Moreover, paint performance is vitally affected by other constituents and the particular formulation, of which plastic may be only a small part.

However, expanding use of the synthetic resins or combinations thereof has produced coatings with superior resistance to a broad range of exposures. Certain properties of these and other more specialized resins can accommodate service conditions beyond the capabilities of older coating materials. A list of resins in broad range coating use would include epoxy, phenolic, vinyl, chlorinated rubber, neoprene, alkyd, acrylic, and urethane. More recently, epoxy resin modified with coal tar has been widely accepted in the industry for immersion and other exposures. Epoxy paints which can be applied and cured under water are examples of the specialized uses to which some of the new resins have been adapted.

True plastic coatings are now available, and some of the more common ones will be discussed briefly. These are composed principally of a particular plastic and have modifiers as minor constituents. They are tough, flexible coatings with high resistance to the natural elements and to many chemicals. They are especially suitable where most other coatings have been generally ineffective because of severe exposure conditions. Today, plastic coatings are expensive, but they can solve some of the more difficult protective coating problems. Costs should decrease with increased use and improved application methods.

Vinyl resins are being increasingly used as protective coatings. These include plastisols, organosols, and dry, generally powdered, vinyl resins. Plastisols are vinyl resins dissolved in liquid plasticizers which remain fluid until heat treated. Organosols are similar to plastisols except that small amounts of volatile solvents are added to improve application properties. Both are high-solids-content materials, the plastisols being essentially 100 percent solids. Fusion of the resins and plasticizers, to form the plastic film, occurs by raising the temperature of the film to 300°F–360°F. Dishwasher racks, dish drainers, plating tanks and racks, piping, and vinyl-on-metal laminates for luggage, instrument cabinets, and furniture are a few uses of these materials. Special primers, usually of the solution kind, are required to obtain adhesion of plastisols and organosols to metalwork.

Powdered vinyl resins can be applied and a plastic protective film formed by several techniques. Again, special primers are required to obtain adhesion of the vinyl resin film to the substrate. Basically, the process heats the article to be coated above the fusion temperature of the vinyl resin, bringing the heated article into contact with the powdered resin causing the resin to melt and cling to the surface. A post-application heating completes the fusion of the plastic film. Methods differ mainly in how the powdered resin is brought into contact with the heated article. Extrusion of a hot melt onto the article, usually a straight piece, is also utilized.

Polyethylene protective films are applied by several different processes. The first and oldest process is flame spray. In this process, powdered polyethylene is carried in a stream of air through an oxygen-propane or oxyacetylene flame, where it melts and is then deposited on the surface of the metal as a continuous film. It is often difficult to obtain a uniform film by this technique. A second method is a dispersion coating application, whereby the polyethylene resin is dispersed in water, followed by evaporation of the water, and heating above the ' .elt temperature of the resin. Polyethylene may also be applied by the previously mentioned method of raising the temperature of the article above the melt temperature of the resin, followed by contact with the powdered resin. Uniform, continuous films result from the two latter processes. Polyethylene also can be extruded onto a straight continuous article.

Of more recent origin is chlorosulfonated polyethylene. This complex resin, unlike straight polyethylene, is soluble in several common solvents and thus can be used in solution coatings. A catalyst, however, is required to set the film. A cured chlorosulfonated polyethylene film has many elastomeric properties. It is used in roof coatings and as a protective top coat over neoprene coatings because it has excellent resistance to the effects of sunlight exposure. Chlorosulfonated polyethylene does not have good abrasion resistance and should not be used in abrasive or erosive environments.

Other plastics, including the cellulosics or acrylics, are used as protective coatings. These are usually applied by heat processes where the dry resin is fused onto the surface to be protected. Many of these plastics are applied as temporary coatings to protect such items as gears, shafts, screws, and other machined parts during shipment and storage. When the item is to be placed in service, the coating is cut and peeled off. For this use, strong adhesion of the plastic film is not desirable, but a continuous film resistant to the elements is essential.

In the fluidized bed process, a heated article is brought into contact with a powdered resin. The article to be coated is heated above the melting temperature of the plastic and then immersed in a fluidized bed of the finely divided material. Coating thickness is controlled by immersion time. The powder contacts the hot metal, fuses and clings to the surface, and gradually accumulates the thickness desired. Often a post-heating cycle completes the fusion. This method is particularly suited to coating small, odd-shaped items. The fluidized bed itself is a mass of finely divided material of controlled particle size within an open container through which air or inert gas under pressure is passed from bottom to top. The velocity of the gas is such that the particles are kept in what could be described as a state of bubbling motion. The gas velocity is near the free settling velocity of the particles in air, so that rapid motion is maintained, yet the material is not blown off. This process is used with both thermoplastic and thermoset resins.

The same effect obtained from the fluidized bed can be produced by directing a stream of powdered resin at an article heated to the necessary temperature. At this writing, the technology of powdered coatings is under active study in the industry, and new developments can be expected. Given the nature of the equipment and heating required, the processes appear most adaptable to in-plant applications to manufactured equipment items rather than field application.

Other thermoplastics are utilized as protective coatings, but because of their high cost, they are used only in certain highly corrosive environments. These include such plastics as vinylidene chloride and the polyfluorocarbons. In addition to thermoplastics, thermosetting plastics are utilized as protective coatings. These include both the heat-set and the catalyst set varieties. Notable among the thermosets used for protective coatings are the phenolics and epoxies. Heat-cured phenolics are among the oldest applications of plastics as protective coatings, and are still used as coatings, and linings for pipe.

Plastic tapes are also used to protect the exterior of steel pipe. Both self-adhering tapes and those requiring a primer or adhesive are available. Polyethylene and polyvinyl chloride tapes are the most common and are available in 10-, 12-, and 20-millimeter thicknesses. Wire brushing is generally used as the cleaning method, and a primer or rubber filler material may be specified for better adhesion and to minimize rust creep. These tapes usually are applied mechanically or by hand in the field just before installing pipe in trenches. Other tapes, such as polyvinyl chloride–butyl rubber combinations, are also available.

Polysulfide compounds have also been used as a protective coating for steel. They are available in both liquid and powder forms and thus may be applied by brushing or spraying.

Synthetic Rubber Coatings

A variety of synthetic rubber polymers meet the needs of the chemical process industries, but except for neoprene (chloroprene), they are little used in ordinary freshwater corrosion control. Neoprene is available in liquid form and thus may be applied by brushing and spraying. A tough, elastomeric film is formed when liquid neoprene cures. It is used in abrasive and erosive environments, and has been found to perform quite well in cavitation-producing conditions. Liquid neoprene, in conjunction with neoprene putty, has successfully sealed leaking construction joints in concrete dams.

Another synthetic rubber gaining widespread use in various coatings is styrene–butadiene. This polymer is compounded into both interior and exterior masonry paints, floor and deck paints, traffic paints, and certain metalwork paints.

Catalyzed Coatings

Catalyzed coatings require the addition of an outside agent (variously called an accelerator, a catalyst, hardener, curing agent, activator, and the like) to produce a chemical reaction that hardens or sets the material. Numerous coatings fall into this class. Probably the most widely known are the catalyzed epoxy resins, the catalyzed phenolic resins, and the polyurethanes. Liquid neoprene might also be classified as such since an accelerator is added to cure it.

With this kind of coating, the chemical reaction which sets the film begins as soon as the catalyst is added to the liquid resin mixture. The time required to complete the reaction varies from material to material and depends on a number of factors that cannot be explained in this limited discussion. The time in which the activated or mixed material remains usable is termed the "pot life" and may be between a few minutes and several hours.

Rust-Preventive Compounds

These coating materials are similar to oils or grease in appearance and physical properties. Grease type compounds do not contain soaps as thickeners, as greases commonly do. Most are formulated from a petrolatum base; some are pigmented for appearance or to harden the film, but most varieties are transparent. Some contain salts, such as chromates, to inhibit rusting. Others contain solvents so they can be applied without heating.

The oil type, commonly referred to as thin-film rust preventive, is used in protecting hydraulic oil cylinder bores and the interior surfaces of hollow castings until they are placed into service. A related product is formulated with microcrystalline wax as a base, rather than petrolatum. Microcrystalline wax is a petroleum product distinguished by its very fine crystalline structure and high softening point when compared with ordinary paraffin wax.

Grease type rust-preventive compounds originated with the primary purpose of temporarily protecting metal surfaces, especially machined surfaces. Since they are soluble in kerosene and a variety of other solvents, the coatings are removed with relative ease when the coated parts are to be placed in service.

Miscellaneous Coatings

Many other special coatings are available for specific end uses. These include heat-resistant enamels, fire-retardant paints, traffic paints, vitreous enamel, and others. Heat-resistant enamels, generally aluminum pigmented, may be formulated with special silicone resins and are utilized for temperatures up to 1200°F. At those high temperatures, the binder is actually destroyed, but a fusion product of the base metal, the silicone, and aluminum pigment occurs. These enamels are quite useful in maintaining boiler equipment, exhaust stacks, and other equipment exposed to high temperatures. Fire-retardant paints are similar to interior oil base paints, except that mineral and intumescent additives are included to retard the combustion rate.

Traffic paints are special, quick-drying paints that are applied to asphalt and concrete surfaces for vehicle and pedestrian traffic control. They are available in white and yellow and may also be reflectorized with minute glass spheres for better night-time visibility.

Vitreous enamel is a heat-fired coating that fuses to the substrate in processing. It is used to a limited extent on small sized, submerged metalwork.

Sheet polyethylene is specified as a cocoon-like coating wrapped around valves, couplings, and fittings in buried pipelines.

ACCESSORY PAINT MATERIALS

Thinners

All the solvents discussed in foregoing sections that form the volatile portion of pigmented-paint vehicles and clear coatings may also be considered thinners. Mineral spirits and turpentine are commonly used as thinners for ordinarily oil and varnish base paints and varnish. Odorless mineral spirits are used as thinners for odorless oleo-resinous paints. Xylene is a thinner for cold-applied coal–tar paints. Lacquer thinner is usually a combination of solvents, such as alcohols, ketones, acetates, and frequently coal–tar distillates. Water is the thinner for cement paint, whitewash, and other water paints.

All solvent thinners are expected to evaporate from the paint film and therefore must be volatile. For this reason, the use of materials with a high boiling point, such as kerosene, as thinners is undesirable unless for some reason you wish to greatly retard drying. The thinner must be compatible with the paint makeup. For example, mineral spirits and turpentine are unsuitable for thinning coal–tar paints and lacquers because they precipitate certain nonvolatile ingredients. One reason for conversion to the practice of preparing and selling paints in ready-to-use form was the frequent trouble on-the-job caused by improper thinning.

Linseed oil may also be considered a thinner since it is used, especially in exterior wood paints, to reduce finish paints to the proper consistency for use as priming paint. Both raw oil and boiled oil are used for this purpose; boiled oil is preferred if atmospheric conditions are such that the use of raw oil would result in excessively slow drying.

Tinting Colors

Oil stains, in effect, are varieties of pigmented paints since they are composed of pigment and vehicle. They have a low pigment content which does not obscure the natural grain of the wood to which they are applied. Their viscosity is low, and they possess high penetrating properties. The vehicle consists of drying oil and solvent.

Paint Drier

Paint drier is a material added in the manufacturing process to paints containing drying oils to improve drying characteristics. As sold over-the-counter, paint drier consists of organometallic drier in a solvent. The active ingredient concentration is low, but even so, paint drier should be used in sparing amounts because an excess impairs paint serviceability. Since most paints are now manufactured with the proper amount of drier, you rarely need to add it on-the-job. (*See* the preceding section on Vehicles.)

Putty and Glazing Compound

Putty is composed basically of calcium carbonate (whiting) and drying oil, predominantly linseed oil. It contains a small percentage of solvent and drier, and sometimes white lead is added. Putty dries and hardens in time and is used for glazing wood sash and for filling holes and cracks before painting.

Glazing compound is used where desired to maintain a seal between the parts of either metal or wooden sash. It is formulated to dry hard on the surface and remain plastic throughout the bulk of the material. To gain this effect, semidrying oil is incorporated with the mineral filler and drying oil that make up regular putty. One important thing to remember about putty or glazing compound is that the surface to which it is to be applied should be prime painted first. Also, wait until the material is dry, at least on the surface, before painting over it.

Calking Compound

Calking compound formulation has undergone considerable change since the development of the polysulfide-based compound in the 1940s. The earlier oil base material is still widely used for sealing joints around windows and doors because of its lower cost. It is similar in composition and properties to glazing compound. The considerably more costly polysulfide kind, is used extensively in building construction where it has, in most instances, shown outstanding resistance to flexing with joint movement, weathering, and penetration by wind-driven water, particularly in masonry structures and curtain-wall construction.

Other sealers are used, including polyurethane foam, silicone rubber, urethanes, epoxy resins, and neoprene rubber, but the polysulfide type generally dominates the field. It is usually supplied as a two-component material with the proper amounts of base material and activating agent. The performance of a good single-component polysulfide may approach that of the two-component materials, particularly if sufficient time and favorable curing conditions prevail. Often a primer is recommended, particularly for masonry joints. Occasionally, the primer is a two-component material, but usually it is a single-component lacquer solution. Laboratory tests indicate that the polysulfide compound is superior to the oil-base material, but its use is generally restricted to joints in dams and power plant roofs and walls or other joints where resistance to weathering is a major consideration. Tests also show that the polysulfide compound should not be used if it is likely to come in contact with bituminous materials since deterioration of the polysulfide compound may result.

Paste Wood Filler

After sanding and before applying varnish or floor sealer to open-grained woods such as oak, material must be worked into the pores of the wood to obtain a smoothly finished job. This material, called paste wood filler, is composed of silica and quick-drying varnish. It is thinned to brushing consistency with mineral spirits or turpentine prior to application. Staining, if desired, should be done before the filler is applied. The filler may be colored with some of the stain to accentuate the grain pattern of the wood.

Surface Filler for Metal

To produce a smooth finish on rough castings, it is often necessary to fill pores and depressions with something more substantial then the usual priming and finish paints. Certain epoxy resins filled with metal powder make excellent surface fillers. These mixtures, when properly catalyzed and cured, adhere tenaciously to metal and may be filed, ground, or machined to surface. As they are 100 percent solids mixtures, no shrinkage is experienced, so they may then be painted like the adjacent metal.

Paint and Varnish Remover

Two general kinds of material are used for removing old paint coatings of the clear and pigmented oleoresinous varieties. One is a strong caustic (lye) solution; the other is a mixture of organic solvents, such as alcohols, acetone, and benzene, with some paraffin wax added to retard evaporation. Both act to disintegrate and loosen the coating so that it can be easily scraped off.

SECTION 2

ESTIMATING QUANTITY OF PAINT; PAINTING TOOLS, ITEMS, AND EQUIPMENT; COLOR AND HOW TO USE IT

In estimating the quantity of paint required it is better to have a little too much material than not enough. Therefore, when figuring square-foot areas, it is better to overestimate than underestimate.

Before starting to paint, make sure you have all the tools, items, and equipment needed to do the job right; especially brushes.

Modern methods of producing ready-mixed paints, enamels, lacquers, varnishes, and stains in a great variety of colors makes it unnecessary and impractical to mix one's own paint.

2

Estimating Quantities of Paint

To estimate the quantity of paint required, first determine the area in square feet that's going to be painted. Then decide the number of coats that will be necessary. A gallon of paint used as a second coat will cover a larger area than a gallon used as a first coat. A first coat is expended in two distinct directions; in addition to adequately covering the surface, it has to penetrate the porous depth of the material. A second coat simply rests on the surface. Different products have various coverage qualities. For this reason, the figures in Table 1 listing the covering power of various paints are average and not exact figures. This table gives the coverage per gallon of nearly a score of finishing materials. The figures were obtained by averaging the claims of different manufacturers of similar products.

In estimating the quantity of paint required it is good practice to provide a little too much rather than not enough. The following methods of figuring areas are sufficiently accurate for all usual requirements.

INTERIOR

Ceilings and Floors

Ceiling and floor areas are determined by multiplying the length of the room by its width.

Table 1
Averages of the Covering Power of Various Paints

Coverage per gallon, in Square Feet

Surface and Product	First (or Primer) Coat	Second Coat	Third Coat
Frame siding			
Exterior house paint	468	540	630
Trim (exterior)			
Exterior trim paint	850	900	972
Porch floors and steps			
Porch and deck paint	378	540	576
Asbestos wall shingles			
Exterior house paint	180	400	
Shingle siding			
Exterior house paint	342	423	
Shingle stain	150	225	
Shingle roofs			
Exterior oil paint	150	250	
Shingle stain	120	200	
Brick (exterior)			
Exterior oil paint	200	400	
Cement water paint	100	150	
Exterior emulsion	215		
Cement and cinder block			
Cement water paint	100	140	
Exterior oil paint	180	240	

Walls

Measure the distance around the room and multiply by the height. Deduct about 15 square feet for each window and single door.

Trim

Windows

One side, sash and frame: 35 square feet
One side, frame only: 20 square feet
One side, sash only: 15 square feet

Surface and Product	Coverage per gallon, in Square Feet		
	First (or Primer) Coat	Second Coat	Third Coat
Medium texture stucco			
Exterior oil paint	153	360	360
Cement water paint	99	135	
Cement floors and steps (exterior)			
Porch and deck paint	450	600	600
Color stain and finish	510	480	
Doors and windows (interior)			
Enamel	603	405	504
Picture molding, chair rails, and other			
trim	1200	810	810
Floors, hardwood (interior)			
Oil paint	540	450	
Shellac	540	675	765
Varnish	540	540	540
Linoleum			
Varnish	540	558	
Walls, smooth-finish plaster			
Flat oil paint	630 Primer	540	630
Gloss or semi-gloss oil paint	630 Primer	540	540
Calcimine	720 Size	240	
Emulsion paint	540	700	
Casein water paint	540	700	

Doors

One side, including frame: 35 square feet
Two sides, including frames: 70 square feet
One side, without frame: 20 square feet
One side, frame only: 20 square feet

Baseboards

Measure length and consider as square feet. This should include any picture molding.

Stairs

The average stairway in a home is 135 square feet, including treads, risers, and stringers.

Stairway including balusters is 300 square feet.

Cabinets

Measure the front area and multiply by 5.

Cornices

Measure the front area and multiply by 2.

Radiators

Measure the front area and multiply by 7.

After computing the total square footage of the area to be painted, see Table 1, to ascertain the number of gallons of paint required, and divide the covering power per gallon in square feet into the total square feet to be covered.

EXTERIOR

Walls

Measure the perimeter of the house in feet and multiply by the height-to-eave line in feet. Do not deduct for windows or doors unless they total more than 100 square feet in area. When windows and doors are average in size, determine the square footage of the four walls as solid areas. Gables must be figured separately.

Gables

The gable on a house or barn is any wall space above the eave line (space indicated by *ACD*, Figs. 1 to 5). To calculate the area of gables in square feet, use the following formulas.

Plain gable roof—Multiply the width at the eave line *AC* by height *BD* and divide by two (Fig. 1).

Gambrel roof—Figure this roof as you would for a plain gabled roof and add 25 percent to the total (Fig. 2).

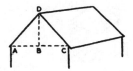

Fig. 1.   Plain gable roof.

Fig. 2.   Gambrel roof.

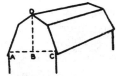

Fig. 3.   Double hip roof.

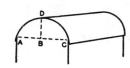

Fig. 4.   Gothic roof.

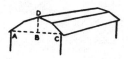

Fig. 5.   Barrel roof.

Double hip, gothic, or barrel roof—Figure the same way as for the plain gable roof and then add 50 percent to the total (Figs. 3, 4, and 5).

Dormers

Dormers are vertical windows that protrude from a roof (Figs. 6 and 7). For quick figuring, count each dormer as 100 square feet regardless of width.

Eaves

Eaves are projecting overhangs of a roof. Frequently, the underparts of eaves are painted. Measure the width and multiply by the perimeter of the house to obtain the square footage of the area. If the eaves are painted the same color as the walls of the house, multiply the total by 1½; if a different color is to be used, multiply by 2.

For eaves with rafters running to the roof line, measure the area and multiply the result by 3.

For eaves over brick or stucco walls, measure the area in square feet and multiply by 3.

Fig. 6. Dormer windows.   **Fig. 7. Dormer window.**

Roof Surfaces

Two steps are used in determining the area of a sloping roof:

1. Determine the flat area by multiplying the width of the roof, including overhang, by the length, including overhang. If the house has wings or porches, measure each of these units separately and add.

2. Add a determined percentage to the total flat area. The percentage to use is determined by the slope, pitch, or kind of roof (Fig. 8). In figuring, always use the slope of the main part of the roof, disregarding dormers.

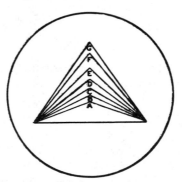

Fig. 8.   Roof slopes.

For slope G—Add 80 percent
For slope F—Add 60 percent
For slope E—Add 45 percent
For slope D—Add 25 percent
For slope C—Add 20 percent

For slope B—Add 12 percent
For slope A—Add 7 percent

Gambrel roof—(*See* Fig. 9). Use average slope *AC* midway between *AB* and *AD*, and add the percentage previously given for a gabled roof.

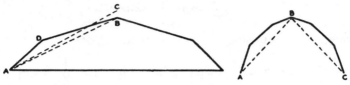

Fig. 9.   **Gambrel roof.**

Fig. 10.   **Double hip roof.**

Fig. 11.   Gothic roof.   **Fig. 12.   Barrel roof.**

Double hip, gothic, and barrel roofs—Draw lines *ABC* and add the same percentage specified for the gabled roof (Figs. 10, 11, and 12.) Then add an additional 20 percent. These roofs are frequently used on barns.

Trim

Since windows and doors are not deducted from the wall area, it is not necessary to calculate the trim area if it is to be painted with the same material. When the trim is to be a different color, figure its area only for the final coat. When two coats are used, paint the first coat of the trim the same as the walls. For the best results, the undercoat for the trim should be tinted to approximate the finish color. After figuring the amount of paint required for the final coat on the walls, it is generally safe to estimate one-quarter of that amount for the finish color for the trim.

To estimate the average surface of trim units separately, use the following figures.

Doors—One side, without frame: 20 square feet.
One side, including frame: 35 square feet.

Windows—One side, including frame: 35 square feet.
One side, sash only: 15 square feet.

Storm sash—Both sides: 15 square feet.

Shutters—Both sides, per pair: 35 square feet.

Screens—*Frame only,* both sides: 15 square feet.
Wire mesh—One pint is sufficient to paint the mesh of approximately eight screens.

Gutters, leaders, and downspouts—Measure the front area and multiply by 2.

Columns—Multiply perimeter by height.

Railings, latticework, and picket fences—Measure the front area and multiply by 4.

3

Painting Tools, Items, and Equipment and Their Uses

WALL AND CEILINGS

Stiff scraping knife—For scraping loose paint and cutting out cracks.

Flexible putty knife or scraper—For filling holes and cracks.

Wall patch (Spackle)—For holes and cracks.

Sandpaper holder

Rags—For cleaning up. (Burn or put outdoors after use.)

Sponges—For washing walls.

Cleaner—For washing walls.

Toner colors or colors in oil—For tinting.

Drop cloths—For protecting floors and furniture.

Thinner—For thinning paint and holding.

Paint pots—For boxing paint and holding for use.

Painter's time saver—A guard to help with cutting in around woodwork.

Ladders and planks—For reaching high places. (*See* Chapter 16, Painting Safety, the section on Ladders.)

Sal soda—To remove excessive gloss.

Masking tape—To protect woodwork if washing walls with sal soda.

Paddles—For stirring paint.

Cheesecloth or strainer—For straining paint or enamel.

41

Glazing liquid—For glazing walls.

Stencils, decals, and wallpaper borders—For decoration.

Toner colors or colors in oil or Japan—For stenciling.

Brushes—Flat wall brushes 3 to 5 inches wide are suitable for all wall work. An open center stucco is particularly good for flat wall paint. To remove brush marks, use a bristle or roller stippler. A stencil brush may also be useful. (*See* Chapter 7, Brush Painting.)

INTERIOR WOODWORK

Sandpaper—For smoothing rough surfaces and light sanding between coats.

Sandpaper holder—A great convenience.

Wall patch or other crack filler—For filling nail holes, cracks, and the like. When using under varnish, tint this material with colors in oil. If you are using stain, always fill after staining.

Paint pots—For boxing paint and holding material for use.

Flexible putty knife—For filling nail holes and cracks.

Paint and varnish remover—For removing old finish.

Thinner—For thinning and clean up.

Drop cloths—For protecting floors and furniture.

Rags—For cleaning up and wiping floor and trim seal. Wiping rags should be burned at once or put outdoors to prevent fire from spontaneous combustion.

Cleaner—For washing woodwork.

Sponge—For washing woodwork.

Toner colors or colors in oil—For tinting.

Ladders and planks—For reaching high places. (*See* Chapter 16, Painting Safety, the section on Ladders.)

Sal soda—To remove excessive gloss. (A cupful to one gallon of warm water. Rinse the surface afterwards.)

Paddles—For stirring paint.

Painter's time saver—A guard to help with cutting in woodwork.

Razor blade holder—For removing paint from glass.

Screwdriver—For removing hardware.

Cheesecloth or strainer—For straining paint or varnish.
Wax—Paste, liquid, or non-rubbing.
Polish—For rubbing final coat of varnish with pumice.
Bleach—For bleaching wood.
Brushes—Varnish brushes 1 to 3 inches wide. For sash work, use a round, flat, or angular sash tool. (*See* Chapter 7, Brush Painting.)

INTERIOR WOOD FURNITURE

Sandpaper—For removing scars, smoothing rough surfaces, and light sanding between coats.
Sandpaper holder—A great convenience.
Crack filler—For filling nail holes, cracks, and the like. (When using varnish, color it with colors in oil. If using stain, always fill holes after staining.)
Paint pots—For boxing paint and holding material for use.
Flexible putty knife—For filling nail holes and cracks.
Paint and varnish remover—For removing old finish.
Scrapers—Various kinds are available for removing old finish.
Thinner—For thinning paint or varnish, and clean up.
Drop cloths—For protecting floors.
Rags—For cleaning up. Burn or put outdoors immediately after use to prevent fire from spontaneous combustion.
Cleaner—For washing furniture.
Sponge—For washing furniture.
Tack cloth—To remove dust from corners.
Screwdriver—For removing hardware and tightening joints.
Wrenches—For dismantling or assembly.
Toner colors or colors in oil—For tinting.
Sal soda—To remove excessive glass. (A cupful to one gallon of warm water. Rinse the surface afterwards.)
Paddles—For stirring paint.
Cheesecloth or strainer—For straining paint or varnish.
Wax—Paste, liquid, or non-rubbing.
Flour pumice and rotten stone—For rubbing.
Polish–For rubbing the final coat of varnish with pumice.

Stencils and decals—For decoration.

Colors in oil or Japan, bronze powders, and the like—For stenciling, decoration, and antiquing.

Masking tape—For striping.

Bleach—For bleaching wood.

Glue—For mending.

Brushes—Varnish brushes 1 to 2-½ inches wide, ½- or ¾-inch fitch for small work; stencil brush; artist brushes for striping and decoration. (*See* Chapter 7, Brush Painting.)

INTERIOR FLOORS

Crack filler—For filling cracks.

Flexible putty knife—For filling cracks.

Thinner—For thinning varnish or enamel, and cleaning up.

Cleaner—For cleaning floors.

Wax remover—For removing wax.

Rags—For cleaning up and mixing floor and trim seal. Wiping rags should be burned at once or put outdoors to prevent fire from spontaneous combustion.

Paint pots—For boxing enamel and holding material for use.

Paddles—For stirring enamel.

Toner colors or colors in oil—For tinting enamel or filler.

Floor broom—For sweeping.

Wax—Paste, liquid or non-rubbing.

Wax applicator—For applying wax.

Masking tape—For striping or designs.

Sponge—For mottling.

Brushes—2-½- to 3-½-inch varnish brush; wide brush or mop for applying floor and trim seal. (*See* Chapter 7, Brush Painting.)

Also Needed for Wood Floors

Sandpaper—For smoothing scars and light sanding between coats.

Sandpaper holder—A great convenience.

Scrapers—Various kinds for removing old finish.

Steel wool—For buffing the final coat of floor and trim seal.

Bleach—For bleaching wood.

Denatured alcohol—For thinning shellac and cleaning shellac brush.

Sanding machine—(Rental) For removing old finish.

Also Needed for Cement Floors

Cement floor patcher—For holes and cracks.

Stiff scraping knife—For scraping off dirt and loose paint.

Wire brush—For removing loose particles and loose paint.

Trisodium phosphate—For removing soaked-in grease. Scrub with a solution of six ounces to one gallon of warm water and rinse. Repeat if necessary.

Commercial muriatic acid—For texturing slick floors.

EXTERIOR WOOD

Stiff scraping knife—For scraping off dirt and loose paint.

Paint and varnish remover—For removing old finish.

Wire brush—For removing dirt, excessive chalk, and loose paint.

Blowtorch or infrared lamp—For burning off paint.

Shellac—(white or orange)—For coating knots and sap streaks.

Denatured alcohol—For thinning shellac and cleaning shellac brush.

Flexible putty knife—For filling nail holes and cracks after first coat is dry.

Stiff putty knife—For glazing windows.

Glazing compound—For filling nail holes and glazing windows.

Calking gun and calking compound—For filling openings around windows, doors, chimneys, and the like.

Sandpaper—For sanding rough or glossy spots.

Sandpaper holder—A great convenience.

Drop cloths—For protecting walks and shrubbery.

Thinner—For thinning paint and cleaning up.

Raw linseed oil—When painting in hot weather.

Ladders and planks—For reaching high places. (*See* Chapter 16, Painting Safety, section on Ladders.)

Cheesecloth or strainer—For straining paint.

Paint pot—For boxing paint and holding material.

Pot hooks—For hanging pot to ladder rung.

Paddles—For stirring paint.

Rags—For cleaning up. Burn or put outdoors immediately after use to prevent fire from spontaneous combustion.

Bar rust penetrating primer—For coating nail heads and other iron to prevent rust stains.

Wood preservative—For protection against rot, termites, and the like.

Zinc dust primer, varnish, or screen paint—For wire screening.

Asbestos roof coating—For inside wood or iron gutters. (To fill holes or cracks, apply on coat, imbed a strip of canvas or burlap when wet. When dry, apply another coat.)

Toner colors or colors in oil—For tinting house paint undercoat and top coat.

Cleaner—For removing dirt or soot.

Hot dipped galvanized nails—For filling back boards and moldings.

Brushes—3½- or 4-inch flat wall or solid center stucco brush for siding; 2½- to 3-inch varnish, sash, or flat wall brush for trim; 1- to 2-inch sash tool or angular sash; ½-or ¾-inch fitch for small work. An additional brush is useful for shellac. (*See* Chapter 7, Brush Painting.)

EXTERIOR MASONRY

Brick and cement coating reducer—For thinning brick and cement coating.

Brick and cement undercoat reducer—For thinning undercoat.

Thinner—For removing form oil or grease, for thinning house paint, and for cleaning up.

Wire brush—For removing dirt, loose particles, efflorescense, and loose paint.

Zinc dust primer or varnish—For coating screen wire and all other metal to prevent staining walls.

Gun and calking compound—For filling cracks and openings around doors, windows, and metal brackets.

Black roof cement—For filling openings around chimney.

Stiff putty knife—For glazing windows.

Glazing compound—For glazing windows; also for filling cavities in mortar joints, after the first coat has dried.

Drop cloths—For protecting walks and shrubbery.

Ladders and planks—For reaching high places. (*See* Chapter 16, Painting Safety, section on Ladders.)

Paint pots—For boxing paint and holding paint for use.

Pot hooks—For hanging pot to ladder rung.

Paddles—For stirring paint.

Rags—For cleaning up. Burn or put outdoors immediately after use to prevent fire from spontaneous combustion.

Asbestos roof coating—For lining the inside of wood or iron gutters. (To fill holes or cracks apply one coat, embed a strip of canvas or burlap while wet and then apply another coat.)

Brushes—3½- to 4½-inch flat wall or solid center stucco for walls; 2½- or 3-inch varnish, sash, or flat wall brush for trim; 1- to 2-inch sash tool, or angular sash. ½- or ¾-inch fitch for small work. (*See* Chapter 7, Brush Painting.)

EXTERIOR METAL

Stiff scraping knife—For scraping off dirt, rust, and loose paint.

Blowtorch—For burning off paint, removing rust and mill scale.

Paint and varnish remover—For removing old paint.

Wire brush—For removing rust and loose paint.

Emery cloth—For removing rust.

Sandpaper—For smoothing rough spots.

Sandpaper holder—A great convenience.

Calking gun and calking compound—For filling openings around metal frames.

Drop cloths—For protecting walks and shrubbery.

Thinner—For thinning paint, cleaning up, and removing greasy film from new copper, tin, and so on.

Ladders and planks—For reaching high places. (*See* Chapter 16, Painting Safety.)

Paint pots—For boxing paint and holding paint for use.

Pot hooks—For hanging pot to ladder rung.

Paddles—For stirring paint.

Rags—For cleaning up. Burn or put outdoors immediately after use to prevent fire from spontaneous combustion.

Toner colors or tinting colors in oil—For tinting.

Asbestos roof coating—For lining the inside of iron gutters. (To fill holes, apply one coat, imbed a strip of canvas or burlap while wet and then apply another coat.)

Copper sulfate—For galvanized iron which has not weathered six months or more. Use one-half pound to one gallon of water. Treat again where there is no black deposit, then rinse.

Brushes—Flat wall brush or solid center stucco for wide surfaces; sash tool or varnish brush for narrow surfaces. The best brush for ornamental iron or around bolt heads is an oval brush. (*See* Chapter 7, Brush Painting.)

EXTERIOR FLOORS

Stiff scraping knife—For scraping off dirt and loose paint.

Paint and varnish remover—For removing old finish.

Flexible knife—For filling holes or cracks.

Thinner—For removing oil or grease, for thinning enamel or varnish, and cleaning up.

Crack filler—For filling holes or cracks.

Rags—For cleaning up. Burn or put outdoors immediately after use to prevent fire from spontaneous combustion.

Paint pots—For boxing paint and holding paint or varnish for use.

Paddles—For stirring paint.

Toner colors or colors in oil—For tinting floor enamel.

Asbestos roof coating—For coating underside of porches or steps to prevent peeling.

Wood preservative—For protecting against rot, termites, and the like. It is preferable to dip or coat joints, and the like, and all four sides and ends of boards before laying.

Brushes—2½- to 3½-inch varnish brush. (*See* Chapter 7, Brush Painting.)

Also Needed for Wood Floors

Sandpaper—For smoothing scars.

Sandpaper holder—A great convenience.

Sanding machine (Rental)—For removing old finish and leveling cupped (warped) boards.

Also Needed for Cement Floors

Wire brush—For removing loose particles and loose paint.

Trisodium phosphate—For removing soaked in grease. Scrub with a solution of six ounces in one gallon of warm water and rinse. Repeat if necessary.

Commercial muriatic acid—For texturing slick floors.

FOR ROOFS

Stiff scraping knife—For scraping off dirt and loose paint.

Calking gun and calking compound—For filling openings around chimney and the like.

Roof cement—For filling holes or cracks where black color is not objectionable.

Trowel—For applying roof cement.

Asbestos roof coating—For lining the inside of wood or iron gutters. (To fill holes or cracks, apply one coat. Embed a strip of canvas or burlap while wet and then apply another coat.)

Drop cloths—For protecting walks and shrubbery.

Thinner—For thinning paint, cleaning up and removing greasy film from new copper, tin, and so on.

Paint pots—For boxing paint and holding for use.

Pot hooks—For hanging pot to ladder rung.

Rags—For cleaning up. Burn or put outdoors immediately after use to prevent fire from spontaneous combustion.

Ladders, planks, and ladder hooks—(*See* Chapter 16, Painting Safety, section on Ladders.)

Paddles—For stirring paint.

Roof paint—For coating gutters.

Also Needed for Wood Shingles

Stiff fibre scrub brush—Use dry brush to remove dirt and loose wood fibre.

Brushes—Wide flat wall brush or inexpensive kalsomine brush. (*See* Chapter 7, Brush Painting.)

Also Needed for Composition Roofing

Aluminum paint—For coating built-up and composition roofs or asbestos roof coating. This paint adds years to a house, and contributes to coolness.

Brushes—For paint, use wide flat wall brush. For asbestos coating use a roof brush. (*See* Chapter 7, Brush Painting.)

Also Needed for Metal Roofs

Wire brush—For removing rust and loose paint.

Copper sulfate—For treating galvanized iron which has not weathered six months or more. Use one-half pound to one gallon of water. Treat again where there is no black deposit, then rinse.

Trisodium phosphate—For cleaning dirt and soot from painted roofs, use six ounces to one gallon of warm water and rinse.

Brushes—Use wide flat wall brush or long handled roof brush. (*See* Chapter 7, Brush Painting.)

4

Color and How to Use It

All reputable American paint manufacturers are members of the National Paint, Varnish and Lacquer Association and maintain products at the high standards set up to protect this important industry. Although many colors are available in ready-mixed form, the painter should have a basic knowledge of the principles and methods of mixing colors to obtain the various tints and gradations necessary to a harmonious color scheme.

COLOR HARMONY

Color Wheel

The simplest method of learning the basic principles underlying color harmony is to make a color wheel. Five simple water colors—red, yellow, blue, black, and white—and a camel's hair brush are all that is required.

Draw a circle four inches or more in diameter and at three equidistant points near the perimeter, paint a spot of color: red at one point, yellow at the second, and blue at the third. These three colors are the primary pigment colors (Fig. 1).

The next step in the construction of a color wheel is to add the secondary colors—orange, green, and purple. They are made by combining the primary colors as follows:

Red and yellow to make orange.
Yellow and blue to make green.
Blue and red to make purple.

51

Experiment with these three combinations and add spots of the secondary colors on the wheel (Fig. 2).

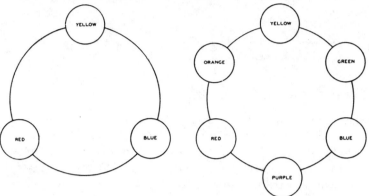

Fig. 1. Primary colors.   **Fig. 2. Primary and secondary colors.**

To complete the color wheel, the six open spaces must be filled in with intermediate colors. Proceed as follows: Mix red and yellow together, then mix in an additional quantity of red; the resultant color will be red–orange. Spot this color on the color wheel between orange and red. Mix red and yellow together again, adding an extra quantity of yellow; the resultant color will be yellow–orange. Spot this color on the color wheel between orange and yellow. Mix yellow and blue to produce green. Repeat with an additional quantity of yellow; the resultant color will be yellow–green. Spot this color between yellow and green. Proceed by mixing yellow and blue a second time to produce green; then add more blue to produce blue–green. Spot this color between green and blue.

Combine red and blue to produce purple; an additional quantity of blue produces blue–purple. Spot this color on the wheel between purple and blue. Combine red and blue again to produce purple and add some red to get red–purple.

The color wheel is now complete with the primary, secondary, and intermediate colors—twelve in all (Fig. 3). These were made with full-strength colors and are classified as pure hues.

Tint. When white is added to any color or hue on the color wheel a tint of that color results. A tint is lighter or higher in value than the original color. In other words, pink is a tint of red, made of red plus white; orchid is a tint of purple and is made by combining purple and white.

Shade. When black is added to any of the twelve colors on the wheel the result is called a *shade* of that color. A shade is darker or lower in value than the original color. For instance, rust is made by combining orange and a larger quantity of black.

Tone. When both black and white are added to any of the colors, a *tone* or "grayed" color is produced.

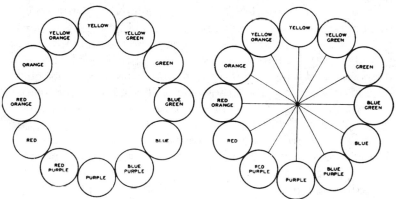

Fig. 3. **Twelve-color wheel.**   Fig. 4. **Lines indicate color**
complements.

Color Formulas

The use of a single color does not create harmony—when two or more colors are combined according to certain basic rules, harmony of color is attained. By applying simple mechanical formulas to the color wheel, colors that harmonize with each other, can easily be determined. The most widely used formulas for selecting harmonious colors are the complement, split complement, double complement, triad, and mutual complement.

True complement. Of all the established patterns or formulas for color harmony, the easiest to use is the true complement or, as it is generally called, the complement. The two colors directly across from each other on the wheel are complements (Fig. 4) and represent all colors in the visible spectrum range or completeness of color. For example, red and green are complements—they are directly opposite each other on the color wheel.

To produce green, both blue and yellow must be combined. Thus, red and green together contain the three primary colors, in other words, completeness of color. The same is also true of orange and blue, yellow and purple, and so on, around the color wheel.

Putting this principle to practical use, let us determine how the color scheme of a room could be based on two true complements. These colors will not be exactly as on the color wheel, but in lighter or darker values which may or may not be grayed.

Picture a room with walls that are painted hyacinth blue (a soft blue–purple), and a cream-colored ceiling. The floor could be covered with a deep blue–purple rug and the furniture might be walnut with fawn tone (yellow–orange) upholstery. Patterned draperies combining yellow–orange tones with cream, and glints of gold on lamp bases and accessories will bring the room to life.

Another room with a color scheme based on true compliments illustrates what could be done with red and green: a rug in two tones of green, and white draperies edged in harmonizing green. The color wheel with these two color schemes charted is shown in Figs. 5 and 6.

Although harmoniously correct, true complements are often unsatisfactory for the decoration of rooms. Two colors alone are likely to become tiresome and monotonous. Unless an unusual effect is desired, efficient color schemes for home decoration generally include three or four colors.

Split complement. For interiors, the principle of the split complement employing three colors (Fig. 7), is likely. The split complement merely expands the single complement by splitting one end of a line, ending in arrows, across the color wheel for finding true complements. If one arrow is set at blue, the true complement would be found by pointing the other arrow directly across to orange. Split the second arrow so that one-half points to the color next to orange on the left, which in this case would be red–orange; the other half would then point to yellow–orange on the right (Fig. 7).

Applying these colors to the decoration of a room, a light tint of yellow—orange, which can be cream color, could be used for the walls and ceiling, combined with a brown carpet, which would be a low value of the yellow–orange. The background of

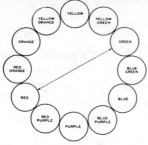

Fig. 5. Red and green are "true complements."

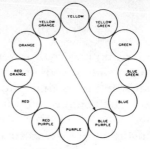

Fig. 6. Yellow–orange and blue–purple are also "true complements."

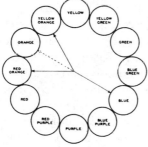

Fig. 7. Split complement.

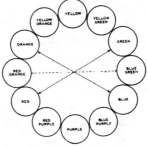

Fig. 8. Double complement.

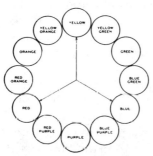

Fig. 9. Triad. Formed by three colors spaced equally.

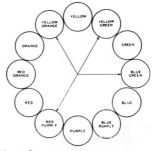

Fig. 10. Mutual complement (analogous scheme).

Fig. 11. Split mutual complement.

the fabric on one chair cover could echo the drapery color—a medium value of red–orange, slightly toned. The wood of the furniture in the room might be a low value red–orange, such as maple. The complement blue could be introduced in the upholstery of a chair, in a lamp base, and in other accessories serving as decorative accents.

Double complement. Another method for achieving color harmony is the double complement. As in the case of the split complement, start with a line drawn through the center of the color wheel indicating true complements. Instead of splitting one end of the line, as for a split complement, both ends are split and the result is a double complement (Fig. 8). A double complement is used for four-color harmony. Note in this illustration that the true complements were originally red–orange and blue–green, the color directly opposite. When divided properly the lines point to red, orange, blue, and green (Fig. 8).

From this color pattern a very pleasant living room can be developed. Pale blue is used for the upper walls above a gleaming white dado, with deep blue for the rug, green in the pattern fabric covering of a sofa or a large chair, and additional tones of green in the leaves of attractive plants. Red, which is the complement of green, appears in the draperies and possibly in the upholstery of a chair, while orange, which complements blue, might appear in a low tone in the furniture.

Triad. The term "triad" means a union of three and aptly describes another very useful formula for color harmony. On the color wheel a triad has the same Y appearance as the split complement, except that the three principal colors are equidistant around the color wheel (Fig. 9). Triads in pure hues, such as red, yellow, or blue or in tones, tints, or shades form some of the most beautiful combinations possible.

The triad is one of the most frequently used color harmony patterns. To illustrate the beauty that can be produced by employing this formula, imagine a living room with wood furniture and a sofa upholstered in a low tone of red. The wall behind the sofa is the same deep tone of red combined with vertical stripes of gray to lend height and dignity to the room. The floor is covered with a gray carpet and the three other walls and woodwork are painted gray. Soft yellow is the background color of fabric covering a wing chair and is used also as a lampshade color, in addition to several soft yellow decorative accessories. A tone of medium blue appears in the upholstery of another chair with approximately the same tone of blue in a pair of Chinese vases on the mantle, which is painted gray.

Mutual complement. Slightly more involved color combination formulas are called mutual and split mutual complements. With the benefit of some experience in planning color schemes described in the preceding, these two formulas will not be as difficult to use as they may seem at first glance.

There are two basic kinds of color harmony. Harmony of contrast has been discussed up to this point. The other color harmony is the harmony of analogy. A mutual complement combines both basic kinds of color harmony (Fig. 10).

Analogous colors are those "linked by resemblance" and are next to each other on the color wheel. Each one has a point of similarity with its neighbor. Thus, yellow–orange is analogous to yellow since there is yellow in it. By the same token, yellow is analogous to yellow–green. Continuing around the wheel, it is apparent that yellow–green is analogous to green, green and blue–green are similarly related, and blue–green is analogous to blue. These relationships apply specifically, at this time, to mutual complements.

The rules of color harmony specify that one must not go more than five steps on a twelve-color wheel in plotting analogous harmonies, to avoid trespassing on the field belonging to the next primary color. It is therefore advisable to stay within the five-step range and then find the mutual complement. To clarify, let us suppose that your eye lights on the segment of the wheel that includes this five-step range: yellow–orange, yellow, yellow–green, green, and blue–green. That is all very well, but what about the contrasting complement from the other side of the color wheel? How is it selected?

If harmonious colors were being plotted for a woman's hat or dress, one would not necessarily bother with mutual complement; analogous colors could be used very effectively. A room, however, is quite a different story. To supply proper color balance, mutual complement is necessary.

To find the mutual complement, focus the eye on the central point of the analogous field selected (the five-color segment previously discussed); the middle or central color would be yellow–green. By looking across the color wheel, one sees that red–purple is the mutual complement (Fig. 10). The foregoing shows that, after a little experimenting, plotting a color scheme of mutual complements is not so complicated. One can go one step farther with a color scheme of mutual complements by splitting it (Fig. 11). Thus, in the case of the yellow–orange, yellow, yellow–green, and blue–green analogy, one would have red and purple instead of red–purple. This color maneuver is called a split mutual complement to an analogous scheme.

Deciding Factors

You will rarely have the opportunity to plan an entire color scheme from scratch. There will almost always be a rug or certain important pieces of furniture, pictures, or draperies to be retained in the redecorated room. Interior decorators call these articles "deciding factors." As a rule, it is not expedient to change the coloring of these particular objects and so they are usually the starting point in determining a new color scheme. Here, the knowledge of the color wheel comes into practical use. The deciding factors in the room are the signposts for the color harmony pattern that the decorative scheme should follow.

As a practical illustration, let us assume that a kitchen and breakfast nook are to be redecorated. The color of the linoleum on the floor is blue, with tiny squares of red and yellow in the design. The breakfast table and chairs are a light bamboo color. In this particular case, both the linoleum and the furniture are deciding factors. The three colors in the linoleum—red, yellow, and blue—clearly indicate the use of a triad. The existing furniture in the breakfast nook, with its yellow bamboo tone, definitely fits into the picture.

Therefore, for the walls and woodwork of this room, there is a choice between red, yellow, and blue. Red for large areas such as walls is out of the question; it is too intense and dominating. If used on small areas, however, it tends to bring life and gaiety to a room. Yellow, in one of its many tints, could be used successfully, but the furniture will not be emphasized if placed against a color so similar to its own.

Well-designed and colorful furniture deserves emphasis by being positioned, when possible, against a contrasting color. In this case, some tone of blue, preferably a light tint, should be used for the walls. If desired, it would not even be necessary to use blue on the entire wall area. A blue dado would be especially effective here with ivory, a tint of yellow, for the upper part of the wall and ceiling. The dado should be high enough to form a suitable background for the breakfast table and chairs. The problem of selecting a suitable background color is also easily solved if the breakfast nook happens to be in an alcove with a definite division from the kitchen. The walls of the alcove could then be painted blue and the balance of the kitchen wall area could be in the yellow range. As for the woodwork, a tint of blue or yellow or even white would be effective.

MIXING AND MATCHING COLORS

Some manufacturers have solved the problem of securing various shades and tints by packaging white paint with a wide variety of tube colors in the quantities required to produce exact hues. Others have developed intermix systems. Two or more containers of paint are intermixed to produce a large number of tints and tones. Consult with your paint dealer or painter to ascertain which method is recommended for your specific purpose.

In the actual mixing and matching of paint, colors-in-oil are used. These are pigments finely ground in oil, available in either tubes or larger containers. Colors-in-oil are used in tinting all kinds of opaque paints except lacquers and water-thinned paints. There are many varieties and kinds of colors-in-oil used for this purpose. To mix colors effectively, it is necessary to be familiar with the names of the pigments and which ones to use to obtain desired results. (*See* Chart 1.)

To produce a desired tone, hue, or shade of any color, it is necessary to combine two or more of these pigments. The principal colors in use, the pigments used to produce them, and descriptions of the colors are listed in Table 2.

Chart 1
Nomenclature for Pigments

Color Name	Description	Pigments to Use
	Indian Red	Purple–red
	Rose Pink	Purple–red
	Crimson Lake	Purple–red
	English Vermilion	Orange–red
Reds	American Scarlet Vermilion	Orange–red
	Venetian Red	Orange–red
	Tuscan Red	Orange–red
	Toludine	Orange–red
	Permanent Red	Orange–red
	Chrome Yellow, Dark (Chrome Orange)	Yellow–orange
Yellows	Chrome Yellow, Light (Lemon Chrome Yellow)	Yellow
	Chrome Yellow, Medium	Yellow
	Golden Ochre	Yellow
	Yellow Ochre	Yellow
	Mitis Green, Light	Yellow–green
	Mitis Green, Medium	Yellow–green
	Mitis Green, Dark	Yellow–green
Greens	Chrome Green, Light	Green
	Chrome Green, Medium	Blue–green
	Chrome Green, Dark	Blue–green
	Cobalt	Green–blue
Blues	Prussian	Blue
	Ultramarine	Purple–blue
	Phthalocyanine	Blue
Purple	Madder Lake	Purple–red
	Burnt Umber, Turkey	Red–orange
	Raw Umber, Turkey	Red–orange
Browns	Vandyke Brown	Red–orange
	Burnt Sienna, Italian	Yellow–orange
	Raw Sienna, Italian	Yellow
	Drop or Ivory Black	Black
Blacks	Lampblack	Blue–black
	Carbon Black	Red–black
	White Lead	White
Whites	Zinc Oxide	White
	Titanium Oxide	White
	Lithopone	White

Table 2

Color Name	Description	Pigments to Use
Apple green	Moderate yellow—green	White for base. Add light chrome green and orange chrome yellow.
Apricot	Pale orange	Medium chrome yellow for base; Venetian red and carmine lake. If a light tint is wanted, add white.
Bottle green	Dark green	Lampblack and Prussian blue for base; lemon chrome yellow.
Browns and brown drabs—all shades	Dusky orange	Venetian red for base; add ochre and lampblack in various proportions according to shades of brown wanted. For the brown drabs, add white to reduce the above brown tints.
Café-au-lait	Light Brown	Burnt umber for base; add white ochre and Venetian red.
Canary	Moderate yellow	Use chrome yellow, yellow ochre, or lemon yellow for base, lightened with white.
Chamois	Weak yellowish-orange	White for base; add ochre, medium chrome yellow to suit, redden with a little burnt sienna.
Chartreuse	Light yellow-green	Medium chrome yellow for base; add some medium chrome green.
Cinnamon	Weak orange	White for base; add burnt sienna, ochre, medium chrome yellow.
Colonial yellow	Moderate yellow	White for base; add medium chrome yellow, tinge with a trifle of orange chrome yellow.
Copper	Weak reddish-orange	Medium chrome yellow; tinged with burnt sienna.
Coral pink	Moderate pink	Vermilion for base; white, medium chrome yellow.
Cream color and all the buffs	Weak yellowish-orange and moderate orange	White for base; add ochre to make the color desired.

Color Name	Description	Pigments to Use
Crimson	Strong red	Deep English vermilion or any of the crimson vermilion reds. If desired very rich, add some of the crimson lakes.
Ecru	Weak yellowish-orange	White for base; add ochre, burnt sienna, lampblack.
Electric blue	Weak blue	Ultramarine blue for base; add white and raw sienna.
Emerald	Strong green	Very light chrome green.
Fawn	Light brown	White for base; add medium chrome yellow, Venetian red, burnt umber.
Flesh color	Weak yellowish-orange	White for base; add medium chrome yellow, French ochre, Venetian red.
French gray	Light gray	White for base; add ivory black with a faint tinge of ultramarine blue and madder lake or carmine.
Golden brown	Moderate brown	Ochre for base; add orange chrome yellow, lampblack. Lighten with white.
Gray green	Weak green	White for base; add ultramarine blue, lemon chrome yellow, lampblack.
Gray stone	Pale brown	White for base; add lampblack, Prussian blue, Venetian red.
Grays, all shades	Gray	White for base; lampblack in various proportions to obtain shade wanted.
Ivy green	Moderate olive green	Ochre for base; add lampblack, Prussian blue.
Jonquil	Moderate yellow	White for base; add medium chrome yellow and a tinge of vermilion.
Lavender	Pale purple	White for base; add ivory black, ultramarine blue, tinge with carmine or madder lake.

Color Name	Description	Pigments to Use
Lemon	Moderate yellow	Use lemon chrome yellow.
Magenta	Deep red-purple	Vermilion for base; add carmine or madder lake with a tinge of ultramarine blue.
Marigold	Strong orange	Medium chrome yellow for base; add white, orange chrome yellow.
Maroon	Very dark red	Tuscan red for base; add orange chrome yellow and some ivory black.
Mauve	Strong red-purple	Ultramarine blue for base; add white, tint with madder lake.
Navy blue	Dusky purple-blue	Ultramarine blue for base; add ivory black.
Nut brown	Weak brown	Lampblack for base; add Venetian red, medium chrome yellow, ochre.
Old gold	Light olive brown	White for base; add medium chrome yellow, ochre and a little burnt umber.
Olive green	Moderate olive	Lemon chrome yellow for base; add about equal parts of Prussian blue and lampblack. Some shades of olive can be made by substituting ochre for lemon chrome yellow. Then, of course, the tone will not be so bright.
Orange	Orange	Orange chrome yellow as it comes from the can.
Peach	Moderate orange-pink	White for base; add pale Indian red.
Pink	Very pale red	White for base; add madder lake or carmine or the crimson shades of vermilion.
Pistachio	Weak yellow-green	Ivory black for base; add ochre, medium chrome green.
Plum	Very dusky purple	White for base; add Indian red, ultramarine blue.

Color Name	Description	Pigments to Use
Primrose	Moderate Yellow	White for base; add lemon or medium chrome yellow according to the color desired.
Purple	Purple	White for base; add dark Indian red and a trifle of light Indian red to suit.
Robin's-egg blue	Pale blue-green	White for base; add ultramarine until the shade is a deep blue, then some pale chrome green.
Russet	Strong brown	White for base; add orange, chrome yellow, a trifle of lamp-black, Prussian blue.
Sage green	Dusky yellow-green	White for base; add medium chrome green until tint is nearly but not quite pea green, then add lampblack to shade it.
Salmon	Moderate orange-pink	White for base; add ochre, burnt sienna, a trifle of vermilion.
Sapphire	Dark blue	White for base; add ultramarine blue.
Sea green	Moderate yellow-green	White base; add Prussian blue, raw sienna.
Scarlet	Deep reddish-orange	Pale English vermilion or any of the scarlet-toned vermilion reds.
Shrimp	Moderate reddish-orange	White base; add Venetian red, burnt sienna, a trifle of vermilion.
Sky blue	Pale blue	White for base; add Prussian blue as desired.
Straw color	Moderate yellow	Medium chrome yellow for base; add ochre, a little Venetian red; lighten with white.
Tan	Dark orange	White for base; add burnt sienna and a trifle of lampblack.
Terra cotta	Dark orange	Ochre for base; add Venetian red and white. Some shades require addition of Indian red. For rich colors, use orange chrome yellow in place of ochre; add Venetian red and a trifle of burnt umber.

Color Name	Description	Pigments to Use
Turquoise	Light greenish-blue	White for base; cobalt blue, pale chrome green.
Violet	Very dusky red-purple	White for base; add pale Indian red, a trifle of dark Indian red.

Procedure

To mix colors properly a definite technique must be followed. Thin the oil color that is being used with a little of the paint, mix thoroughly. Add a little more paint, and again stir or mix thoroughly. Combine the mixture with the paint and blend well. Be sure that the last streak of color is blended in, or it will reappear as ugly marks when least expected.

It is important to mix enough paint for the entire job, especially if a large surface is to be covered. It is extremely difficult to duplicate a color exactly if a small additional quantity of paint is required to finish the job.

It is well to remember that different colors dry in different ways. Some dry lighter, some darker, and some change quite a bit. Consequently, be sure to brush out a sample and permit it to dry to confirm that it is the exact color required. If a particular hue or tint is desired, it is advisable to brush out a large sample, preferably on a surface similar to that on which the paint will be used, and allow it to dry thoroughly. Study the resultant color under artificial as well as natural light and study its appearance in relation to other colors in the room.

Effects of Light on Color

Light tints on walls and ceiling areas serve as reflectors and help take advantage of both natural and artificial lighting. Dark colors soak up light as a sponge soaks up water. Thus, it is very easy to understand that a certain amount of illumination might be adequate in a room with light-colored walls and yet be insufficient in a room with dark red and blue walls. In some instances, there is another method of exploiting the supply of natural light.

Dark porches are apt to cast a shadow on the rooms they adjoin. Painting porch ceilings in light tints reflects a maximum amount of light into the house. The light-reflecting powers of various paint colors for both exterior and interior use are as follows:

Color	Light Reflected (Percent)
White	70–90%
Ivories and Creams	55–71%
Light yellows	65–70%
Light buffs	40–56%
Light greens	40–50%
Medium greens	15–30%
Oranges	15–30%
Medium blues	15–20%
Dark blues	5–10%
Medium grays	15–30%
Reds and Maroons	3–18%
Medium and Dark browns	3–18%
Black	1– 4%

Another important point to consider when mixing and matching colors is the lighting. Fluorescent tubes have unusual effects on colors. A color sample that looks good under fluorescent lighting may not under incandescent lighting or natural light. The reverse is also true. It is well worth any additional work or trouble involved to test colors under actual lighting conditions.

In making a final decision about color, it is important to remember that a finished job will look darker than the sample, especially if a large area is painted, for the size of the painted area greatly influences the value of colors. Wall areas reflect each other, thus intensifying color. Therefore, it is always a good idea to choose a lighter tint than the finished effect desired.

To achieve complete harmony, check the color sample against the various color factors in a room and also against any colors in adjoining areas that are visible through open doors.

Warm and Cool Colors

The adjective "warm" is usually applied to those hues seen in natural objects that are associated with the feeling of heat, for example, fire or the sun. Yellows, oranges, and reds are classified as warm colors. They merit careful consideration in planning color schemes for rooms that seem either cold, dark, or both.

On the other hand, the term "cool" describes hues seen in natural objects that have an air of coolness about them, for instance, water, snow, ice, and shadows. Cool colors are the blues, greens, and certain tones of neutral gray. They are excellent selections for rooms exposed to the warm afternoon sun. A kitchen on the southwest corner of the house which receives the heat of the sun when the hot stove is cooking dinner can easily be visually transformed into a cool room with tones of blue or green.

Although there has been some dispute among decorators as to whether the exposure of a room can be used as a guide in color planning, you can't go wrong using the suggested colors for various exposures given in Table 3.

Table 3
Suitable Colors for Northern-Hemisphere Exposures

Exposure	Suggested Colors for Walls and Decorative Accents
Northern (Receives no direct sunlight)	Warm colors such as yellow, gold, rose, beige, bittersweet, buff, burgundy, café-au-lait, canary, chamois, cinnamon, coral, cream, daffodil, dusty rose, ecru, fawn, flesh, henna, maize, peach, primrose yellow, russet.
Southern (Has warmer light)	Cool colors such as green, light blue, light gray, turquoise, sky blue, robin's-egg blue, jade, French gray, chartreuse, Alice blue, apple green, aqua green, leaf green, lettuce green, lime, mint green, Nile green, emerald green.
Eastern (Light is hard; gives a harsh look to some colors)	Colors such as light gray, ivory, cream, buff, fawn, French gray, taupe. (Some of the warm colors suitable for northern rooms can also be used, especially if rooms are small.)
Western (Warmest light received by any section of house)	Cool soft colors such as sky blue, powder blue, oyster white, mint green, Alice blue, apple green, Nile green.

PAINT STYLING

Paint styling is a modern method of employing colorful paints to emphasize the good features of a room, house, building, piece of furniture, or any object and minimize the not-so-good features. To emphasize a good feature, surround it with a different color, tint, or shade so that it stands out more prominently. To minimize a bad feature, surround it with a matching color so that it will blend in and thus become less noticeable. In other words, this is the art of camouflage.

Those who wish to take advantage of the many developments of paint styling should study the use of colors on the exteriors of new homes and in model rooms that are publicly exhibited in stores, model homes, and illustrated in many magazines. These homes and rooms shape the trends in color styling.

Color experts, designers, and decorators are aware of the way color can deceive the eye. Look across a field at a light-colored house and then at one that is dark-colored. Although they are equidistant and exactly the same size and construction, the light-colored house will appear larger. The same principle can be applied inside a house. Paint the walls and ceiling of one room in a light tint, and the walls and ceiling of another room of equal size in a much darker color, and you will find that the light-colored room seems much larger than the dark-toned one. The "largest" color is yellow, next is red, then green, blue, and finally black.

Then there is the matter of the colors that convey a feeling of warmth: reds, oranges, yellows, and yellow–greens, all of which seem to advance toward you and bring things nearer. The exact opposite is true of the so-called cool colors: blues, violets, blue–greens, and blue–grays seem to retreat and push things away.

Some colors seem heavier than others, for instance, deep colors compared to pale colors. The lightest color of all, of course, is white, and the heaviest is black. Same-sized objects painted in white seem to be much lighter in weight than those painted in black or dark colors.

All of these factors are taken into consideration when employing the principles of paint styling. The most important point of all, however, is the emphasizing of good features and the minimizing of bad ones.

Paint Styling Exteriors

Paint styling as a method of minimizing defects can be applied effectively to the selection of a color scheme for the outside of a house (Fig. 12). Protruding chimneys that are visible from the outside as they rise from the ground to the roof are usually large at their base. If a chimney is too large in proportion to the size of the house, painting it the same color as the house will make it blend with the background color. Its size will then be less noticeable (Fig. 13).

Fig. 12. Examples of how intelligent paint styling will improve the appearance of houses.

A chimney that is too small and weak-looking in comparison to the house will also benefit visually from being painted the same color as the house.

When the roof line of the house is cut up by too many gables, paint everything on the roof dark to offset the disadvantage. Do not paint dormers or chimneys in colors that will draw

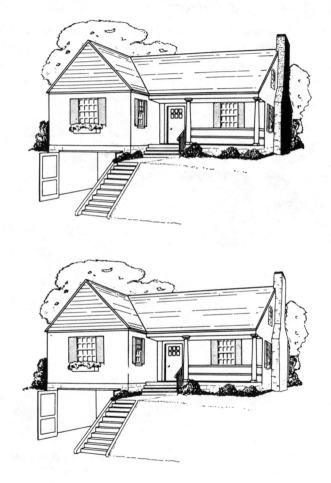

Fig. 13.   Upper illustration shows a house with a chimney that is too large; lower illustration shows the same house with camouflaged chimney.

the eye to this area of least attractiveness. In addition, draw the eye away from the roof by featuring the front door and the shutters on the lower floor with eye-holding hues of some attractive color.

If dormers stick out too much or not enough they can be visually lost by painting them the same color as the roof. Should it not be necessary to conceal the dormers, a small house can be made to seem larger by painting the dormer faces the color of the side wall. This carries the wall color right up into the roof and gives the appearance of additional height (Fig. 14).

Dormers on a tall house should be painted the same dark color as the roof, so that they visually become part of the roof and not the side walls. This tends to make the house seem lower.

Fig. 14.   Painting dormers the same color as the roof helps considerably.

When a house seems too high for its width, it can be lowered visually by painting the roof a darker color (Fig. 15). Dark roofs seem to sink toward the ground. If a tall house has shutters, those of the upper story should be the same color or tone as the roof. This visually brings the roof lines still lower, as the eye will travel to the bottom line of the dark upper shutters. Paint the remaining shutters the color of the body of the house. If the second-story windows are directly above those on the first floor, as is usually the case, painting all the shutters the same dark tone will give vertical lines to the house, accentuating its height just as vertically striped wallpaper tends to make a room seem higher.

The dark shutters upstairs and the light ones downstairs tend to emphasize the horizontal, ground-hugging lines.

A house with different sized window openings or shapes is likely to look jumbled if the windows are emphasized by a color different from the walls. Conceal this defect by painting windows the same color as the house and removing the shutters from all small windows that are dissimilar in area, leaving only those that are larger and more uniform in size (Fig. 16).

Fig. 15.   A small house that appears too high (top) may be "lowered" by painting the roof and shutters of the upper story a dark color.

Fig. 16. A simple color effect helps conceal windows of various shapes.

Introducing too many varied building materials can also break up the overall unity of a house. The exterior of a house can be greatly improved by applying established principles of paint styling. The house shown in the lower right inset of Fig. 17 looked smaller than it actually was because its surface was broken up with too many kinds of materials and colors. The foundation and garage were gray cinder blocks. The wing and chimney were constructed of red brick. A clapboard gable appears on the wing of the house, and the body is stucco. White shutters added little visual interest to the house, while the dark door woodwork and dark chimney further broke up the surfaces. To give the house unity, to increase its apparent size, and to make it look up-to-date, it was paint styled in the following manner:

Parts of the house	*New color*
Entire body and chimney	white
Roof	gray
Shutters (to center interest)	maroon
Front door, new window box, garage interior	straw color
Chimney top	Maroon band (a modern touch

Fig. 17.   Upper illustration shows how paint styling has improved the appearance of the house shown in lower illustration.

The improvement made in the appearance of this house, shown in the upper illustration of Fig. 17, requires no further comment.

The lower left illustration in Fig. 18 shows a house that seemed too high in proportion to its width. The body of this house was white; the roof, light in tone, seemed to take the house up and up, blending it with the light-colored sky. The dark shutters on both floors looked like vertical lines, carrying the line upward and enhancing the impression of height.

By paint styling this house to make it seem lower, the roof was darkened, visually pushing the house closer to the ground. The upper shutters were painted a dark rose tone of the same color depth as the roof, with the lower shutters a light gray. This broke the vertical lines and brought the dark roof still nearer the earth. The body of the house was toned down to a light gray so that its bulk would not be quite so prominent. The definite improvement accomplished by paint styling is shown in upper illustration, Fig. 18.

In paint styling, the way dark and light areas are allocated is the first importance of color. It specifies, in other words, where color interest should be stressed, on what areas it should be modified, and where it should be accentuated. Every house is a separate problem and should be treated as such. If paint styling has been properly planned and executed, the advantages gained will be self-evident.

Fig. 18. Intelligent paint styling improved the appearance of the house shown in the lower illustration.

Paint Styling Interiors

The paint industry, through its Council for Paint Styling, has publicized that certain little-known precepts of color usage can make all the difference. The Council points out that we need no longer be bound by painting and decorating rules that used to seem unbreakable. For instance, it was once thought that all walls in a room had to be given the same color treatment because they were in the same room.

The new conception of the use of color presented by the Council stresses that surfaces should be colored so as to contribute the maximum beauty and utility to a room or the exterior of a house. Among its many suggestions, the following should interest the home owner:

1. If a room seems too small, employ the illusion of increased size made possible by using light colors on the larger surfaces. Paint walls and woodwork in a light color to make them seem larger.

2. If a room seems too large and is well lighted, use the knowledge that dark colors seem to come toward you. Paint the walls in a darker tone. It will make the room seem smaller, friendlier, and more inviting.

3. Then, of course, remember that light tints make rooms lighter by reflecting more of the light that falls upon them, while cool colors make warm rooms seem cooler and vice versa.

The Council for Paint Styling has worked to demonstrate how color can be used as a means of untangling the knotty puzzles caused by unfortunate planning in architecture and decoration. It has shown, for instance, that:

1. Long, narrow rooms can be made to look wider by putting a dark color on the wall at each of the narrow ends and a lighter color on the remaining walls and ceiling (Fig. 19).

2. Rooms that are square and uninteresting in shape can be improved by featuring one wall with a color or pattern that is different from the other three walls, thus providing a focal point of interest. This distinctive color is usually put on the wall that includes a fireplace, if the room has one.

3. Ceilings that look too high can be made to seem lower by painting them in a color darker than the walls (Fig. 20).

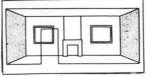

Fig. 19.   Narrow rooms look wider when end walls are painted a darker color.

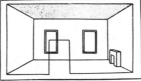

Fig. 20.   High ceilings can be made to seem lower by painting them a darker color than the side walls.

In paint styling interiors, the same technique is employed as for exterior surfaces. Emphasize the good features in a room by painting them in a color, shade, or tint different from the adjoining surfaces. For example, let us assume that the windows and doors in a room are well placed and well proportioned. Paint the woodwork in a lighter tint if the wall surfaces are dark, or dark if the walls are light. Attention will focus on the windows and doors. On the other hand, if the windows and doors are ill proportioned and badly placed, make these defects less noticeable by painting them the same color as the walls.

Radiators and risers benefit by this treatment. When they are painted the same color as the wall against which they are placed they are not nearly as noticeable as when they stand out in contrast to their background.

COLOR DO'S AND DON'TS

DO—Use light colors in a small room to make it seem large.

DO—Aim for a continuing color flow, from room to room, throughout your home by using harmonious colors in adjoining areas.

DO—Paint room ceilings a deeper color than walls if you want them to appear lower; paint ceilings in lighter shades for the opposite effect.

DO—Study color swatches in both daylight and nightlight. Colors often change under artificial lighting.

DON'T—Paint the woodwork and trim of a small room in a color that is different from the background color, or the room will appear cluttered and smaller.

DON'T—Paint radiators, pipes, and similar projections in a color which contrasts with walls or they will be emphasized.

DON'T—Choose neutral or negative colors just because they are safe, or the result will be dull and uninteresting.

DON'T—Use glossy paints on walls or ceilings of living areas since the shiny surface creates glare.

SECTION 3

PREPARING SURFACES FOR PAINTING AND METHODS OF APPLYING PAINT

Since the painting of interior surfaces is most important from the decorative standpoint, care must be taken that a uniform and smooth surface is obtained.

Study the outside of your house thoroughly and carefully. Although you may need a roofing specialist to check your "topside" surfaces, you can discover much for yourself by studying the other materials of your dwelling—wood, cinder block, stucco, brick, tin, iron, copper, or steel.

In order to do a good job with a minimum of trouble, choose the right tools and learn how to handle them properly. The brush, the roller, and the sprayer are the basic tools.

5

Preparing Surfaces
for Painting

Before you brush, roll, or spray a drop of paint, you should perform certain preparations to ensure a good job with a minimum of effort, errors, and spattering. The precautions may seem obvious, but they are often overlooked.

PROTECT OTHER SURFACES

Cover floors and furnishings with drop cloths (Fig. 1.) You can use tarps, old cloth sheets, or inexpensive plastic sheets designed for this purpose.

Fig. 1.   Using a drop cloth.

Clean up as you paint. Wet paint is easy to remove; dry paint is hard to remove. Use turpentine or other thinner to remove oil paint; use water to remove latex.

Caution: If paint is dropped on an asphalt tile floor, *do not* attempt to remove it with mineral spirits or turpentine since this may permanently damage the tile. If the paint will not come off with a dry cloth, let it dry and then scrape it off.

Rub protective cream onto your hands and arms. A film of this cream makes it easier to remove paint from your skin when the job is done. Old gloves or throwaway plastic gloves and aprons are also useful.

CHECK THE CONDITION OF THE PAINT

When you buy new, good quality paint from a reputable store, it is usually in excellent condition. However, after stirring the paint thoroughly (if it should be stirred), you should examine it for lumps, curdling, or color separation. Do not use the paint if any signs of these conditions remain.

Old paints which, when opened, release a foul odor (especially latex paint) or show signs of lumps or curdling, are probably spoiled. Such paint should be discarded.

If there is a "skin" on the surface of the paint when you open the container, remove as much of the hardened film as possible with a spatula or knife (Fig. 2) and strain the paint through cheesecloth or fine wire mesh such as window screening. If you fail to do this, bits of the skin will show up with exasperating frequency to spoil the appearance of your paint job.

FOLLOW DIRECTIONS ON MIXING

New paints are usually ready for use when purchased and require no thinning except when they are to be applied with a sprayer. Ask the advice of the paint store salesman when you buy the paint, *and check the label before you mix or stir.* Some man-

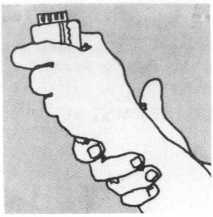

Fig. 2.   Using a scraper.

ufacturers do not recommend mixing as it may introduce air
bubbles. If mixing is required, it can be done at the paint store
by placing the can in a mechanical agitator—or you can do it at
home with a paddle or spatula.

If you open the can and find that the pigment has settled,

Fig. 3.   Stirring pigment.

use a clean paddle or spatula to gradually work the pigment up from the bottom of the can, using a circular stirring motion (Fig. 3). Continue until the pigment is thoroughly and evenly distributed, with no signs of color separation.

If the settled layer proves to be hard or rubbery, and resists stirring, the paint is probably too old and should be discarded.

PROTECT THE PAINT BETWEEN JOBS

Between jobs, even if only overnight, cover the paint container tightly to prevent evaporation and thickening, and to protect it from dust. Oil base and alkyd paints may develop a skin from exposure to the air.

When you finish painting, clean the rim of the paint can thoroughly and put the lid on tightly. To ensure that the lid is airtight, cover the top and rim of the can with a piece of cloth or plastic film (to prevent spattering) and tap the lid firmly into place with a hammer (Fig. 4).

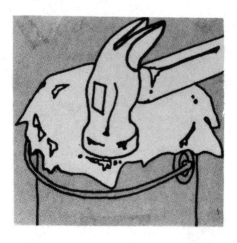

Fig. 4.   Airtight lid.

PREPARATION OF SURFACE

The finest paint, applied with the greatest skill, will not produce a satisfactory finish unless the surface has been properly prepared. The basic principles are simple although they vary somewhat with different surfaces and, to some extent, with different paints. The goal, however, is always the same—to provide a surface with which the paint can form a strong, permanent bond.

In general, proceed as follows:

1. The surface must be clean, smooth, and free from loose particles such as dust or old paint. Use sandpaper, a wire brush, or a scraper to accomplish this. (*See* Figs. 5, 6, and 7.)

2. Oil and grease should be removed by wiping the surface with mineral spirits. If a detergent is used, a thorough rinse with clean water should follow. (Fig. 8).

3. Chipped or blistered paint should be removed with sandpaper, a wire brush, steel wool, or a scraper.

4. Chalked or powdered paint should be removed with a stiff bristled brush, or by scrubbing with water mixed with household washing soda or TSP (trisodium phosphate, sold in hardware stores). If the old surface is relatively firm, an oil primer can be applied without the prior use of a stiff brush. The primer rebinds the loose particles and provides a solid base for the paint.

5. Loose, cracked, or shrunken putty or calk should be removed by scraping.

6. If new putty, glazing compound, calking compounds, and sealants are used, they should be applied to a clean surface and allowed to harden before paint is applied. (*See* Figs. 9 and 10.) If the calk is a latex type, latex paint can be applied over it immediately without waiting for the calk to harden.

7. Damp surfaces must be allowed to dry before paint is applied, unless you are using a latex paint.

8. Make sure *wallboard panels* are securely nailed or adhered in place. If the panel joints have not been taped and filled, this should be done before painting. When joint cement and/or

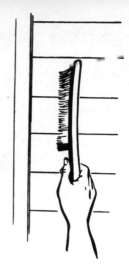

Fig. 5.   Use of brush.

Fig. 6.   Using sandpaper.

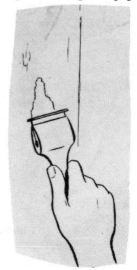

Fig. 7.   Using scraper.

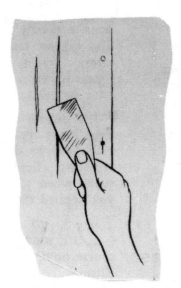

Fig. 8.   Removing oil or grease.

Fig. 9.   Filling cracks and nail head indentations.

patching materials are thoroughly dry, sand them smooth. Some paints require a primer before use on new wallboard. Check label directions.

Wood

Preparations especially for wood are as follows:

1. Scrape clean all areas where sap (resin) has surfaced on the wood and sand smooth prior to application of knot sealer. Small, dry knots should also be scraped and thoroughly cleaned, and then given a thin coat of knot sealer before applying wood primer.

2. Fill cracks, joints, crevices, and nail holes with glazing compound, putty, or plastic wood and sand lightly until the surface of these spots is flush with the surface of the wood. (*See* Fig. 9.) Always sand in the direction of the grain—never across it.

3. New wood surfaces to be stain-finished should first be sanded smooth. Open grain (porous) wood should be coated with paste filler before the stain is applied. (Paste fillers come in various matching wood colors.) The surface should then be re-sanded. Read the manufacturer's instructions carefully before applying paste fillers.

As soon as **new wood** is exposed to weather it should be primed. If unpainted wood has been allowed to weather for any length of time (even as short as one week), it should be sanded down to fresh wood and undercoated for the best adhesion.

Seal all open joints, seams, and corners with calking compound to keep water and bugs out, heat and air-conditioning in. (*See* Figs. 10, 11, and 12.)

Masonry

Preparations especially for masonry are as follows:

1. Surfaces such as plaster, gypsum, cement, and drywall should be dry and clean. If the surface is cracked, sand it smooth and then fill with spackling compound or some other recom-

Fig. 10.   Calking.

Fig. 11.   Calking.

Fig. 12.   Calking.

mended crack filler. After the repaired surface is dry, sand
lightly until smooth—then wipe clean.

2. Allow new plaster to dry for 30 days before painting.

3. Roughen unpainted concrete and stucco with a wire
brush to permit a good bond between the surface and the paint.

4. Wash new concrete surfaces with detergent and water to remove any film left by oil, or the compound used for hardening the concrete during the curing process.

5. Remove efflorescence, the crystalline deposit which appears on the the mortar between bricks, by using undiluted vinegar or a 5-percent muriatic acid solution. After scrubbing with acid, rinse the surface thoroughly. *Caution:* When using muriatic acid, wear goggles and gloves for protection.

Metal

1. Clean new metal surfaces such as galvanized steel, aluminum, or tin with a solvent such as mineral spirits to remove the oil and grease applied as a metal preservative by manufacturers.

2. Remove rusted or corroded spots by wire-brushing or with coarse sandpaper. Chemical rust removers are also available from paint and hardware stores. Paint will not adhere well when applied over rusted or corroded surfaces.

3. Allow galvanized steel, such as that used for roof gutters, to weather for about six months before painting. If it is necessary to paint sooner, wash the surface with mineral spirits or VM&P (Varnish Makers & Painters) naphtha, then apply a primer recommended specifically for galvanized surfaces.

Before you paint exterior surfaces, thoroughly inspect and check the surface condition of window and door frames and the surrounding areas, the bases of porch and entranceway, steps, siding, downspouts, under-cave areas, and any areas where moisture is likely to collect.

Check the Weather

You can easily ruin your paint job if you forget to consider the weather. Excessive humidity or extremely cold weather can cause trouble. Good ventilation, regardless of the weather, is essential.

Specifically, follow these guidelines:

1. Unless you are using latex paint, you should not paint on

damp days. A moist painting surface may prevent good bonding.

2. If humidity is high, check the surface before painting. If you can feel a film of surface moisture, it would be better to wait for a drier day. If you are painting inside and the area is air-conditioned, however, neither rain nor humidity will affect the job.

3. Exterior painting is not recommended if the temperature is below 50°F or above 95°F, since extreme temperatures may prevent a good bond. This is especially critical if you are using latex paint.

4. If conditions are borderline, good ventilation will help paint to dry. Allow more drying time in damp or humid weather. The label on the can will tell you the normal drying time, but test the surface by touch before you apply another coat. When paint is thoroughly dry, it is firm to the touch and not sticky.

6

Paint Application Methods

The most common methods of applying paint are by brush, roller, and spray. Of the three, brushing is the slowest method, rolling is much faster, and spraying is usually the fastest of all. The choice of method is based on many additional factors such as environment, substrate, the kind of coating to be applied, finish desired, and skill of the personnel involved.

Roller coating is most efficient on large flat surfaces. Corners, edges, and odd shapes, however, must be brushed. Spraying also is most suitable for large surfaces, except that it can also be used for round or irregular shapes. Brushing is ideal for small surfaces or for cutting in corners and edges. Dip and flow coat methods are suitable for the volume production painting of small items in the workshop.

The surroundings may prohibit spray application because of possible fire hazards or potential damage from overspray. Adjacent areas, not to be coated, must be masked when spraying is performed. This precaution takes time and, if extensive, may offset the advantage of the speediness of spraying.

Spraying nevertheless has particular advantages. Rapid drying, lacquer products such as vinyls should be sprayed. Application of such products by brush or roller may be extremely difficult especially in warm weather or outdoors on breezy days. Coatings applied by brush may leave brush marks in the dried film; rolling leaves a stippled effect, while spraying yields the smoothest finish, if done properly.

INTERIOR SURFACES

Flat paint gives the most uniform appearance, for the low sheen helps hide surface irregularities. Gloss gives the longest lasting finish and is easiest to clean.

WALLS, WOODWORK, CEILINGS, AND FLOORS

Interior Paint

Walls. Latex and oil and alkyd paints, in flat and gloss, for use on walls are available at several price levels. Latex can be applied directly to wallboard, wood, masonry, and walls previously painted with latex or oil and alkyd. You can use oil and alkyds directly on wood and previously painted walls. Always prime plaster and any loose and powdery or badly worn areas. Sound wallpaper may be painted over, although it should be removed to avoid any changes from peeling or bubbling.

Woodwork. Bare or previously finished woodwork can be coated with latex or oil and alkyd paints. Because gloss paint is more durable than flat, it is often chosen for woodwork, which takes more abuse. However, painting woodwork with the same flat paint used on the adjacent walls gives a perfect color match and is very satisfactory for moderate wear and tear.

Ceilings. Ceilings look best when painted with specially formulated ceiling paint. Important features are that this flat finish paint minimizes lap marks and glare; has minimum spatter; is non-yellowing; hides surface irregularities; and fills hairline cracks. Ceiling paint may also be used on walls, when a dead flat, white paint is desired.

Floors. Floor enamel can be used on wood, concrete, and metal surfaces. Both latex and oil and alkyd enamels are available. They tolerate abrasion, heavy traffic, and repeated scrubbing, as well as providing some slip resistance.

Special Finishes

Metal paints. Iron and steel must be primed for best results, then finished with either latex or oil and alkyd paint. A variety of special metal finishes, which combine primer and topcoat, are also available.

Masonry paints (For cement, concrete block and brick). Rubber-base paint and cement paint are both good for basement walls; rubber base paint being the best for waterproofing. Ordinary latex wall paint is fine for masonry walls above ground.

Texture paint. Texture paint is a heavy paint that hides small cracks, bumps, and hollows on a wall or ceiling. It can easily be textured into a variety of patterns.

Fire-retardant paint. The prime purpose of this paint is to delay the advance of fire to allow sufficient evacuation time; preventing structural damage is secondary. In contact with fire or extreme heat, this paint puffs up to form an insulation which prevents the surface underneath from reaching its burning point for a certain period of time.

Interior Stains and Varnishes

Interior stain enhances the beauty of natural wood. It lets grain and texture show through while tinting the wood to the color or wood tone of your choice. Inexpensive wood can often be matched, by staining, to rare, exotic, and expensive wood. Stain is for use on bare wood or wood that has been treated only with a sealer. After staining, coat the surface with varnish to make it more durable and easier to clean.

Interior varnish produces a clear, tough film that protects wood surfaces. There are three basic kinds of varnish: alkyd, urethane, and spar. Alkyd is excellent for surfaces that receive little or moderate wear, such as furniture, cabinets, paneling. Urethane has the best durability and chemical resistance. It is ideal for use on floors and other areas that get abuse. Spar has the best sun and water resistance. Use it on surfaces such as window sills. Varnish comes in both gloss and satin (dull) finishes so that it can be either obvious or unobtrusive.

Primers, Sealers, Wood Fillers

Primers and sealers are built to do what a finish coat just cannot do well—stick to plaster and loose or powdery paint and rust; seal wallboard, brick, masonry, wood, stucco, and stone; and dry very fast.

Wood filler is used on open-grained woods (like oak) to fill tiny cracks so the surface is absolutely smooth, and to prevent dust and dirt from settling in the cracks and discoloring the finish.

Tools for Interior Painting

For a detailed discussion of the tools used for interior painting, refer to Chapter 3.

Figuring the Amount of Paint You Need

Use the following instructions to determine the amount of paint you need, or have your dealer calculate for you, free of charge.

The perimeter of a room (the total distance around the edges of a room) multiplied by the height (floor to ceiling) gives the total area in square feet. If you are using a different coating for the trim, subtract from your total the area of doors (approximately 21 square feet each) and windows (approximately 15 square feet each). Ceiling area is the length times the width of the room.

Divide your total wall area by 400 square feet, which is the area one gallon of paint will cover. The result will be the number of gallons required for one coat. Use the same procedure to figure out how much trim paint and ceiling paint you will need.

Example:
    A room is 12 by 15 feet, with an eight-foot high ceiling. It has two doors and two windows. The walls are to be painted in a flat paint, the trim in a glossy paint, and the ceiling in ceiling paint.

Wall area including doors and windows is:

$$54 \quad \times \quad 8 \quad = \quad 432 \text{ square feet}$$
$$\text{(perimeter)} \qquad \text{(height)}$$

Trim area is:

$$42 \quad + \quad 30 \quad = \quad 72 \text{ square feet}$$
$$\text{(2 doors)} \qquad \text{(2 windows)}$$

Wall area excluding doors and windows is:

$$432 - 72 = 360 \text{ square feet}$$

Ceiling area is:

$$15 \quad \times \quad 12 \quad = \quad 180 \text{ square feet}$$
$$\text{(length)} \qquad \text{(width)}$$

Amount of paint required is:

For walls: Approximately 1 gallon

$$400 \overline{)360}$$

For trim: Approximately 1/5 gallon (buy 1 quart)

$$400 \overline{)72}$$

For ceiling: Approximately 1/2 gallon (buy two quarts)

$$400 \overline{)180}$$

Order of Painting a Room

Where to start. If ceiling and walls of a room are to be painted, do the ceiling first. Start in a corner and cut in (apply a 2-inch strip of paint) where walls and ceiling meet (Fig. 1).

Ceiling. Use a ladder or long-handled roller to paint ceilings. Always start in a corner and work parallel to the shortest side of the room, but paint as wide a strip as possible. Avoid spinning the roller by going too fast.

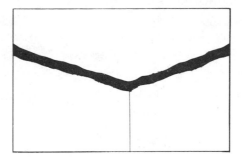

Fig. 1.   Where to start painting ceiling and walls.

Woodwork, then walls. If woodwork and walls are to be painted, paint the woodwork first. Then cut in around the edges of the woodwork and where the walls meet the ceiling. Use a roller to apply paint to walls. (*See* Fig. 2.) Roll as close to the edge of the woodwork as possible, since a roller coating has a different texture and color effect from a brush.

Floor. Start in a corner diagonally across from the room exit. Use a brush to cut in where walls and floor meet. Then use either a wide brush (4 inches) or a roller with an extension handle to paint the floor. (The roller is easiest and fastest.)

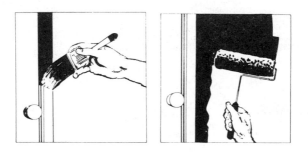

Fig. 2.   Painting woodwork and walls.

Interior Painting Methods

Cover furniture and floors with plastic drop cloths. Remove draperies, pictures, mirrors, switch and receptacle plates, and all hardware. Loosen lighting fixtures or cover with masking tape.

Correct brush use. Dip half the length of the bristles into the paint. Tap the brush gently against the side of the can, but do not wipe it across the tip. (*See* Fig. 3.)

Hold the brush comfortably near the base of the handle,

Fig. 3. Correct brush use for interior painting.

Fig. 4. Holding a brush.

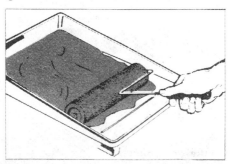

Fig. 5. Correct roller use for interior painting.

exerting light pressure with your fingertips (Fig. 4). Do not bear down, but exert enough pressure to make the bristles flex slightly toward the tip as you begin the brush stroke.

Correct roller use. Roll slowly into the well or deeper end of tray. Roll back and forth until roller is well covered with paint. Then, roll onto the ridges in the upper, more shallow portion of the tray and lightly roll back and forth to remove excess paint. (*See* Fig. 5.)

Cover about four square feet (.4 square meters) with each full roller load. That is about 400 square feet (36 square meters) per gallon. This application rate can be best judged by using the "N" roller pattern technique. (*See* Fig. 6.)

1. Roll out the letter "N" as shown.

2. Cross roll to spread paint.

3. Finish with light roller strokes in one direction, but at a right angle to the cross roll.

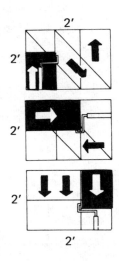

Fig. 6. Roller pattern technique.

Windows. See Fig. 7a for the parts of a window. Raise the inside sash and lower the outside sash. Paint the inside sash; first the crossbars, then the frame. Do not paint the top edge of the inside sash, as you will use that surface to move the sash. Next, paint the outside sash (crossbars, then frame), but do not paint the bottom edge. (*See* Fig. 7.)

Fig. 7. Interior of a window.

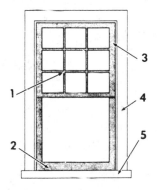

**Fig. 7a. Parts of a window and the correct painting order:
(1) mullions, (2) horizontal of sash, (3) verticals of sash, (4) verticals of frame, (5) horizontal frame and sill.**

Move the sashes to within about one inch of their closed positions. Paint the parts of the outside sash that were previously obstructed. Also paint the top edge of the inside sash. Next paint the window casing and then the sill. (*See* Fig. 8.)

When the paint is dry, move both sashes down as far as they will go. Paint the upper part of the check rails. When the paint is thoroughly dry, raise both sashes and paint the lower check rails. (*See* Fig. 9.)

For casement windows (windows that open out or in, rather than up), open them and paint the top, side, and bottom edges first. Finish with the cross bars, frames, casings, and sills. (*See* Fig. 10.)

Fig. 8.   **Painting a window.**

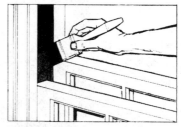

Fig. 9.   **Painting a window.**

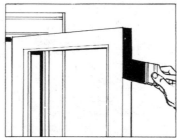

Fig. 10.   **Painting a casement window.**

Doors. Start by painting the top panels. Paint the molding edges and then do the remaining panel area by brushing first across, then up and down. (*See* Fig. 11.)

After doing all panels, paint the remaining area. (*See* Fig. 11.) and finish with the door edges. If the door swings in, paint the lock-side edge. If it swings out, paint the hinged edge.

Paint doors that are flush the same way you would do a wall or other flat surface, painting the edges first.

Fig. 11.   Painting the inside of a door.

Cleaning Up

To keep your paint tools and accessories in good condition and ready to reuse requires only a little extra attention at the end of the day or the job.

If latex paint was used, clean brushes, rollers, other tools and hands with soap and water (Fig. 12). If an oil/alkyd paint,

Fig. 12.   Cleaning paint tools and accessories.

stain, or varnish was used, clean with paint thinner. In either case, first wipe all excess paint from the brush or roller onto newpaper to be discarded.

Keep left-over paint for touch-ups. The air trapped inside covered cans of paint can cause a skin to form, but this is easily removed when you are ready to use the paint again. To provide the best seal and minimize skin formation, place a sheet of thin plastic wrap or other light plastic under the can lid before replacing it. Be sure the lid is tapped down securely.

If one-third or less of the paint is left in the container, transfer it to a smaller receptacle that will be completely filled. Label the new container. For safety, never leave an unlabelled container of paint around the house.

Maintenance

Paints, stains, and varnishes can be cleaned with a mild detergent and water. Avoid using abrasive cleaners since they usually remove paint as well as dirt or stains.

EXTERIOR SURFACES

You can add beauty and protection to your house with minimal effort using exterior finishes for siding and trim, plus special paints for masonry, metal, and floor surfaces.

Exterior Coatings

A variety of latex and oil and alkyd paints in flat and gloss are available. Flat paint gives the most uniform appearance, for the low sheen helps hide surface irregularities. Gloss paint gives the longest lasting finish and is easiest to clean.

Exterior Paint

Wood surfaces. Latex and oil and alkyd paints in flat and gloss for use on wood are available at several price levels. They can be used on siding and trim, on smooth or rough sawn wood, on houses, fences, tool sheds, and so on.

Masonry surfaces. Masonry surfaces such as concrete, cement, brick, stucco, and asbestos can be painted with latex paints, which have excellent resistance to alkali and moisture.

Metal surfaces. Latex paints can be applied to metal surfaces such as gutters, flashing, and aluminum siding.

Floors. Floor enamels can be used on wood, concrete, and metal surfaces. Both latex and oil and alkyd enamels are available. They resist abrasion, heavy traffic, repeated scrubbing, and weather.

Exterior Stains and Varnishes

Stains. Stains are the finish for you if you want the beauty of natural wood. Exterior stains are used on wood siding, shingles, fences, garden furniture, and the like, and they are available in semi transparent and solid (opaque) colors.

Latex stains are more durable and retain their color longer than oil and alkyd stains. Oil and alkyd stains, however, take to wood evenly and leave a more uniform appearance.

Solid color stains are like thin house paint. They can hide a previous color stain but are not thick enough to hide the texture of rough wood. Semi transparent stains are a tint—they give color to wood without hiding texture or grain. They can only be used over bare wood or wood previously given a semi-transparent stain.

Varnishes. Exterior varnishes produce a tough, flexible film that protects the surface from severe weather conditions while not hiding the surface's appearance and color. There are different varieties for wood and metal surfaces. Since varnish is clear and lets light through to the surface, eventually there is a loss of adhesion between varnish and surface. As a result, varnish on exterior surfaces must be stripped after a number of years and reapplied.

Primers, Preservatives, Water Repellents

Primers are made for wood, masonry, and metal. Wood primers give extra protection against moisture, cracking, splitting, and staining. Metal primers help prevent corrosion. Primers will stick to surfaces that a top coat will not. The dried primer film provides outstanding flexibility over surfaces subject to contraction and expansion from temperature change.

Preservatives can only be used on bare wood. This clear finish protects against insect and fungus damage. Some preservatives are also waterproof and will protect the surface from warping. Certain preservatives can be painted over.

Water repellents are clear coatings which help prevent water seepage through exterior wood and masonry surfaces. They are especially important for stucco and brick.

Tools for Exterior Painting

For fast painting, spraying equipment may be rented or purchased. (*See* Chapter 3.) In less than a day an average-sized house can be sprayed with paint or stain. Written operating instructions are a must, and it is helpful to practice first on an inconspicuous part of the house. Two kinds of sprayers are available: the kind which mixes air and paint, and the "airless" sprayer, generally considered best for house exteriors.

Figuring the Amount of Paint You Need

Use the instructions here to determine the amount of paint you need, or have your paint store calculate for you, free of charge.

The perimeter of a house (distance around the house) multiplied by its height gives the total area (in square feet) below the roof line. For each pitched roof or gable, multiply the height of the peak, from the roof base, by half the base. Add the peak area square footage to the square footage below the roof line for a total.

In our example (*See* Fig. 13), the perimeter is 40 + 20 + 40 + 20 = 120. The total area to be painted is calculated as follows:

Area below the roof line:

$$120 \times 12 = 1440$$
(perimeter)   (height)

Gables:

8 ×	10 × 2	=	160
(height of peak)	(1/2 length of base)		
(no gables)			

Total   1,600 square feet

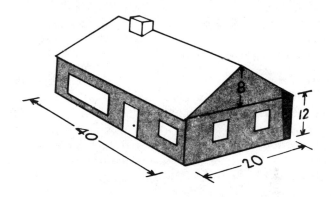

Fig. 13.   Figuring out the amount of paint needed for your house.

If you are using a different coating for the trim, subtract from your total the area of doors (approximately 21 square feet each) and window frames (approximately 15 square feet each).

If you intend to paint gutters, assume that each running length equals a square foot of area. Add that square footage to either the house paint square footage or trim square footage.

Divide your total by 400 square feet, which is the area one gallon of paint will cover. The result will be the number of gallons required for one coat.

Example:

$$
\begin{array}{r}
4 \text{ gallons} \\
400 \overline{\smash{)}1600} \\
\underline{1600} \\
0
\end{array}
$$

Exterior Paint Problems

Paint problems must be corrected before repainting or they will probably recur. The most common problems (peeling, flaking, blistering, redwood and cedar staining, checking, cracking, alligatoring, nailhead staining, peeling gutters, flaking and chalking on masonry, and pollution) are discussed in Chapter 14, *Paint Failures.*

Preparing the Surface

A properly prepared surface is essential not only because the paint job will look better but because it will adhere better, and last longer. The paint needs a clean, solid, dry surface to stick to.

New wood. As soon as new wood is exposed to weather it should be primed. If unpainted wood has been allowed to weather for any length of time (even as little as one week), it should be sanded down to fresh wood and undercoated for best adhesion.

Seal all open joints, seams, and corners with calking compound to keep water and bugs out, and to hold heat and air-conditioning.

Previously painted wood. Check for areas in need of repair, and take the steps necessary to remedy. Remove dirt by dusting or washing. Scrubbing with detergent may be necessary on areas where dirt is embedded. Areas protected from weather (under eaves, overhangs, porch ceilings, and others) should be washed with detergent and rinsed well, even if they look clean. This removes the invisible salt deposits leached out of paint by dew or condensation. Remove and replace loose, worn out, or dry putty around glass.

Concrete and concrete block. Clean off loose dirt and other foreign matter. All cracks, breaks, and voids should be filled with the proper patching materials before applying a finish coat. Primer is generally not required.

Allow newly poured concrete to weather for a few years. Fill new concrete block with latex filler and coat with latex house paint.

Stucco. Remove any loose or powdery material. Seal new,

weathered, and powdery stucco with a clear conditioner before painting.

Brick. Remove and replace any loose mortar. Allow new brick to age one year before applying two coats of latex house paint.

Metal. Metal surfaces must be clean and free of loose paint and rust. Prime cleaned iron and steel with metal primer. New galvanized metal or aluminum should be wiped with mineral spirits and coated with latex house paint.

Order of Painting a House

Paint the siding of a house first, then the trim. Railings, porches, steps, and the foundation should follow. Finally, paint shutters, screens, and storm windows that can be removed.

Start on the side that is not in direct sunlight. Be sure that no rain clouds are in sight and, if you are using an oil/alkyd paint, that there is no dew on the surface. Begin at the very top and work down. Paint horizontal siding in horizontal strips; vertical siding in vertical strips. Paint as wide an area as you can reach safely and comfortably from your ladder.

Next, paint trim, railings, and so on, as previously described. In this way, you will avoid paint splattering and achieve the neatest possible job.

Exterior Painting Methods

Correct brush use. Dip half the length of the bristles into the paint. Tap the brush gently against the side of the can (Fig. 14), but do not wipe it across the lip.

Hold the brush comfortably near the handle base, applying light pressure with your fingertips. The bristles should flex slightly toward the tip as you begin the stroke, but you should not bear down on the brush.

Correct roller use. A roller speeds application on flat surfaces such as masonry and floors. First, paint the edges with a brush. Paint with a roller up to the edged strip. Roll as close to the edge as possible (Fig. 15), since a roller leaves a different appearance in texture and color from a brush. Paint should be rolled on in

Fig. 14.   Correct brush use for exterior painting.

light, even strokes in different directions. If paint is rolled on too fast, it will spatter.

Side walls. Paint the underside of siding first. Then immediately paint the surface, always working from an unpainted area back into the still-wet paint from immediately preceding strokes. (Failure to maintain a wet edge can lead to unsightly "lap" marks that only an entire second coat of paint will hide.) Spread out the paint with smooth, even strokes. (*See* Figs. 16 and 17.)

Finish a complete side, or at least to a door or window, before stopping for the day. More important, do not start a new can of paint in the middle of a board or large wall area. If the remaining paint in a can will not finish an area, mix it with some new paint with the partially filled can before starting the area. This will help blend the color.

Fig. 15.   Correct roller use for exterior painting.

Windows. Raise the inside sash and lower the outside sash. Paint the outside sash, first the crossbars, then the frame. Do not paint the bottom edge of the outside sash as you will touch its surface to move the sash. Next, paint the inside sash (crossbars, then frame), but do not paint the top edge. (*See* Fig. 18.)

Move the sashes to within about one inch of their closed positions. Paint the parts of the inside sash that were obstructed. Also paint the bottom edge of the outside sash. Next, paint the window casing and then the sill. (*See* Fig. 19.)

When the paint is dry, move both sashes down as far as they will go. Paint the upper part of the checkrails. When the paint is thoroughly dry, raise both sashes and paint the lower checkrails. (*See* Fig. 20.)

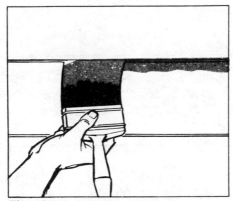

Fig. 16. Painting exterior side walls.

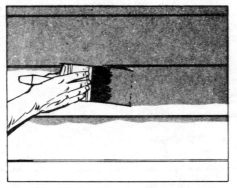

Fig. 17. Finishing exterior side walls.

Fig. 18. Painting the outside sash of a window.

Fig. 19. Painting window sashes.

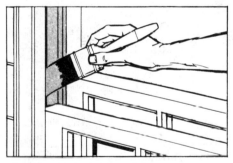

Fig. 20. Painting a window.

For casement windows (windows that open out or in, rather than up), open them and paint the top, side, and bottom edges first (Fig. 21). Finish with the crossbars, frames, casings, and sills.

Doors. Start by painting the top panels. Paint the molding edges first. Then do the remaining panel area by first brushing across, then up and down.

After doing all the panels, paint the remaining area and finish with the door edges. (*See* Fig. 22.) If the door swings out, paint the lockside edge with exterior paint. If it swings in, paint the hinged edge with exterior paint.

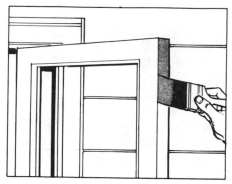

Fig. 21.   Painting a casement window.

Fig. 22.   Painting doors.

Fig. 23.   Painting porch and steps.

Paint flush doors as you would do a wall or other flat surface, painting the edges first and then filling in the large area. Complete the job by doing the door frame and jambs.

Porches and steps. Start at the back, farthest from the steps or entrance. Paint the edges first, then work toward the center and front. (*See* Fig. 23.)

On steps, paint the underside of the step extension first, then do the back panel (Fig. 23.) Finish with the horizontal surface.

Cleaning up

To keep your paint tools and accessories in good condition and ready to reuse requires only a little extra attention at the end of the day or the job.

If latex paint was used, clean brushes, rollers, other tools, and your hands with soap and water. If an oil/alkyd paint was used, clean with paint thinner. In either case, first wipe all excess paint from brush or roller onto newspaper to be discarded.

Keep left-over paint for touch-ups. The air trapped inside covered cans of paint can cause a skin to form, but this is easily removed when you are ready to use the paint again. To provide the best seal and minimize skin formation, place a sheet of thin plastic wrap or other light plastic under the can lid before replacing it. Be sure the lid is tapped down securely.

If one-third or less of the paint is left in the container, transfer it to a smaller receptacle that will be completely filled. Label the new container. For safety, never leave an unlabeled container of paint around the house.

Maintenance

Paints, stains, and varnishes can be cleaned with a mild detergent and water. Avoid using abrasive cleaners since they usually remove paint as well as dirt or stains.

7

Brush Painting

The use of a brush assures good contact of paint with pores, cracks, and crevices. Brushing is particularly recommended for applying primer coats and exterior paints.

BRUSH AND PAINT APPLICATION

In selecting a *brush*, you should choose one that is wide enough to cover the area in a reasonable amount of time. If you are painting large areas such as exterior or interior walls or a floor, you will want a wide brush—probably 4 or 5 inches in width. If you are painting windows or trim, you will want a narrow brush so that you can efficiently cover comparatively narrow surfaces —probably 1 to 1½ inches in width.

The bristles should be reasonably long and thick, so that they will hold a good amount of paint, and flexible, so that you can stroke evenly and smoothly.

Generally speaking, a medium-priced brush is the best investment if you only have occasional jobs of painting.

Select the best kind of *paint pot* for brush painting—a one-gallon paint can from which the lip around the top has been removed. (The lid of the can is fitted to the lip around the top.) You can cut this lip off with a cold chisel. If you leave the lip on the pot, it will fill up with paint as you scrape the brush, and this paint will continually drip down the side of the pot.

Dip the brush to only one-third the length of the bristles, and scrape the surplus paint off the lower face of the brush, so there will be no drip as you transfer the brush from the pot to the work.

Here is how to apply paint by brush. For complete coverage, first "lay on," then "lay off." Laying on means applying the paint first in long, horizontal strokes. Laying off means crossing your first strokes by working up and down. (*See* Fig. 1.)

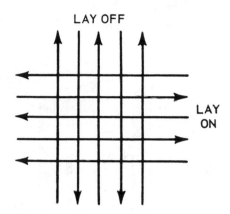

Fig. 1. **Laying on and laying off.**

By using the laying on and the laying off method of crossing your strokes, the paint is distributed evenly over the surface, the surface is completely covered, and a minimum amount of paint is used. A good rule is to "lay on" the paint the shortest distance across the area and "lay off" the longest distance. When painting walls, or any vertical surface, "lay on" in horizontal strokes, "lay off" vertically.

Always paint ceilings first and work from the farthest corner. By painting the ceiling first, you can keep the walls free of drippings by wiping up as you go along.

When painting ceiling surfaces, you will find that ceiling coats should normally be "lay on" for the shortest ceiling distance and "lay off" for the longest distance.

To avoid brush marks when finishing up a square, use strokes directed toward the last square finished. Near the end of the stroke, while the brush is still in motion, gradually lift it from the surface. Every time the brush touches the painted surface at the start of a stroke, it leaves a mark. For this reason, never finish a square by brushing toward the unpainted area; always end by brushing toward the area already painted.

When painting pipes and stanchions and narrow straps, beams, and angles, "lay on" paint diagonally as shown in Fig. 2. "Lay off" along the long dimension.

Always carry a rag for wiping drips or smears.

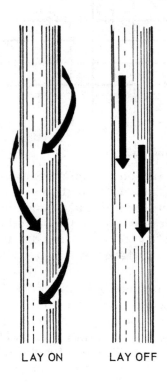

LAY ON   LAY OFF

Fig. 2.   Painting pipes and stanchions.

TYPES OF BRUSHES

Natural Bristle Brushes

Natural bristle brushes are made with hog hair. This kind of brush was originally recommended for applying oil base paints, varnishes, lacquers, and other finishes, because natural fibers resist most strong solvents.

Synthetic Bristle Brushes

Synthetic bristle brushes are made from a synthetic fiber, usually nylon. Today's nylon brushes are recommended for both latex (water soluble) and oil base paints, because this tough synthetic fiber absorbs less water than natural bristles, while also resisting most strong paint and lacquer solvents. In addition, nylon bristles are easier to clean than natural bristles.

Brush Quality

Brush quality determines painting ease, as well as the quality of the finished job. A good brush holds more paint, controls dripping and spattering, and applies paint more smoothly, insuring a minimum of brush marks.

To assure that you are buying a quality brush, check the following factors.

Flagged bristles (Fig. 3) have split ends that help load the brush with more paint, while contributing to a smooth paint flow. Cheaper brushes have less flagging, or none at all.

Tapered bristles (Fig. 4) also help paint flow and release paint smoothly. Check that the base of each bristle is thicker than the tip. This helps give the brush tip a fine painting edge for more even and accurate work.

Fullness is important, too. As you press the bristles against your hand, they should feel full and springy. If the divider in the brush setting is too large, the bristles will feel skimpy, and there will be a large hollow space in the center of the brush.

Bristle length should vary. As you run your hand over the

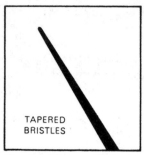

Fig. 3. Tapered bristles.   Fig. 4. Flagged bristles.

bristles, some shorter ones should pop up first, indicating a variety of bristle lengths for better paint loading and smoother release.

A strong setting is important for bristle retention and maximum brush life. Bristles should be firmly bonded into the setting with epoxy glue, and nails should be used only to hold the ferrule to the handle. (*See* Fig. 5.)

The size and shape of a brush are also important. The choice of brush width is determined by the amount of open or flat area to be painted. (*See* Fig. 6.)

CLEANING BRUSHES

A good rule to follow is to clean brushes with the same solvent you used to thin the paint. In other words, oil base paints, enamels, and varnishes generally require turpentine or mineral spirits. Shellacs should be removed with alcohol. Water base paints, such as latex, acrylic, and calcimine paints, should be removed with soap and water. Soak the brush for a few minutes in the appropriate solvent and then squeeze solvent through the brush until it is clean and free of paint.

The proper cleaning procedure is as follows:

1. Remove excess paint by scraping, soak the brush in the proper thinner, and work it against the bottom of the container (Fig. 7).

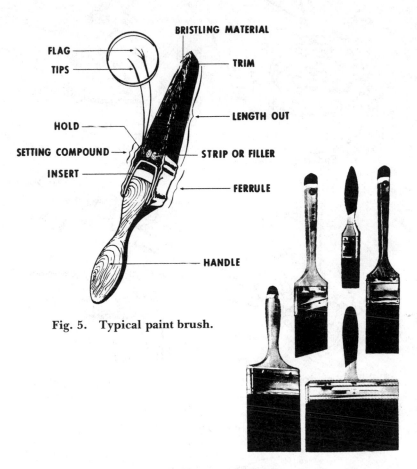

FLAG

TIPS

BRISTLING MATERIAL

TRIM

HOLD

LENGTH OUT

SETTING COMPOUND

INSERT

STRIP OR FILLER

FERRULE

HANDLE

Fig. 5. Typical paint brush.

Fig. 6. Kinds of brushes.

2. To loosen paint in the center of the brush, squeeze the bristles between thumb and forefinger, then rinse again in thinner. If necessary, work the brush in mild soap suds and rinse in clear water (Fig. 8).

3. Press out the water with a stick (Fig. 9).

4. To further remove water, twirl the brush in a container so you will not get splashed (Fig. 10).

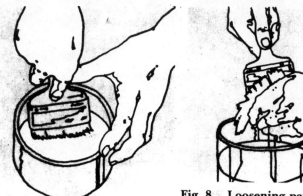

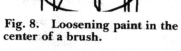

Fig. 7. Soaking a brush.

Fig. 8.   Loosening paint in the center of a brush.

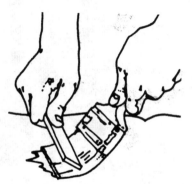

Fig. 9.   Pressing out water from a brush.

Fig. 10.   Twirling a brush in a container.

Fig. 11.   Combing brush bristles.

5. Comb the bristles carefully, including those below the surface (Fig. 11). Allow the brush to dry by suspending it from the handle or by laying it flat on a clean surface. Wrap the dry brush in the original wrapper or in heavy paper to keep the bristles straight. Store suspended by handle or laid flat.

8

Roller Painting

Rollers are being used more and more for painting, especially since a wide variety has become available for different jobs. A roller is a cylinder attached to and rotating around a metal bar which, in turn, is connected to a handle. Rollers range from 1½ to 18 inches long and from ½ to 2½ inches in diameter. The fabric used to cover the cylinder varies according to the paint used; the length of the fuzz or "nap" depends on the texture of the surface. Lamb's wool works well with oil base paints, but becomes matted if used with waterbase paints. Nap lengths can range up to 1½ inches with longer naps most useful for very rough surfaces. Mohair, made from the hair of Angora goats, has nap lengths of $^3/_{16}$ to ¼ inch and it is especially effective with enamels and on smooth surfaces. Two artificial fibers are used on rollers; dynel, with nap lengths of ¼ to 1¼ inches, is extremely good for latex paints; dacron, which is softer than dynel, is suitable for outdoor oil or water (latex) paints. Dacron comes in nap lengths ranging from $^5/_{16}$ to ½ inch. (*See* Table 4, Roller Selection Guide.)

Table 4

Roller Selection Guide

Type of Paint	Smooth (1)	Semi-Smooth (2)	Rough (3)
Aluminum	C	A	A
Enamel or semigloss (Alkyd)	A or B	A	
Enamel undercoat	A or B	A	
Epoxy coatings	B or D	D	D
Exterior house paint			
Latex for wood	C	A	
Latex for masonry	A	A	A
Oil or alkyd—wood	C	A	
Oil or alkyd—masonry	A	A	A
Floor enamel—all types	A or B	A	
Interior Wall paint:			
Alkyd or oil	A	A or D	A
Latex	A	A	A
Masonry sealer	B	A or D	A or D
Metal primers	A	A or D	
Varnish—all types	A or B		

Roller Cover Key*	Nap Length (Inches)		
A—Dynel (modified acrylic)	$\frac{1}{4}-\frac{3}{8}$	$\frac{3}{8}-\frac{3}{4}$	$1-1\frac{1}{4}$
B—Mohair	$\frac{3}{16}-\frac{1}{4}$		
C—Dacron polyester	$\frac{1}{4}-\frac{3}{8}$	$\frac{1}{2}$	
D—Lamb's wool pelt	$\frac{1}{4}-\frac{3}{8}$	$\frac{1}{2}-\frac{3}{4}$	$1-1\frac{1}{4}$

(1) Smooth surface: hardboard, smooth metal, smooth plaster, drywall, etc.

(2) Semismooth surface: sand finished plaster and drywall, light stucco, blasted metal, semismooth masonry.

(3) Rough surface: concrete or cinder block, brick, heavy stucco, wire fence.

*Comprehensive product standards do not exist in the paint roller industry. Roller covers vary significantly in performance between manufacturers and most manufacturers have more than one quality level in the same generic class. This table is based on field experience with the first-line products of one manufacturer.

USING A ROLLER

For a large, flat surface, painting with a roller is easier than brush painting for the average do-it-yourself painter. Select a roller that is comfortable to hold and practice with several dry strokes across the surface. When you buy a roller you will find that it comes as part of a set—the roller itself, and a sloping metal or plastic tray (Fig. 1).

Roller Method

Pour the premixed paint into the tray to about one-half the depth of the tray. Immerse the roller completely, then roll it back and forth along the ramp to fill the cover completely and remove any excess paint. As an alternative to using the tray, place a specially designed galvanized wire screen into a 5-gallon can of the paint. This screen attaches to the can and remains at the correct angle for loading and spreading paint on the roller. (*See* Figs. 1 and 2). The first load of paint on a roller should be worked on newspaper to remove entrapped air from the roller cover. It is then ready for application. As the roller is passed over a surface, thousands of tiny fibers continually compress and expand, metering out the coating and wetting the surface. This is in sharp contrast to other application methods that depend upon the skill and technique of the painter. The uniformity of roller application is less susceptible than other methods to the variable ability of the painter.

Basic rules must still be followed, however. Always trim around ceilings, moldings, and the like, before rolling the major wall or ceiling surface. Then, roll as closely to this edge as possible to maintain the same texture. Trimming is usually done with a 3-inch wall brush. Always roll paint onto the surface, working from the dry area into the just painted area. Never roll completely in the same or one direction. Do not roll too fast and avoid spinning the roller at the end of the stroke. Always feather out the final strokes to pick up any excess paint on the surface. This is accomplished by rolling the final stroke out with minimal pressure.

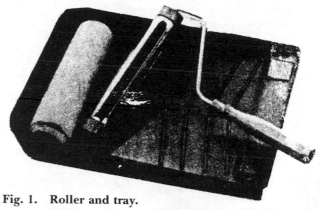

Fig. 1. Roller and tray.

Fig. 2. Can and screen.

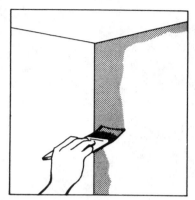

Fig. 3. Brushing a strip.

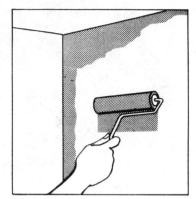

Fig. 4. Using a roller.

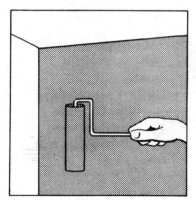

Fig. 5. Using a roller.

Fig. 6. Using a brush at the bottom of a wall.

To paint walls with a roller, proceed as follows:

1. Starting at the upper left-hand corner, brush a strip just below the ceiling line for a width of 2 feet. Also paint a strip along the left edge from the ceiling to the floor. (*See* Fig. 3).

2. Starting in an unpainted area, roll upward toward the painted area (Fig. 4).

3. Complete an area about 2 feet wide and 3 feet deep at a time (Fig. 5).

4. At bottom of the walls, cut in with the brush where you cannot reach with the roller. Use a cardboard guard to protect the woodwork. (*See* Fig. 6.)

ROLLER CARE

Rollers used with alkyd or oil base paints should be cleaned with turpentine or mineral spirits. When latex paint is used, soap and water will clean satisfactorily. If any paint is allowed to dry on the roller, paint remover or a brush-cleaning solvent will be needed.

9

Spray Painting

Paint sprayers are particularly useful for large areas. Spraying is much faster than brushing or rolling and, although some paint is likely to be wasted through overspraying, the savings in time and effort may more than compensate for any additional paint cost. Once you have perfected your spraying technique, you can produce a coating with excellent uniformity of thickness and appearance.

The sprayer can readily cover surface areas accessible to the brush or roller only with difficulty. All coats can be applied satisfactorily by the spray technique *except for the primer coats.* Spraying should be done only on a clean surface since the paint may not adhere well if a dust film is present.

Complete instructions for the care, maintenance, and operation of a spray gun are included in the manufacturer's manual, and these instructions should be carefully followed. Only a few of the major spray painting techniques are given here, as follows:

Spray painting utilizes a pump and, usually, an electric motor to force paint through a nozzle and onto the surface to be painted. In the most common paint sprayer, paint is poured into a closed container called a pot. Compressed air forces the paint through a hose to a spray gun. A separate hose is connected to the spray gun. The paint is then atomized by air blown through an opening in the caps of the spray gun. (*See* Fig. 1.)

A second spraying process is called the airless spray. Airless spray equipment utilizes a hydraulic pump rather than air pressure to force the paint. The pressures are much higher. Atomizing is done by forcing the paint through a fine strainer at

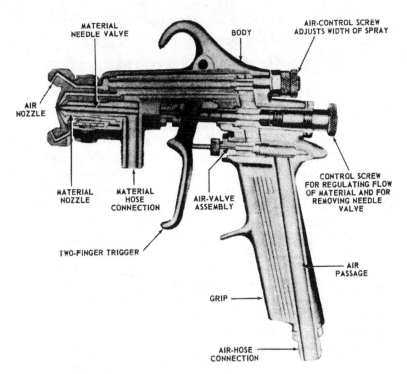

Fig. 1. Cross section of a spray gun.

pressures ranging from 1,500 to 3,000 pounds per square inch. Paint leaves the sprayer at a very high speed and the sudden release of pressure causes the paint to atomize. With this sort of equipment a more uniform paint job is possible.

There are several things to keep in mind when setting up and using spray equipment. The paint must be thin enough to be atomized into a spray, but thick enough to stick to a surface without running or dripping. The air pressure on the pot of paint determines exactly how much paint will flow into the nozzle. If too much air is fed in, the paint will atomize too much and a fine dry spray will be produced. If too little pressure is applied, the paint spatters and leaves a speckled, almost gritty, coat. The air cap on the spray gun controls the amount and distribution of air and how it mixes with the paint. The nozzle on the spray gun controls the amount of paint and air delivered to the surface. The paint's thickness should be changed only if necessary.

SPRAY GUN ADJUSTMENT

Correct adjustment of the air control and material control screws is the first essential in producing the spray best suited to the work at hand. The air control screw adjusts the width and density of the spray. Turning the screw clockwise concentrates the material into a round, more dense spray; turning it counterclockwise widens the spray into a fan-shaped, more diffuse spray. As the spray is widened, the flow of material must be increased; if it is not, the spray will break into a fog. Turning the material control screw clockwise increases the flow of material; turning it counterclockwise decreases the flow. Which spray (ranging from round and solid to fan-shaped and diffused) is most desirable depends upon the character of the surface and the material being sprayed. Experience and experiment are the only real guides here. Practice on waste material, using different adjustments, until a spray is obtained which covers uniformly and adequately.

OPERATIONAL DEFECTS OF THE SPRAY GUN

The clogging of one or more of the air outlets or incorrect adjustment of the air and/or material controls causes uneven distribution of the spray.

Spitting is the alternate discharge of paint and air. Common causes are dried out packing around the material control needle valve, a loose material nozzle, and dirt in the material nozzle seat. To remedy dry packing, back off the material control needle valve and place two drops of machine oil on the packing. To correct looseness of the material nozzle and dirt on the nozzle seat, remove the nozzle, clean both nozzle and seat with thinner, and screw the nozzle tightly back into place.

Air leakage from the front of the gun is usually caused by an improperly seated air valve in the air valve assembly as shown in Fig. 1. Improper seating may be caused by foreign matter on the valve or seat, wear or damage to the valve or seat, a broken valve spring, or a sticky valve stem in need of lubrication.

Paint leakage from the front of the gun is usually caused by improper seating of the material needle valve. Improper seating may be caused by damage to the valve stem or tip, foreign matter on the tip or seat, or a broken valve spring.

SPRAY GUN STROKE

Figure 2 shows the correct method of stroking with a spray gun. Hold the gun six or eight inches from the surface to be painted, keep the axis of the spray perpendicular to the surface, and stroke back and forth in horizontal lines. Pull the trigger just after you start the motion, to avoid applying excess paint at the beginning and end of the stroke.

Figure 3 shows right and wrong methods of spraying an outside corner. If you use the wrong method shown, a good deal of paint will be aimed into thin air and wasted.

SPRAYER CARE

Clean the sprayer promptly after use, before the paint dries. After using oil base or alkyd paints, clean the sprayer with the same solvent used to thin the paint. After using latex paint, clean with detergent and water. Fill the sprayer tank with the cleaning liquid and spray it clean.

If the fluid tip becomes clogged, it can be cleaned with a broom straw. *Never* use wire or a nail to clear clogged air holes in the sprayer tip.

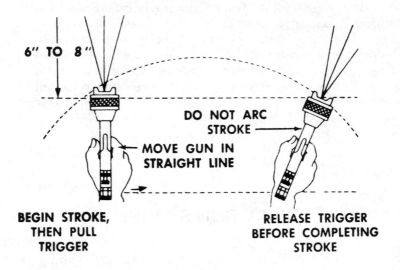

6" TO 8"

DO NOT ARC STROKE →

← MOVE GUN IN STRAIGHT LINE

BEGIN STROKE, THEN PULL TRIGGER

RELEASE TRIGGER BEFORE COMPLETING STROKE

Fig. 2.   Stroking with a spray gun.

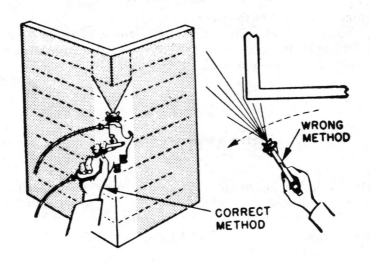

WRONG METHOD

CORRECT METHOD

Fig. 3.   Spraying an outside corner.

LUBRICATION OF THE SPRAY GUN

Your spray gun also needs lubrication. The fluid needle packing should be removed occasionally and softened with oil. (*See* Fig. 4.) The fluid needle spring should be coated with grease or petrolatum.

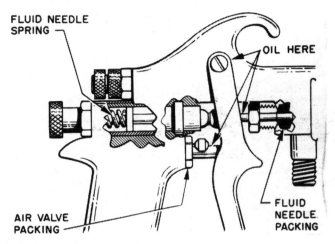

Fig. 4. Lubrication points of a spray gun.

SECTION 4

PAINTING WOODWORK, PAINTING METALWORK, AND PAINTING CONCRETE, MASONRY, AND MISCELLANEOUS SURFACES

Before you brush, roll, or spray a drop of paint, there are certain preparations you should make. These steps will ensure a good job with a minimum of effort, errors, and spattering, whether the surface is woodwork or metalwork; or concrete, masonry, or other surfaces.

Protective coatings are the principal means of controlling metalwork corrosion. The effectiveness of coatings on equipment and structures has considerable influence on the life, safety, operating efficiency, appearance, and economy of projects.

In most instances, the painting of concrete and masonry is done mostly for decorative, lighting, or sanitary purposes rather than to protect and preserve the construction material. Coatings are also used on concrete for waterproofing and dampproofing, and for algae control.

135

10

Painting Woodwork

The expense of maintaining coatings on the woodwork of buildings and residences is not a small item. This chapter tells what materials to use and how to use them for economical woodwork painting.

SELECTION OF PAINTS

Practically all paints and accessory materials required for painting woodwork are adequately covered by federal specifications. Exceptions are sometimes made when small quantities of paint are involved. For these exceptions, good quality stock paints should be procured from well-established paint companies.

In using federal specifications it is necessary to consider amendments and revisions. These are implemented from time to time to keep abreast of developments in formulation and raw materials. The use of materials conforming to the latest revision or amendment is recommended. A list of federal and other specifications for paints and paint materials will be found in Appendix 1.

Paint for Exterior Surfaces

Pigmented paints for exterior wood surfaces are mostly ready-mixed, linseed oil vehicles, although emulsion paints are gaining acceptance. (*See* Appendix 1.)

Light Tints. Exterior oil paint (federal specification TT-P-

102) is used for white and light tints, class A for white and class B for tints. Fume-resistant white paint (federal specification TT-P-103) is pigmented without lead to avoid discoloration from sulfide fumes. The primary pigments of class A and B paints (federal specification TT-P-102) are white lead, zinc oxide, and titanium dioxide. If factory tinted, extender pigments and tinting pigments for class B paints are also included in the total pigment content. When combined in proper proportions these pigments provide optimum hiding power, durability, and repainting characteristics.

Class B differs from class A in that nonchalking titanium dioxide is used in class B. Some chalking is desirable to produce self-cleaning and a good surface for repainting, but chalking must be controlled to obtain a balance with good durability. There should be less chalking in tinted paints than in white paint because it tends to make light colors look faded. The addition of zinc oxide reduces chalking, but too high a proportion introduces early checking and cracking since this substance tends to harden the film. Titantium dioxide substantially adds to the hiding power of the paint and, because of its effectiveness in deflecting the sun's rays from the vehicle binder, adds to durability. Class B paint can be factory tinted or can be obtained as a white base to be tinted on-the-job with pigments in oil.

Although paint pigmented only with white lead has been used successfully in the past, it is now considered less satisfactory than the lead–zinc–titanium mixed-pigment paint. The same applies to paint pigmented with a mixture of white lead and zinc oxide without titanium dioxide. A straight white lead paint lacks hiding power and becomes dirty more rapidly than the mixed-pigment paint.

Pigments in oil and tinting colors (TT-P-381) include a variety of tinting pigments in blacks, browns, greens, oranges, reds, and yellows. These are the colors that your paint store will add to make the stock color conform to the shade you desire. These are concentrated mediums for tinting interior and exterior finishes such as paints, enamels, lacquer, and the new synthetics. In specifying a tinting color or medium, if you cannot give a color number given in the specification as well as the name of the color, you can use a color sample for matching.

Priming paint for use on unpainted wood may be prepared by adding one pint of linseed oil to one gallon of exterior oil paint (TT-P-102) to be used as the finish paint. Raw linseed oil is normally used but boiled oil may be used for faster drying. A special primer (TT-P-25) for exterior wood painting is generally preferred to primer prepared from finish paint. Specially mixed primers give excellent performance and are recommended especially if only two coats of paint are to be used.

Lead-free paint for dwellings may become mandatory in the near future. In this case, suitable materials are covered by federal specifications TT-P-25 (primer) and TT-P-102 (top coat).

Emulsion paints achieved wide popularity for exterior house painting in the 1960s because of their simplicity, good handling qualities, and ease of cleanup. Concurrently, roller application also gained wide usage. These developments speeded application and permitted the average householder to produce better results. However, early latex paints proved markedly less durable than oil base paints in weathering exposures. Thereafter, steady improvement in resins, particularly acrylic resins, and paint formulations have narrowed the gap so that the serviceability of *latex paints* is now believed to approach that of oil base paints. Latex breathing characteristics may also prove advantageous in instances where small amounts of moisture in wood might cause oil paints to adhere poorly. Allowing the moisture vapor to escape through the paint film may forestall peeling, flaking, and blistering. This would apply only to painting new wood, the surface of which lacks an existing impermeable membrane.

Many name-brand latex house paints are available, and most are suitable for both wood and metal (TT-P-96). Wood surfaces should be primed with oil base primer (TT-P-25) because, when applied directly, the water base paint may raise the grain of the wood, and may also dry too rapidly to bond well.

Dark Paints. A variety of pigments, owing to their deep colors, usually impart more hiding power than white and tinted paints. The durability of dark paints is, on the whole, superior to that of light paints because dark pigments are better able to protect the vehicle binder from sunlight. However, some dark paints, especially some greens and blues, are prone to fading that detracts from appearance before the film has otherwise deteriorated seriously. Also, for areas with high exposure to heat, a lighter colored coating may provide longer service than a darker coating because it will reflect more heat, an important factor in surface deterioration. Ready-mixed dark paints for exterior woodwork are described here briefly. Where a close color match is required, it is necessary to provide a sample of the desired color for matching or refer to a specific color number from federal standard No. 595. The following colors are a sample from this standard.

1. *Red and Brown, (TT-P-31)*—This is an iron oxide pigmented paint, often referred to as barn paint. It is suitable for both wood and metal and is noted for excellent durability in ordinary atmospheric exposure.

2. *Yellow, (TT-P-53)*—This paint is available in bright colors ranging from light to medium chrome yellow. It is a durable paint frequently used on signs.

3. *Orange, (TT-P-59)*—The color of this paint is orange–red, commonly referred to as international orange. It is a durable paint, but it is inclined to fade on exposure. It is used on high towers and elevated tanks in an alternating or checkerboard pattern with white paint for aircraft warning.

4. *Black, (TT-P-61)*—This is a very durable paint for outside exposure, and, being black, it has exceptionally good hiding power.

5. *Chrome–Green, (TT-P-71)*—This is a trim enamel, with a large percentage of spar varnish in the vehicle. It dries smooth and glossy, retains its gloss well, and is better than the average green paint in resistance to fading. However, this is usually a rather slow drying paint and ample time for thorough drying should be allowed.

6. *Deep Colors, (TT-P-37)*—This alkyd resin paint is available in a variety of deep colors for application to properly primed wood and metal surfaces.

7. *Enamels, (TT-P-489), Class A*—Occasionally, a full gloss enamel finish is desired on exterior woodwork. This specification covers a high-grade alkyd enamel in black, brown, maroon, reds, oranges, greens, blues, yellows, and grays that is suitable for woodwork, although it is intended primarily for metal

painting. Class A, the air-drying kind, should be specified. Class B is a baking enamel for use on metal.

8. *Enamels, (T-E-529)*—Semigloss enamel is suitable for use on wood surfaces when a mid-range gloss is desired.

Stains. Under federal specification TT-S-708, there are stains suitable for either smoothly planed or roughly surfaced exterior woods where it is desirable for the grain and texture of the wood surface to be visible more clearly than is possible with more highly pigmented coatings.

For wood shingles, stain is usually preferred to paint as a decorative and protective coating, because it does not form as tight a film and thus permits breathing for better drying after rains and snowfall. Federal specifications generally cover only the brown and red colors. However, other colors may be secured by using other pigments suggested by the Forest Products Laboratory (FPL). The pigment suggested in federal specifications and by the FPL is approximately doubled for all shingle stains.

The stain, as furnished, is more in the nature of a thin paint and is recommended, as is, for staining planed wood. Good shingle stains in light colors may be prepared by thinning tinted exterior oil paint (TT-P-102) with the mineral spirits in about equal parts. Also, an oil alkyd paint (TT-P-52) is available in white, light and medium tints, and deep tones for use on wood shakes and rough siding.

Varnish for exterior hardwood. Frequently, thresholds and sometimes handrails and doors are made of hardwood. Customarily, these surfaces are varnished, rather than painted, to avoid obscuring the grain of wood. A high-grade spar varnish, such as can be formulated with phenolic resin and tung oil, should be used for maximum durability in sun and rain exposure (TT-V-121). For open-grained woods, such as oak and ash, paste wood filler (federal specification TT-F-336) should be applied before varnishing. Semitransparent exterior stains (federal specification TT-S-708) can also be used on these surfaces either before or in lieu of spar varnish.

Paint for Interior Surfaces

Pigmented paints for interior surfaces are commonly formulated with quick-drying vehicles such as varnish or a mixture of varnish with boiled or heat-bodied linseed oil. Alkyd vehicles are especially suitable. These vehicles enable faster work and create smoother films that hold their color better, are easier to wash, and stand up better under washing than the soft, linseed oil vehicles used in exterior wood paints.

A semigloss finish is usually desirable for interior woodwork, particularly an excellent semigloss, alkyd vehicle enamel in white or light tints (TT-E-508) or an odorless, semigloss interior enamel (TT-E-509). For a high-gloss finish, which is frequently desired in kitchens and bathrooms because of better washability, a high-grade alkyd in enamel white or light tints (TT-E-506) is preferable, or an odorless enamel of the same type (federal specification (TT-E-505) may be used. Flat paint is not usually considered desirable for woodwork because of relatively poor durability and washability. There are some flat paints (TT-P-47), in white and light tints, that are suitable for interior woodwork when these factors are not important. Tints in these paints may be secured by furnishing a color sample to the manufacturer or by adding pigments in oil (TT-P-381) or tinting medium, (TT-T-390) to the white paint on-the-job. Interior latex base paint (TT-P-29) can also be used if a flat finish is desired. However, this paint has to be obtained tinted, as pigments in oil are incompatible with it. This paint has much better washing and scrubbing resistance than the oil base flat paint.

Priming paints for the gloss and semigloss paints are available (TT-E-543 or TT-E-545) or it may be mixed on-the-job by thinning the semigloss enamel you're going to use with turpentine or mineral spirits, or thinning odorless enamel (TT-E-509) with odorless thinner, at the rate of one pint of thinner to one gallon of paint.

Normally, the odorless enamels are not used because of higher expense. However, if the volatile fumes which are characteristic of ordinary enamels are obnoxious, the odorless varieties may be used.

Increasingly, water emulsion paints are replacing oil base

paints for many interior surfaces. The industry is making rapid strides in upgrading their durability and appearance. The easy application and cleanup make these paints highly attractive, especially to anyone of limited experience and expertise.

Dark paints are somewhat difficult to obtain because the general preference is for light paints, for better lighting, in interior woodwork. Somewhat deeper colors than ordinarily expected in the full gloss and semigloss paints previously described can be achieved by incorporating additional pigments in oil. However, care must be taken not to add too much pigment because it can interfere with gloss and leveling properties. Deep colors in flat and eggshell finish can be prepared satisfactorily by use of pigments in oil in paint conforming with federal specification TT-P-47.

Full gloss enamel (TT-E-489) is available in a variety of dark colors and is suitable for interior wood painting. (*See* the section on Paint for Exterior Surfaces, Dark Paints.) Semigloss machinery paint, such as semigloss alkyd paint (TT-E-529), is available in numerous colors and is suitable for interior woodwork. Lusterless enamels (TT-E-527) can also be used.

Clear coatings for interior woodwork are used for interior woodwork, such as hardwood trim and floors, where it is desirable to retain and enhance the natural beauty of the grain.

Interior varnish (TT-V-71) gives a good clear finish for trim. If a rubbed finish is desired, cabinet rubbing varnish (TT-V-86) should be used. Boiled linseed oil (TT-L-190) thinned with about 25 percent mineral spirits (TT-T-291) or turpentine (TT-T-801) is used with nice effect for some purposes; for example, its use on knotty pine. Bleached shellac is often used for finishing light-colored wood to avoid darkening of the surface. It is not generally as satisfactory as a good varnish because of its brittle character and poor resistance to some liquids, notably alcohol. Bleached, refined, 4½-pound cut shellac (TT-S-300) is a grade of shellac varnish suitable for interior woodwork finishing.

Another system for interior woodwork that does not appreciably darken the surface is made of one coat of lacquer sanding sealer (TT-S-190) followed by two coats of clear gloss brushing lacquer (TT-L-26) after sanding. This system is often used on interior doors and other woodwork, including plywood paneling, where a clear, high-gloss, light-colored coating is desired. It is not recommended for refinishing previously coated woodwork unless the old coating is completely removed first; the solvents in the sealer and lacquer soften old coatings, resulting in an unsatisfactory job. An exception would be an old coating of the same sort of lacquer coating.

Stains are frequently used in clear finish systems to intensify or modify the original color of the wood. Nonbleeding, oil stains (TT-S-711) in cherry, light oak, dark oak, mahogany, and walnut, or the nongrain raising, solvent dye-type (TT-S-720), are generally preferred. Good stains of this sort also can be prepared on-the-job by mixing pigments in oil (TT-P-381) with a vehicle liquid composed of one part raw linseed oil (TT-L-215), one part turpentine (TT-T-801), and one-half part drier (TT-D-651) (lead and manganese type). About one gallon of this liquid is used with one-half pint of pigment in oil. Variations in color and intensity of pigments indicates the desirability of trial mixtures to establish the desired color. The time before wipe-off also governs the depth of staining achieved. As a guide, raw sienna and ochre are the basic pigments for light oak stain, burnt sienna for mahogany, burnt sienna and ochre for cherry, a mixture of burnt umber and vandyke brown for walnut, and raw sienna shaded with burnt umber for dark oak.

For floors, a special penetrating varnish called floor sealer is designed for effective penetration into the wood. It leaves a thin but durable coating on the surface. Where this material is used, worn areas in traffic lanes are much less prominent than when a relatively thick coating of regular varnish is applied (TT-S-176, class I for oaks, class II for maple and birch). Paste wood filler, (TT-F-336) is used for treating open-grained wood, such as oak, before the sealer is applied. A special lacquer floor sealer (TT-S-171) is often used for sealing floors that have been oil treated before varnishing. The lacquer sealer prevents the oil from being absorbed and marring the finish coating.

It is a good practice to wax a clear finish surface for protection and to improve appearance. A polishing wax for trim, floors, and furniture is covered by federal specification P-W-158, type I for liquid consistency, type II for paste. A simple, inexpensive, no-buffing treatment for floors is accomplished with wax emulsion (P-W-155).

Paint for Softwood Floors

At best, pigmented paint cannot be expected to endure very long in the traffic lanes of floors. Linseed oil vehicle paints are unsatisfactory. A serviceable paint is known to the trade as porch and deck paint. This is prepared with a tough medium- or long-oil varnish vehicle for optimum wearing qualities and good resistance to moisture. Federal specification TT-E-487 covers such an enamel in brown, gray, oak, and red. It is recommended for porches, steps, and floors made of softwood, both inside and outside.

Priming paint is made by thinning one gallon of the ready-mixed paint with one quart of a mixture composed of two parts boiled linseed oil and one part turpentine. For the second coat, the paint is thinned with one pint of this mixture to one gallon of paint. If a third coat of the ready-mixed paint is applied, the paint may be thinned slightly with turpentine or mineral spirits to facilitate spreading.

Accessory Materials

Appropriate specifications for various accessory materials used in woodwork painting are shown in Table 5.

PREPARATION OF WOOD SURFACES

Properly conditioning the surface to be painted is of utmost importance for an effective paint job. No matter how good the paint may be or how suitable it is for the work, it cannot give good service if applied over a dirty or otherwise improperly conditioned surface.

The preparation of wood surfaces for painting requires consideration of the effects of moisture in the wood. Excessive moisture in the cells and pores of lumber interferes with the penetration and bonding of paint and may cause blistering. Wood that has not been properly seasoned before construction, or that has become damp in wet weather afterwards, should be permitted to dry before a priming coat is applied. On the other hand, the prolonged exposure of unpainted wood results in

Table 5

Specifications for Various Accessory Materials

Item	Specification	Remarks
Turpentine	TT-T-801	Normally no preference need be indicated as to type; all three types are satisfactory.
Mineral spirits	TT-T-291, light grade.	The heavy grade is used where it is desired to slow the drying of paint.
Linseed oil Raw Boiled	 TT-L-215 TT-L-190	Occasionally, linseed oil is thinned with turpentine and the mixture used as the thinner for certain paints.
Paint drier	TT-D-651, lead and manganese type.	The lead-free type is used where the use of lead-free paint is necessary.
Putty	TT-P-791, whiting type or white-lead whiting type.	The two types are used interchangeably for glazing wood sash and filling holes and cracks. Some preference is given the white lead whiting type for the latter purpose.

Item	Specification	Remarks
Glazing compound for steel sash.	TT-G-410	This material is also satisfactory for glazing wood sash.
Calking compound.	TT-C-598, plastic	The gun grade is soft in consistency for use in a calking gun. The knife grade is of glazing compound consistency for use with hand tools.
Sealer compound	TT-S-227	This is a two-component rubber base calking material for sealing joints or cracks.
Knot sealer	WP-578	This is a Western Pine Association formula. A second choice is shellac, TT-S-300; either orange or bleached, in a light body, is suitable.
Paint-and-varnish remover.	TT-R-251, nonflammable, wax free, thick liquid or semipaste.	This is a nonflammable, organic solvent remover. For some uses, the wax type may be satisfactory and more economical. The flammable type may be used where there is no fire hazard.

warping, cracking, dirt accumulation, and sometimes fungus growth. About one week of clear, warm weather should be allowed if the wood is green or becomes wet. When the woodwork has been properly prime coated, the moisture content of the wood is fairly stabilized and finish painting may be deferred as desired but not long enough for the prime coat to deteriorate or weather. Finish painting should be deferred, if possible, until the fresh plaster in the building is relatively dry. This applies to painting exterior as well as interior woodwork because excess moisture in the plaster will be drawn into the outside wood. The priming coat itself is not so tight that it will prevent such moisture from escaping. The reduced permeability produced by one or two finish coats will, however, prevent moisture from spreading and blistering and peeling can result. It is apparent that concern over the proper dryness of wood before painting applies mostly to exterior woodwork. Interior wood is largely protected from the weather. Furthermore, especially in millwork products, the wood used for building interiors is more carefully seasoned before it becomes part of the job.

Surfaces should be free of dust, dirt, oil, grease, or other contamination at the time of painting. Where dirt or mortar scale adheres tightly, use a scraper. Dust can be brushed off, and grease and oil may be removed by washing with mineral spirits or other solvents. (*See* Chapter 14, Paint Failures.)

Sanding

For the most part, sandpapering exterior wood surfaces is unnecessary. The finished paint coating is not expected to be paper smooth, and little if any increase in paint durability would result. However, unusally rough spots in exterior woodwork should be worked out to secure good continuity in the paint film.

Sanding interior woodwork is generally necessary for a satisfactory paint job. Doors, casings, moldings, and other trim are usually sanded by hand or with a small power sander; No. 0 sandpaper is used. The use of No. 1 first may be expedient if the wood surfaces have not been smoothed sufficiently at the mill. Fine steel wool is often preferred for rounded and irregularly shaped surfaces.

Floors are sanded most efficiently by machine. It is wise to employ an experienced operator for this work, because a floor surface can be easily damaged if the machine is not operated properly. For new oak and maple floors, No. 2½ sandpaper is used for cutting high spots and joints, No. 1 for intermediate sanding, and No. 0 for finishing. For new pine and fir floors, No. 2½ or No. 3 sandpaper is used for the first cutting and No. 1 or No. 1½ for finishing. Finer paper is not used on pine and fir because the resins in these woods cause gumming. Floors should be sanded before the shoe is placed around the baseboard to permit the machine to work as closely as possible to the edges of the floor. Even so, sanding by hand will be required for areas that cannot be reached by the machine sander, as in corners.

Puttying

Although puttying should not be done until after the priming coat has been applied and dried, it is discussed here as a step in preparing wood surfaces for the application of finish coats of paint.

Putty is applied with a putty knife or with the fingers, whichever is most convenient, to fill nail holes and cracks in the wood. It should be pressed firmly in place and finished off (sanded, scraped, or brushed) flush with the surface. It should not be painted over until it has become dry and firm because a paint film over damp putty will dry slowly and subsequent checking of the paint film may result. For shallow nail holes and cracks, allow at least 48 hours for the putty to harden. For deep fillings or for putty applied in glazing, at least one week and preferably two or three should elapse before painting. It is usually desirable to smooth the puttied area with light sandpapering before painting.

For small nail holes and cracks and other areas which need filling, particularly in interior woodwork, plastic wood, a mixture of resins, rapid drying solvents, and finely divided wood particles, may be faster and easier to use than putty. Generally, this material can be sanded the day after application. Various colors to match different woods are available.

Sealing Knots and Pitch Streaks

Any sap on wood surfaces should be removed by scraping, then washing with turpentine. Sealer is then applied by brushing in one thin coat to completely cover the affected area as well as a few inches of overlap. Sealer for this purpose dries very fast and a wait of two hours to overnight is adequate before applying the priming paint. (*See* the sections on Sealers, and Accessory Materials, later in this chapter for a discussion of sealers and recommendations.)

PREPARATION OF PAINTS

Proper preparation of paints is too often overlooked in the desire to get on with the job. Full value from the paint cannot be realized if it is inadequately mixed or improperly thinned. It should be remembered that the manufacturer has carefully proportioned the pigment and vehicle ingredients in good quality paint to obtain the best results. The cost in time and effort required for proper paint preparation is insignificant in relation to the cost of the entire paint job. It is an inexcusable waste to apply paint that will not give the best service simply because it has not been prepared properly.

Mixing

The pigments of all ready-mixed paints left standing for a while tend to settle to the bottom of the liquid. In some paints settling results in a soft paste at the bottom of the container. In others, the settled material is dense and hard. The variation, as might be expected, is due largely to differences in the specific gravity of pigments. For example, red lead with a specific gravity of 8.7 tends to settle into hardness, and Prussion blue with a specific gravity of 1.8 tends to settle softly. In any case, the settled pigment must be distributed evenly throughout the liquid.

Pigmented paints used in woodwork painting are nearly always furnished in a range of small containers—one-half pint to five-gallon cans. Mixing paint in containers of this size is commonly accomplished by hand, although the use of power stirrers for the larger containers and automatic shaking devices is becoming more common. In shaker mixing, the container is placed unopened in the shaker and agitated until the contents are uniformly mixed, which requires from 3 to 15 minutes. Mixing is checked by opening the container and inspecting for undispersed pigment lumps with a paddle.

Proper mixing by hand or power stirring is performed as follows:

1. Remove the top of the container and pour off most of the thin supernatant material into a clean can.

2. Stir the remaining paste with a clean, broad, flat paddle or power stirrer until a uniform consistency is obtained, thoroughly incorporating pigment that has accumulated along the sides and on the bottom of the container.

3. Return the liquid that was originally poured off, a little at a time, with continual stirring, until the paint has been recombined to a smooth, even consistency.

4. The final step in proper mixing is to *box* the paint. This is done by pouring the paint back and forth several times from the one container to the other.

Where pigment settling is very light, about half of the paint may be poured off into a clean container. The paint is stirred in each of the two containers to uniformity, and the mixing then completed by thorough boxing. It is not a good practice to attempt to stir paint to uniformity in a filled container. Two containers should be used since the mixing can be accomplished in much less time and with more assurance of a thorough job.

It is not usually a good practice to order ready-mixed paints in large drums. The principle reason is that it is difficult and time-consuming to mix so large a volume of paint to uniformity. Also, skin formation tendencies and evaporation losses, both of which deteriorate the paint, are encouraged when paint from a large container is used. These factors add up to increased costs and a low-quality job, especially when paint from a large container is used gradually.

If pigmented paint is furnished in drums, the mixing procedure is essentially the same as described for hand or power stirring the contents of small containers. The advantage of power stirring in this case is evident. Rolling drums of pigmented paints is not considered a practical method of mixing because for densely settled pigment, the process would have to be continued for an unreasonable period to be thorough.

Clear coatings, such as varnish and floor sealer, normally do not require mixing because they are true solutions and therefore normally include no significant amounts of settled material. This should be investigated, however, by inspection with a paddle. If there is some settling, recombine, if possible, by stirring or shaking the container. If there is considerable settled material that does not recombine, even though warmed, the coating material is defective and should not be used. (*See* the section on Warming.) Vigorous stirring, and especially shaking, introduces air bubbles that are particularly objectionable in clear coatings because they disrupt the smoothness of the film. Therefore, it is best to minimize stirring and, if vigorous agitation is required, the material should be allowed to stand for some time before use to permit the air bubbles to escape.

Tinting

Before adding pigments in oil for tinting, base paints should be mixed to uniform composition as described in the section on Mixing. The paste pigment in oil should be thinned to about paint consistency with turpentine or mineral spirits before being added to the paint to facilitate mixing. The tinting liquid should be added slowly and stirred into the paint until the color is uniform throughout. Care should be taken so that the tinting color is not permitted to remain concentrated on the walls of the container.

There are no exact rules governing the proportion of pigments in oil to give desired tints. Shade and intensity in pigments in oil and tinting susceptibility of the base paint vary enough to make each tinting job an individual case. Tinting is an art, in which good judgment in selecting combinations of pigments in oil and quantities is gained from experience. There is a tendency to underestimate the tinting strength of pigments in oil. It is wise to proceed slowly to avoid overtinting and need for additional base paint to tone down the mixture. Factory-tinted paints are preferred, because more uniform color matching is assured.

Thinning

With the exception of floor enamel (TT-E-487) all ready-mixed paints used in painting woodwork, as described in the sections on Paint for Exterior Surfaces; Paint for Interior Surfaces; Paint for Softwood Floors; and Accessory Materials; are designed for use in finish coats without thinning. Thinning these paints will result in coatings that are spread too thin for good durability. In rare cases, pigmented paints of these kinds, left standing, may thicken enough to warrant the addition of a small amount (not over one pint per gallon) of mineral spirits or turpentine. As a rule, thinning is not intended and should not be done, except as specifically required.

Thinning is required for the preparation of priming paints from exterior oil paint (TT-P-102) and interior semigloss enamels (TT-E-508 and TT-E-509). (*See* the sections on Paint for Exterior Surfaces and Paint for Interior Surfaces.) Thinning, up to a maximum of one pint of mineral spirits (odorless if required, TT-T-295) or turpentine to one gallon of paint, is permissable for the second coat of three-coat systems of either exterior oil paint (TT-P-102) or interior enamels (TT-E-505, TT-E-506, TT-E-508, and TT-E-509). Thinning requirements for porch and deck paint are covered in the section on Paint for Softwood Floors. Thinning liquids and the amount of thinning for the preparation of shingle stain on-the-job are covered in the preceding section on Paint for Exterior Surfaces.

Before thinning, the paint should be mixed to uniform consistency as described in the section on Mixing. The quantity of paint to be thinned is transferred in an approximately measured amount to a clean container (usually a painter's bucket) large enough to hold both paint and thinner. The proper amount of thinner is then measured, poured into the paint, and the mixture stirred to uniform consistency.

Warming

When paint becomes chilled, its viscosity increases, and there may be precipitation of nonvolatile vehicle ingredients. The viscosity increase may be sufficient to cause difficulty in brushing; it also tends to reduce wetting and penetration properties. It is common practice to warm chilled paint (as a guideline, when the temperature is below 50°F) before mixing for use.

Storing in a heated room is the simplest method of warming paint. Where this is impracticable, the use of a hot water bath or an electrically heated blanket is recommended. It must be remembered that most paints, including all those used in wood painting, are *flammable* and heating over an open flame is extremely hazardous and should not be permitted. Moreover, localized overheating caused by direct heat is injurious to paint. In warming paint in a hot water bath or blanket, the lid of the container must be loosened and left ajar to allow the escape of solvent fumes; otherwise, the lid is apt to be blown off or the container may be distorted or even ruptured by the increase in internal pressure. Warming the paint to about 90°F is good procedure, but heating should not extend beyond the period of time necessary to reach this temperature. The temperature should not exceed 100°F because of fire hazard, an increased settling tendency, and lose of solvent.

PAINT APPLICATION

Painting normally should commence as soon as the surfaces are properly conditioned and atmospheric conditions are suitable. (*See* the sections on Sanding; Puttying; Sealing Knots and Pitch Streaks.)

For outside painting, the warm and clear weather is preferable. Outside painting should never be done in rain or snow or when the wood is damp or covered with frost. Outside painting in freezing temperatures is undesirable, even if the weather is clear. If painting must be done in near-freezing weather, the paint should be warmed to improve application and wetting properties. Thinning should be restricted to the normal requirements. It must be recognized that, although paint dries more slowly in freezing weather, adding paint drier on-the-job is not a satisfactory solution.

In interior painting, good ventilation must be provided to avoid a concentration of dangerous fumes that may cause an explosion or be injurious to health. The best conditions for interior painting are clear, warm weather, when doors and windows can be comfortably left open. If heating the house's interior is required, precautions must be taken to make certain paint materials and fumes are kept away from an open flame. Open flame heating, as from salamanders, is also undesirable because the water formed by combustion and prolonged burning will introduce excessive moisture into the air and onto the surface being painted.

Paint is commonly applied to wood by brush or roller. Ready-mixed paints supplied for woodwork painting are designed to have the proper consistency for brushing. Brush application to wood is advantageous because the paint can be worked to fill fine cracks and open pores and a small amount of contamination can be tolerated since it will be worked up with the paint. (*See* Chapter 7, Brush Painting.) Large areas, where a slight orange peel effect on the finish is not objectionable, are best coated with a roller. Roller coating is more rapid, deposits a more uniform film, and works the paint into the surface as does brushing. (*See* Chapter 8, Roller Painting.)

Paint is sometimes applied to wood by spray in new construction. (*See* Chapter 9, Spray Painting.) The surface must be very clean for a good spray painting job because any film or other foreign material will impair the bond of the paint. Spray painting trim and cabinet work may be more time-consuming than brush painting because of the elaborate masking required. Also, in interior painting, spray application produces excessive fumes. Although spray painting woodwork is not always undesirable or will not necessarily result in less durable coatings, better results are usually obtained by brushing.

It is false economy to use mediocre brushes. With proper care, a good brush can be used over and over, and each time satisfaction in the quality of the work will result. Long, soft bristles hold more paint and leak less on overhead work, facilitating the job because less time is required for dipping and wiping the ferrule. Especially in interior woodwork painting with enamels and varnishes, the use of a high-quality brush is important. Such brushes give a smooth, level coating, free of brush marks. A good brush, like many tools of high quality, is expensive. The length of the bristles should at least equal the width of the brush.

In brush painting, the paint should first be laid on with the brush strokes in one direction, followed by lighter, smoothing-off strokes at an angle. The latter strokes are usually parallel to the grain of the wood. Exterior linseed oil paints are best applied with a minimum of brushing. This paint loses its leveling ability quite rapidly, and brush marks will remain in the film if it is brushed too much. Furthermore, unsightly lap marks result if progress is broken or delayed on large areas because the paint applied first will set to the point where it will not blend properly with fresher paint.

Inside work, especially, should be planned to minimize lapping. In lapping, the final brush stroke should be from the freshly painted area into and over the lap, with the brush lifted away from the area being lapped, forming a neat featheredge. If the final brush stroke begins in the area being lapped and ends in the newly applied paint, a mark will be visible where the brush was first set down. (*See* Chapter 7, Brush Painting.)

Painting Exterior Woodwork

Three-coat painting of exterior woodwork was considered the standard in good painting procedure for years. It is now recognized, however, that a properly executed two-coat job will serve very nearly if not fully as well. Even though repainting is required somewhat sooner with a two-coat system, the cost of applying a later, additional coat will not greatly exceed that of applying a third coat in the initial painting.

Whether a two-coat or three-coat system is used, the total coating thickness should be approximately the same. The priming paint in the two-coat system should be applied at about 450 square feet per gallon and the finish paint at 550 square feet per gallon. In the three-coat system, the priming paint should be applied at about 550 square feet per gallon and the second and third coats of finish paint at 650 square feet per gallon. The hiding ability of dark-colored paints makes it especially easy to spread this paint farther. This possibility should be guarded against, however, because it adversely affects durability.

Each coat of paint should be allowed to dry thoroughly to a firm film before the succeeding coat is applied. For exterior paints of the linseed oil vehicle type, the drying time should be at least 48 hours, even in warm and clear weather. Under less favorable conditions, the drying time should be extended accordingly. For enamels of the alkyd vehicle type, 24 hours drying time is normally adequate.

Staining Shingles

Dipping is probably the most effective method of applying shingle stain. The stain is poured into a suitable, clean container deep enough to immerse shingles resting on the botton, butt end down. This depth should be enough to completely cover the area that will be exposed to weather, plus a few inches to spare. If more than one shingle is dipped at a time, the shingles should be adjusted so that the stain will reach all immersed surfaces. Cedar shingles take the stain quickly and can be removed promptly after immersion. Shingles made of cypress, yellow pine, and other resinous woods require soaking until all portions of the grain have taken up the stain. Upon removal, the shingles should be placed so that excess stain will drain back into the container—a rack draining into a sloped trough is a good example. New stain is added as required to maintain the level of immersion. Occasional stirring remixes settled pigment. One gallon of stain will be required for about 50 square feet of exposed shingle area.

Stain is also commonly applied by brushing after the shingles are installed. The work can be done most efficiently with a long-handled daubing brush. The stain should be applied liberally to enable it to soak into the shingles. Runs should be brushed out. About 100 square feet of exposed shingle area can be covered with one gallon of stain, as applied by brushing in a one-coat operation.

Painting Interior Woodwork

Pigmented paint on interior woodwork is usually applied in three coats to obtain the best appearance and durability. However, two-coat systems using good-quality paints may frequently be satisfactory.

It is not considered necessary or practicable to determine set rules for paint coverage rates used on interior woodwork. For estimating purposes, a coverage of about 500 square feet per gallon per coat may be expected. In three-coat work, the paint should be spread somewhat farther in each coat than in two-coat work. In the latter, each coat should be close to maximum thickness without running and sagging. Enamels must be watched with special care for runs and sags, and these should be brushed out promptly before the paint has time to set.

In a three-coat system, the priming paint is followed by two coats of finish paint. The finish paint should be applied as furnished, without thinning. If desired, paint for the first finish coat may be thinned with not more than one pint of mineral spirits or turpentine to one gallon of paint. In the two-coat system, the priming coat is followed by one coat of finish paint, applied as furnished. Each coat should be allowed to dry thoroughly and should be lightly sanded before the succeeding coat is applied. A minimum of 24 hours' drying time is required; more is often necessary for the film to acquire adequate hardness for sanding without gumming.

Painting Softwood Floors

Whether inside or outside, the objective in painting softwood floors and steps is to provide good protection and appearance without leaving an excessively thick coating on the surface. Eventually, the coating in a *traffic lane* will be worn away and a better repainting job will be obtained if the original coating is reasonably thin.

A two-coat paint system is recommended, each coat spread to cover 600 to 800 square feet per gallon. Drying time between coats should be at least 24 hours. (*See* the section on Paint for Softwood Floors.)

Staining and Varnishing

Except for the use of different varnishes, as discussed in the sections on Paint for Exterior Surfaces and Paint for Interior Surfaces, staining and varnishing operations are essentially the same for interior and exterior hardwood.

Where stain is to be used, it is applied as the first coat to new wood. It is applied liberally by brushing and allowed to stand for a while. The excess is then wiped off with cloths. The porosity of the wood and the depth of color desired determine the length of the soaking period, which is established by trial. A drying period of 24 hours is recommended before proceeding to the next operation.

In the case of open-grained wood, such as oak, a filler coat is applied after staining. If staining is omitted, the filler coat is applied as the first operation. It may be desirable, for appearance's sake, to add some of the same stain to the filler. The paste filler is thinned with turpentine or mineral spirits to brushing consistency before use. The thinned filler should be applied liberally and brushed well into the surface. After setting for about 15 minutes, excess filler is taken up by vigorous rubbing across the grain with burlap or other rough cloth. Drying time for the filler coat should be at least eight hours. A limed oak effect can be obtained by substituting white paint for paste wood filler. After the excess is wiped off, the open spaces in the grain retain a white coloration.

After application of the filler coat, the surface is ready for the first coat of varnish. (If staining is omitted and the wood is close-grained, such as birch or maple, varnishing the new wood will directly follow sanding.) Smooth, thin coats of varnish are recommended for the best appearance. Brush strokes across the grain should be followed by leveling-off strokes with the grain. At least three coats will be required for either interior or exterior work to provide good appearance and durability. Five and six coats are often used to achieve the desired effect on furniture. Thorough drying and smoothing with very fine sandpaper or steel wool between coats are essential to fine work. Surfaces should be carefully dusted immediately before the application of each coat. If a low-gloss, satiny finish is desired, the completed

coating, after drying hard, is rubbed, using soft cloths and powdered pumice in water or linseed oil.

The use of bleached shellac and clear lacquer in interior
woodwork finishing entails much the same procedure. The
shellac varnish or lacquer is substituted for regular varnish. The
work can be done faster with these materials because they dry
much faster. However, they do not provide as satisfactory a
finish as varnish and are recommended only where varnish is
considered to introduce excessive coloration.

An oil rubbed finish is obtained by repeated rubbing of new
wood, such as walnut or mahogany, with linseed oil. Either raw
oil used alone or boiled oil thinned with turpentine is satisfactory. Heating the oil is advantageous. The oil is rubbed in, using
a soft cloth, then the excess is wiped off each time. Repeated
applications over a period of time produce an attractive, resistant finish.

A pleasing clear finish for knotty pine paneling is obtained
with boiled linseed oil thinned with turpentine or mineral spirits.
Two coats are usually adequate to provide a smooth finish without excessive discoloration. A drying period of 48 hours is recommended between coats.

Sealing Hardwood Floors

Ordinarily, hardwood floors are not stained in order to retain
the desirable natural coloration of the wood. Paste wood filler is
applied first, where required, as discussed in the section on
Staining and Varnishing.

Floor sealer may be applied in the conventional manner by
brushing in two coats, or by flooding and squeegeeing off the
excess. In brush application, the first coat should be well
brushed into the surface to secure maximum penetration. The
coverage rate is about 500 square feet per gallon. The finish coat
should be thin—applied at 800 to 1,000 square feet per gallon.

In the flooding method, the sealer is poured directly on the
floor and spread with a lamb's wool applicator. Additional sealer
is worked into the dull spots appearing in more porous areas,
until the entire surface is uniformly sealed. The workman
should wear clean, solvent-resistant rubber-soled shoes or over-

shoes in this operation. The excess sealer is removed with a floor squeegee and pickup pan, and the work finished with a clean buffing mop to remove footprints and other irregularities in the coating. This excess may be recovered by straining through a fine screen or cheesecloth. After it is thinned with mineral spirits or turpentine to its original consistency, it is ready for reuse.

It is a good practice to burnish the floor after the seal coat is thoroughly dry (at least 24 hours after application) to remove highlights and smooth any raised grain resulting from the sealing treatment. Burnishing may be accomplished with No. 0 steel wool in a power-driven floor machine. This machine and the special equipment used in the flooding method of applying sealer are available from dealers in floor maintenance supplies.

Waxing

Wax polish may be applied at any time to a clean finished surface after the finish has completely dried and hardened. Polishing wax, in either paste or liquid form, should be spread in a uniformly thin coating, allowed to dry, and then rubbed with a soft cloth or polishing pad. A machine polisher is advantageous for floors, especially if large areas are involved.

Wax emulsion, which is especially appropriate for asphalt-, vinyl-, and rubber-tiled floors, is also suitable for wood floors. It is applied by mopping, spread carefully in a thin, even coat. When applied for the first time, two coats are recommended with 30 to 45 minutes drying time between coats. The coverage for wax emulsion may be estimated at 1,200 to 1,500 square feet per gallon per coat. Wax emulsion coatings normally are not polished. The gloss is not as high as that obtained with a polishing wax, but the floor is less slippery.

MAINTENANCE PAINTING

The maxim for economical maintenance of coatings, whether on woodwork or other surfaces, is "do it before it is too late." Too frequently the old coating is permitted to deteriorate excessively before it is renewed. This means that an unnecessarily large portion of the repainting expense must go to surface preparation. In most cases, it also means the new coating will be less satisfactory than if the old coating had been sound and intact. There are no rigid rules as to how long an old coating on woodwork will last before a fresh coat is required. Some interior finishes will last virtually a lifetime; conversely, some exterior finishes may require renewal every year. The former category includes varnish finishes not in direct sunlight or subjected to mechanical damage. The latter category would again be varnish finishes that deteriorate quite rapidly when directly exposed to the elements. It is therefore necessary to examine coatings at regular intervals to determine repainting needs.

Exterior Woodwork

Closely observing the condition of paint films is required to judge properly the need for repainting. Viewed from a distance, old paint may appear to be satisfactory even though it is considerably deteriorated, or it may appear to be in poor condition only because of dullness or dirt accumulation. In the latter case, washing may be sufficient to restore a satisfactory appearance.

Usually, the first sign of paint weathering is reduced gloss, followed by chalking of the film. Both are to be expected before the serviceability of the coating is vitiated. A reasonable amount of chalking is desirable for several reasons: it permits self-cleaning of the coating; it produces a full surface that is best for the adhesion of new paint; and it reduces film thickness. (*See* Chapter 14, Paint Failures.) Where no chalking occurs, the built-up thickness over years of repainting aggravates cracking and scaling. Most exterior wood paints are formulated to control chalking to an optimum degree. (*See* the section on Paint for Exterior Surfaces.)

Repainting should be done when chalking has proceeded to the point where bare wood just begins to show or when minute checks or cracks appear. The film has then been damaged and, if deterioration is left unchecked, flaking and scaling or serious loss of the protective coating will soon develop. New paint can be applied directly over a coating that shows only checking, fine cracking, or chalking, but when the edges at cracks curl and the paint begins to flake off, considerable extra expense in surface preparation will be incurred.

Surface Preparation. In areas where the old coating is intact, only the removal of dust and dirt is necessary before paint is applied. Usually brushing with a painter's duster is adequate. If washing is needed, hosing may be sufficient. If soap or detergent is used, it is important that the surface be rinsed with clear water to remove any residue.

Loose paint and curled edges of paint require removal by scraping and wire brushing. Sometimes, particularly if large areas are involved, defective coating is burned off with a torch. Paint-and-varnish remover can also be used, but this procedure is more often confined to interior surfaces where the utmost in a smooth repainting job is desired. (*See* Chapter 1, Basis for Selecting Coatings, section on Paint and Varnish Remover; *see also* Table 5, in this chapter.) Areas that have been treated by scraping and wire brushing or burning should be sandpapered, taking care to featheredge the boundary of the intact coating. Old coatings that are glossy should be dulled to assure good adhesion of the new paint. This may be done by sandpapering or by treating with dilute ammonia or trisodium phosphate solution. One part commercial ammonia to 20 parts of water or one-half pound trisodium phosphate to one gallon of water are recommended concentrations. After treatment, the surfaces should be rinsed with clear water.

Loose boards should be nailed firmly in place; those that are badly defective should be replaced. Cracks in the wood should be filled with putty, and gaps around window and door casings should be filled with calking compound. Loose putty or glazing compound on windows should be replaced with fresh material.

If mildew is present (usually only in warm, damp climates), it is recommended that the infected surfaces be thoroughly scrubbed with a solution of trisodium phosphate (1½ ounces of the powder to one gallon of water), followed by rinsing with clear water. There are commercial fungicides available in paste form that may be directly added to paint to prevent mildew.

Precautions regarding atmospheric conditions and dryness of the wood, as discussed in the sections on Sanding; Puttying; Sealing Knots and Pitch Streaks; Mixing; Tinting; Thinning;

and Warming; apply to maintenance painting as well as to new work. Attention should also be given to paint that shows blistering, which is caused by excessive moisture beneath the paint film. Before repainting, the source of such moisture should be eliminated, if possible. Spaces between boards where moisture could enter from a driving rain should be closed by renailing or filling with putty or calking compound. If the building interior is unusually damp, it is likely that ground water drainage needs improving. Unless the source of moisture is eliminated, blistering will recur in the new paint film.

Repainting. Paints used in the maintenance of old coatings on exterior woodwork and the procedures for preparing paints are the same as for new work. (*See* the sections on Selection of Paints; and Preparation of Paints.) General practices in the application of paint are also the same. (*See* the section on Application of Paints.)

When pigmented paints are used, bare areas of wood should be given a priming coat before applying new finish paint. A single coat of finish paint is all that is normally required, but an additional coat or coats may sometimes be needed where a light paint is inadequate to cover a dark paint.

In revarnishing exterior woodwork, bare areas should be given two coats of varnish and, after they are smoothed by sandpapering, an additional overall coat should be applied. Shingles which have previously been stained should be restained; painted shingles cannot be stained satisfactorily because the paint film prevents proper penetration of the stain.

Interior Woodwork

If treated with reasonable care, a good paint job on interior woodwork will last many years before repainting is required. The checking and chalking found in exterior paint films seldom develop. In many cases, a fresh coat of paint is applied simply to brighten the surface or to change its color. In others, mechanical damage to the film or cracking in the underlying surface makes repainting necessary. Repeated washing will eventually erode an interior coating to the point where repainting is necessary.

Surface Preparation. The condition of the old surface determines the steps necessary to prepare it properly for a new finish. It should, first of all, be clean. Any grease scum, such as that found in kitchens, should be removed with mineral spirits, turpentine, or an effective commercial remover; otherwise, the old wax film will interfere with the adhesion and drying of the new finish. (This is particularly important when refinishing floors.) If the old coating is glossy after cleaning, it should be sandpapered lightly. Any cracks and small holes should be filled with putty. Plastic wood, a preparation available in paint and hardware stores, is useful in repairing deeply gouged spots. In sanding chipped areas of paint, the edges of the intact paint should be featheredged into the bare spots. Loose dust and dirt and the powder left by sandpapering may be removed by brushing.

An old surface marred by numerous chipped spots and deep scratches must be completely removed for a good refinishing job. For floors, this is accomplished by machine sanding, using coarse sandpaper (No. 3 or No. 4) to minimize gumming. Following removal of the old coating, the floor is smoothed with finer sandpaper, as described in the section on Sanding.

Paint-and-varnish remover is used for removing the old finish from cabinet work, trim, doors, and furniture. The liquid or semipaste remover is brushed over surfaces and allowed to stand until the coating softens and can be readily scraped off. In some cases, if the old coating is very thick or resistant to softening, more than one application of remover may be required. This should be followed by washing with mineral spirits or turpentine to remove any wax residue left from the remover (unless a wax-free remover is used).

If pigmented paint is to be applied to a stained, clearfinished surface, there is a possibility that the stain will be taken up by the solvent in the paint and bleed through the new finish, producing a streaked discoloration. This will occur only if the stain is of the organic-dye type sometimes used in cherry and mahogany stains. Bleeding may also result if paint is applied over an old pigmented type coating containing soluble colors.

This is most apt to happen where red is present in the old coating. If a trial application of paint over a few square inches shows bleeding, it is desirable to seal the surface with a coat of shellac before repainting.

Repainting. The paints used in repainting interior woodwork and the procedures for preparing paints are the same as for new work. (*See* the sections on Selection of Paints; and Preparation of Paints.) General painting practices also are the same. (*See* the section on Application of Paints.)

Normally, a single coat of pigmented paint over an intact, previously painted surface is adequate. Areas where the old coating has been removed to bare wood should be given a preliminary coat of priming paint. Two coats of finish paint may be required in some cases to produce satisfactory hiding, especially if the new paint is light-colored and the old coating is dark.

In revarnishing interior trim and furniture, it may be necessary, for a uniform appearance, to restain areas where the old coating has been removed completely. Also, when puttying it is desirable to mix stain with the putty before it is placed. Two coats of varnish are recommended as a preliminary application to bare areas, followed by a single coat over all.

In refinishing floors with floor sealer, where the old coating has been completely removed, two thin coats of sealer over the entire area are recommended. Spots where the old coating is worn or dressed down should be given a preliminary coat of sealer, followed by a coat over all. If cracks have developed in the flooring between boards, paste wood filler should be worked into them before resealing.

TIMBER PRESERVATION TREATMENT

Structural timbers used as fence posts, utility poles, piling, subflooring, wood framing, small bridges, or below subflooring and other floors, require preservative treatments to protect the timber from living, wood-destroying organisms, such as insects, marine borers, and fungi. This is accomplished by processing the timber with chemical substances (preservatives) that reduce susceptibility to deterioration by these organisms. Selection of a proper preservative treatment depends not only on the final use of the timber but also on the kind of wood.

High retention of preservatives is most effectively accomplished by pressure methods which force the liquid to penetrate deeply into the grain of the wood. In the new construction, pressure-treated timbers should also be painted with a preservative.

Recommended practices in treating timbers with various preservative oils, oil-borne preservatives, and water-borne preservatives are given in Federal specification TT-W-571. Various standards of the American Wood Preservers' Association (AWPA) form a part of this specification. The AWPA manual is the standard of the industry.

Preservative Oils and Oil-borne Preservatives

Preservative oils, such as coal–tar creosote (TT-C-655), creosote–coal–tar solutions (TT-C-650), and creosote–petroleum solutions (TT-W-568), are ordinarily used in treating posts, poles, ties, and any wood material that will be in water (sea or fresh), in contact with the soil, or in any other situation where high-moisture conditions prevail. If oil-treated material is to be used in buildings or where bleeding is especially undesirable, straight creosote (TT-C-655), or either pentachlorophenol (TT-W-570) or copper naphthenate (AWPA specification P-8) dissolved in a distillate petroleum oil should be used.

For subflooring and wood framing below the subfloor, but above grade, a water-repellent wood preservative (TT-W-572) should be used. This is a solution of one or more toxic chemical and water-repellent materials dissolved in a liquid that will not swell wood. It is particularly useful in resisting decay and retarding changes in dimensions by controlling moisture content.

Waterborne Preservatives

Waterborne preservatives are often used in buildings when oil-treated wood is unacceptable because of color or odor. These include acid-copper chromate, ammoniacal copper arsenite, and chromated copper arsenate. Waterborne preservatives should not be used in marine environments, in freshwater, in contact with ground subject to high annual rainfall, or under other severe leaching conditions. Various waterborne preservatives, such as acid-copper chromate, ammoniacal copper arsenite, and chromated copper arsenate, are available under a federal specifications.

Painting of Treated Timbers

As a general rule, wood treated with coal–tar creosote or solutions containing this substance cannot be painted satisfactorily with oil paints, with the possible exception of aluminum paints. Some success has been reported in painting treated timbers with emulsion paints. Wood treated with waterborne preservatives and well seasoned after treatment can be painted satisfactorily, however. It is doubtful that wood treated with copper naphthenate solutions can be painted unless the treating solution has been specially prepared. Wood treated with petroleum solutions of pentachlorophenol can be painted depending on the solvent and the thoroughness with which the residual oils are removed by seasoning after treatment. (*See* Chapter 11, Painting Metalwork; Chapter 12, Preparation of Metal Surfaces and Paints, and Application of Paints; and Chapter 13, Painting Concrete, Masonry, and Miscellaneous Surfaces.)

11

Painting Metalwork

The traditional red lead paints still have their place, but today the protective coating industry offers a large variety of paints for use in various exposures. No one paint is a cure-all. Although exposure is the most important criterion in choosing paint for iron and steel, there are other factors involved, such as the kind of structure, accessibility for maintenance painting, and job conditions. Moreover, cost is and should be an ever-present consideration. (*See* Section 1, Paint and Paint Materials.)

CORROSION

Extent of Corrosion

All structural metals corrode to some extent in natural environments. Bronzes, brasses, stainless steels, zinc, and aluminum corrode so slowly that they are expected to survive for long periods without protection. Corrosion of structural grades of iron and steel, however, proceeds quickly unless the metal is protected. Iron and steel's susceptibility to corrosion is a large concern because vast quantities of these metals are used in construction. However, plastics with corrosion resistance and other properties are increasingly being used and may, in time, significantly replace iron and steel. Annual losses due to corrosion have been variously estimated at upwards of $10 billion dollars, depending considerably on the costs included. It is apparent that protection against iron and steel corrosion is an indispensable phase of sound engineering.

The urgency of controlling corrosion is further emphasized by the escalating costs of heavy equipment and construction. The engineering profession recognizes this, evidenced by the concerted effort that has been and is being made to solve the problem. Until the perfect coating or other method of protection is found, best advantage must be taken of available means to reduce waste from corrosion to a practicable minimum.

Cause of Corrosion

Before addressing the means of mitigating corrosion, the conditions under which it occurs should be considered. Iron and steel are man-made refinements of natural substances and their existence, as such, is contrary to the process of nature. In other words, these metals are created from stable natural oxides and have a compelling tendency to revert to their oxide forms. The oxide of iron, ferric oxide, and its hydrated form, ferric hydroxide, are familiar to all as common rust.

Although the same corrosion processes account for rusting in atmospheric exposures as in submerged environments, the effect ordinarily is less damaging in the atmosphere because the loss of metal occurs more uniformly over the surface. Corrosion prevention measures for such surfaces, therefore, are as often cosmetic as protective. Since corrosion in buried, submerged, or alternately submerged exposures usually proceeds continuously and rapidly, constituting the more serious threat to the function of structures, the following discussion emphasizes these more critical aspects. Understanding the fundamental corrosion process often enables more perceptive analysis of field corrosion. Thus, the corrosion can more readily be related to basic causes, enabling more effective mitigation.

The cell shown in Fig. 1 illustrates the corrosion process in its simplest form. This cell includes the following essential components:

1. A metal anode.
2. A metal cathode.
3. A metallic conductor between the anode and cathode.
4. An electrolyte (water containing conductive salts), in

contact with anode and cathode but not necessarily of the same composition at the two locations.

In addition, oxygen is usually present as a depolarizing agent. As can be seen in Fig. 2, these components are arranged to form a closed electrical path or circuit. In the simplest case, the anode would be one metal, perhaps iron; the cathode another, say copper; and the electrolyte may or may not have the same composition at both electrodes. Alternatively, the electrodes can be the same metal if the electrolyte composition varies.

If the cell shown were constructed and allowed to function, an electrical current would flow through the metallic conductor and the electrolyte. The anode would corrode (rust, if the anode were iron). Chemically, this is an oxidation reaction. Simultaneously, a nondestructive chemical reaction (reduction) would proceed at the cathode, usually producing hydrogen gas on the cathode. When the gas layer insulates the cathode from the

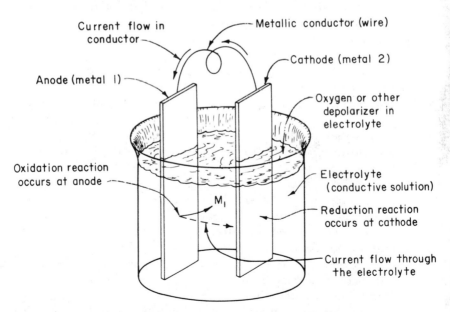

Fig. 1.   A simple cell showing the components necessary for corrosion.

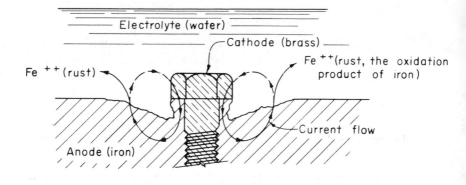

Fig. 2. Brass bolt in an iron plate in immersion creates a galvanic couple (corrosion cell).

electrolyte, the current flow stops, thus polarizing the cell. However, oxygen or some other depolarizing agent is usually present to react with the hydrogen, reducing this effect, and so the cell would continue to function. If the metallic conductor were replaced with a voltmeter, a difference of potential could be measured between the electrodes.

Basically analogous conditions prevail in the corrosion of field structures and some typical cells are depicted in Figs. 2, 3, 4, and 5. These are all practical examples of the simple cell in Fig. 1.

Corrosion in these cells is an electrochemical phenomenon, which means it is a chemical reaction involving the flow of electrical current. The tendencies of different metals to go into solution in their particular environments are fundamental properties of these materials, reflected as measurable electrical potentials. The differences in potential between anodic and cathodic areas may be regarded as the driving force initiating corrosion and controlling its magnitude. Under this influence, the anode metal corrodes (i.e., oxidizes and passes into solution); simultaneously a related but nondestructive reduction reaction occurs at the cathode. When this process occurs in the absence of external sources of potential and current, the result is referred to as local cell corrosion.

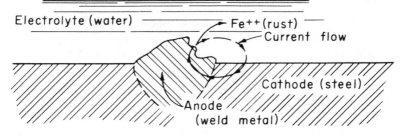

Fig. 3. Weld metal may be anodic to steel, creating a corrosion cell when immersed.

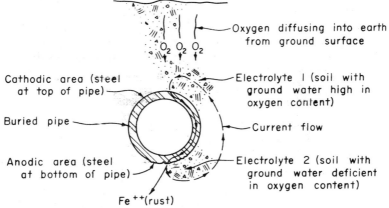

Fig. 4. A metal pipe buried in moist soil may corrode on the bottom. A difference in oxygen content at different levels in the electrolyte will produce a difference of potential. Thus, anodic and cathodic areas will develop and a corrosion cell, called a concentration cell, will form.

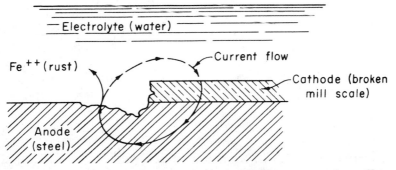

Fig. 5. Mill scale is cathodic to steel, establishing a corrosion cell.

Thus, for the rusting of ferrous metals to proceed in natural environments, there must be, simultaneously: moisture; a combination of metallically connected anodic and cathodic areas; and oxygen or some other depolarizing agent. If one or more of these three are absent, corrosion will not take place. Unfortunately, this is seldom the case. Moisture is nearly always available, whether the metal is submerged, buried in soil, or exposed to the atmosphere. Metal submerged in water is exposed to oxygen because of dissolved air. Aerating conditions determine the amount of oxygen in water; but even stagnant water has some, however slowly it is diffused.

Anodes and cathodes may be created in so many ways that they are virtually always present. The most obvious formation is by contact of dissimilar metals, as will be discussed in the following. If mill scale is present, it is cathodic to base metal. Even though metal is polished, chemical and physical differences in localized areas create anodes and cathodes on the surface. Differences in soil conditions, such as moisture content and resistivity, are commonly responsible for creating anodic and cathodic areas. Different concentrations of oxygen in water or in moist soils in contact with metal at various locations results in cathodes at points of relatively high oxygen levels and anodes at relatively low points. Strained portions of metal reportedly tend to be anodic and unstrained portions tend to cathodic. Thus, under all ordinary circumstances where iron and steel are exposed to natural environments, the conditions essential to corrosion are more or less present.

Pitting deserves special mention because it is the local cell corrosion that is predominantly responsible for the functional failure of iron and steel hydraulic structures. Pitting may perforate water pipe, rendering it useless, even though less than five percent of the total metal has been lost through rusting. Even when confined water is not a factor, pitting can cause structural failure from localized weakening effects while considerable sound metal remains.

Pitting develops when the anodic (corroding) area is small in relation to the cathodic (protected) area. For example, it can be expected when much, but not all of a surface is covered by mill scale, applied coatings, or deposits of various kinds. Pitting may also develop on bare, clean metal surfaces because of irregularities in the physical or chemical structure of the metal. Localized, dissimilar soil conditions at the steel surface can also create conditions which promote pitting.

Galvanic Couples. When the electrodes of a corrosion cell are composed of two dissimilar metals, the result is called a galvanic couple. A galvanic couple may cause the premature failure in metal components of hydraulic structures or may be advantageously exploited. Galvanizing iron sheets is an example of the useful application of galvanic action. In this case, iron is the cathode and is protected against corrosion at the expense of the zinc anode. Alternatively, a zinc or magnesium anode may be located in the electrolyte close to the structure and still be connected metallically to the iron or steel. This is termed cathodic protection. On the other hand, iron and steel becomes the anode when in contact with copper, brasses, and bronzes, and corrodes rapidly while protecting the latter metals. Corroded steel, partially covered by mill scale, can be thought of as a form of galvanic couple since steel becomes an anode when coupled with mill scale.

The driving force (difference of potential) available to promote the electrochemical corrosion reaction is reflected by the galvanic series. This lists a number of common metals and alloys arranged according to their tendency to corrode galvanically. Metals grouped together do not have a strong effect on each other, and the farther any two metals are separated, the stronger the corroding effect on the one higher in the list. It is possible for certain metals to reverse their positions in some environments, but the list given generally holds in natural waters and the atmosphere. (The galvanic series should not be confused with the similar electromotive forces series which shows exact potentials based on highly standardized conditions which rarely exist in nature.)

GALVANIC SERIES
Corroded end (anodic)
    Magnesium
    Magnesium alloys
    Zinc

Aluminum 2 S

577686°—61—6

Cadmium

Aluminum 17ST

Steel or iron

Cast iron

Chromium-iron (active)

Ni-Resist

18-8 Chromium-nickel-iron (active)

18-8-3 Chromium-nickel-molybdenum-iron (active)

Lead-tin solders

Lead

Tin

Nickel (active)

Inconel (active)

Hastelloy C (active)

Brass

Copper

Bronzes

Copper-nickel alloys

Monel

Silver solder

Nickel (passive)

Inconel (passive)

Chromium-iron (passive)

18-8 Chromium-nickel-iron (passive)

18-8-3 Chromium-nickel-molybdenum-iron (passive)

Hastelloy C (passive)

Silver

Graphite

Gold

Platinum

Protected end (cathodic)

Although the preceding galvanic series represents the driving force generally available to promote a corrosion reaction, the actual rate may be considerably different from that predicted from the driving force alone. Electrolytes may be poor conductors, or long distances may introduce a large resistance into the corrosion cell circuit. More frequently, scale formation forms a partially insulating layer over the anode. A cathode having a layer of absorbed gas bubbles resulting from the corrosion cell reaction is said to be polarized. The effect of such conditions is to reduce the theoretical consumption of metal by corrosion. The area relationship between the electrodes also may strongly affect the corrosion rate; a high ratio of cathode area to anode area produces rapid corrosion, but in the reverse case the cathode polarizes and the rate soon drops to a negligible level.

The passivity of stainless steels is attributed to the presence of a corrosion-resistant oxide film over the surfaces. In most natural environments, stainless steel remains in a passive state and thus tends to be cathodic to ordinary iron and steel. The change to an active state usually occurs only where chloride concentrates are high, as in sea waters, or in reducing solutions. Oxygen starvation also causes the change to an active state. This occurs where there is no free access of oxygen, such as in crevices and beneath contamination on partially fouled surfaces.

Stray Currents. The accelerated corrosion of steel and iron can be produced by stray currents. Direct currents in the soil or water associated with nearby cathodic protection systems, industrial activities, or direct current electric railways can be intercepted and carried for considerable distances by buried steel structures. Corrosion takes place where the stray currents are discharged from the steel to the environment, and damage to the structure can occur very rapidly.

Suppression of Corrosion

Rarely is structural iron and steel located so that corrosion will not take place. For the most part, fresh waters are well aerated, and stifled corrosion because of oxygen deficiency cannot be expected. Some corrosive conditions are worse than others, but even in the milder exposures some anticorrosion measures are nearly always warranted.

When ferrous metal is to be exposed more or less continuously to water, accurate prediction of the corrosion problems to be encountered assists immeasurably in selecting appropriate protective measures. Much investigative effort has been devoted to evaluating the many parameters of any given situation, such as the chemical composition, temperature, turbulence, and flow rate of the water, as well as the composition of the corroding medium, presence of mill scale, stress in the metal, and bimetallic couplings. Studies of water properties, in particular, have led to various methods for predicting whether water at a structure will tend to form a carbonate scale or be corrosive.

Field corrosion surveys are frequently performed and supplemented by laboratory tests if corrosive conditions are expected on new projects or unusual corrosion problems have arisen on existing projects. Results of these tests of various physical and chemical properties are used to evaluate the corrosive tendencies of the soil or water environment. One of the most common properties tested is electrical resistivity. It has been found that severe corrosion is usually associated with soils and waters of low resistivity. The following table shows a commonly accepted overall relationship between soil resistivity and corrosion.

Resistivity (ohm-centimeters)	Corrosivity
Less than 1,000	Very corrosive
1,000 to 5,000	Moderately corrosive
5,000 to 10,000	Mildly corrosive
Greater than 10,000	Slightly corrosive

Differences of resistivity also result in corrosion, and severe corrosion can occur in soils of high resistivity if there is sufficient variation in the resistivity of adjacent soil areas.

Another method of determining the corrosive properties of soil and water employs an electrical-resistance corrosion meter. This instrument measures corrosivity directly by determining the amount of metal lost by corrosion from a standard specimen.

These and other investigative methods can aid in developing data that can be especially useful in analyzing serious problems on existing structures. It may also forestall problems on planned structures by disclosing potentially corrosive locations or situations. However, in the present state-of-the-art, the results may not predict definitely the minimum corrosion control measures required for the best economy. Accordingly, most corrosion control practices are predicated on the basis of successful experience with methods which cope with a wide range of conditions at reasonable cost. The following are examples.

Control of Oxygen. In closed water-circulation systems such as a hot-water heating system, it is often practicable to remove the dissolved oxygen from the water to stop corrosion. This principle has also been applied, to some extent, to control corrosion in cold-water pipelines.

Control of Moisture. In dry air, iron and steel will not rust. Under ordinary circumstances, corrosion stops if the relative humidity is not much greater than 30 percent. This characteristic can be applied advantageously to control corrosion in confined areas. In operating galleries and other places where the humidity is high and considerable condensation occurs on cold-water pipes, dehumidifying equipment is frequently the most satisfactory method of controlling corrosion and adding to the life of decorative and protective coatings on machinery and other equipment.

Water Treatment. Chemicals called rust inhibitors—typically chromates, phosphates or silicates—are sometimes dissolved in small amounts in water, rendering it noncorrosive to iron and steel. A protective film that suppresses progressive corrosion is produced or maintained on the metal surface. This method is especially applicable where water is recirculated, as, for example, in a gasoline-engine cooling system. It is not economically feasible to treat a large column of flowing water such as that passing through a power pen-stock or outlet pipe. Rust-inhibiting salts must be used carefully because insufficient amounts may intensify rather than inhibit the corrosive attack in localized areas.

It is sometimes possible to treat certain waters with chemicals that react to form a hard, dense film of calcium carbonate on the inner surface of the pipes. If properly developed, the coating affords excellent protection against corrosive agents in the water.

Cathodic Protection. Corrosion can be suppressed by applying an electric current to metal so as to render it entirely cathodic.

Thus, the possibility of corroding is eliminated.

The cathodic protection current may be supplied galvanically or as impressed current. The metals for the simple cell in Fig. 6 can illustrate. In this case, the ferrous metal (representing the metal in the structure to be protected) would be made the cathode by selecting a metal higher in the galvanic series (magnesium) than the other electrode (anode). This anode would be located at some distance from, but wired to, the structure. When consumed by corrosion, it would be replaced to maintain protection.

Figures 7 and 8 show cathodic protection supplied by impressed current. Here, the polarity of the current is selected to

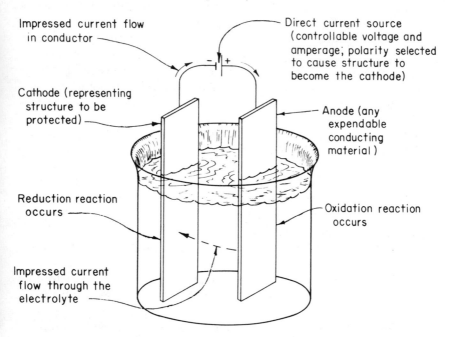

Fig. 6.   Impressed-current cathodic protection is effected by reversing the direction of current flow shown in the cell illustrated in Fig. 1 by means of an external current source. The natural potential is overridden by voltage from the external source, forcing the current to flow from the anode through the electrolyte to the cathode.

make the structure cathodic, and the choice of anode material is determined by its durability rather than its position in the galvanic series. The current and voltage can be as high as necessary to afford protection to large structures while overcoming soil or other resistances in the electrolyte (wet soil).

Cathodic protection is applicable only if metal is in contact with an electrolyte, as when buried in moist soils or immersed in water. It is especially suitable in proximity to waters with good conductivity and dissolved salts that will precipitate a carbonate film on the cathodic metal surface. The carbonate film is effective in reducing current requirements and tends to take over this function as the initial protective coating fails.

The choice of anodes depends on job conditions. Magnesium is most commonly used for galvanic anodes. However, zinc can also be used. Galvanic anodes are seldom used when the resistivity of the soil is over 3,000 ohm-centimeters; impressed current is normally used for these conditions. Graphic, high-silicon cast iron, scrap iron, aluminum, and platinum are used as anodes with impressed current. The availability of low-cost power is often the deciding factor in choosing between galvanic or impressed current cathodic protection.

Protective coatings are normally used in conjunction with cathodic protection and should not be neglected when this approach is contemplated. Since the cathodic protection current must protect only the bare or poorly insulated areas of the surface, coatings which are highly insulating, very durable, and free of discontinuities lower the current requirements and system costs. Moreover, a good coating enables a single impressed current installation to protect many miles of piping. Coal–tar enamel and vinyl resin are examples of coatings which are most suitable for use with cathodic protection. Certain other coatings may be incompatible. For instance, phenolic coatings may deteriorate rapidly in the alkaline environment created by the cathodic protection currents. Although cement mortar initially conducts the electrical current freely, polarization (formation of an insulating film on the surface as a result of the protective current) is believed to moderately reduce the current requirement.

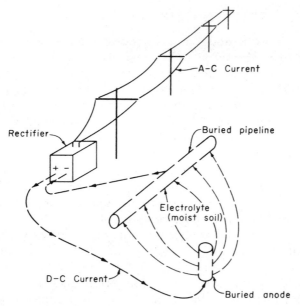

Fig. 7.   Field installation of impressed-current cathodic protection.

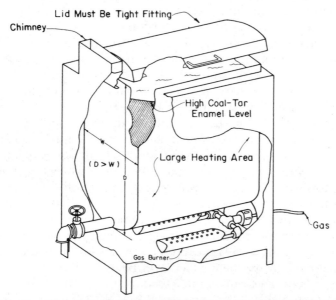

Fig. 8.   Diagram of the essential features of a properly designed small-sized coal–tar–enamel heating kettle suitable for field use.

Cathodic protection is being used increasingly to protect buried and submerged metal structures in the oil, gas, and waterworks industries. Specialized applications include the interiors of water storage tanks. Cathodic protection also should be considered a means of prolonging the life of old, corroded steel pipelines rather than replacing the lines. In addition, pipelines are now routinely designed to ensure the electrical continuity necessary for effective functioning of the cathodic protection system, if necessary later. Thus, electrical connections or bonds are required between pipe sections in lines with mechanically coupled joints. Insulating couplings may be employed at intervals to electrically isolate some parts of the line. Leads may be attached during construction to facilitate needed cathodic protection installation.

Corrosion-Resistant Alloys. Despite their high cost, corrosion-resistant alloys are increasingly in use. They are applicable where there is no satisfactory method of controlling the corrosion of ordinary iron and steel. With the new developments and decreased costs that may be expected, no doubt even greater use will be made of these alloys.

Stainless steels and nickel–copper alloys typify these corrosion-resistant metals, of which there are many. They must be selected with discrimination, according to environment. It should be remembered that although alloys are generally much more resistant to corrosion than ordinary iron and steel, they are not always immune. Also, these metals must not be used in conjunction with mild steel. In the passive state, they are cathodic to mild steel and can cause corrosion by galvanic action.

Protective Coatings. Paint is the oldest and still the most widespread means of combating corrosion. The paint film is a barrier between the corroding environment and the metal. In other words, it minimizes the contact of moisture and oxygen with the metal surface. Effectiveness depends not only on paint's moistureproof quality, but also on its ability to adhere and its own immunity to the corroding environment. (*See* Chapter 10, Painting Woodwork; Chapter 12, Preparation of Metal Surfaces and Paints, and Application of Paints; Chapter 13, Painting Concrete, Masonry, and Miscellaneous Surfaces.)

12

Preparation of Metal Surfaces and Paints, and Application of Paints

The first requisite for effectively painting iron and steel is proper cleaning of the surface. It is true that some coatings are more tolerant than others to the presence of foreign matter; however, nearly all coatings will last longer if applied to a truly clean surface. In many cases, this rigid requirement is the difference between success and failure of the coating job. The degree of cleaning will vary with the method and the conscientiousness and thoroughness with which it is applied. Cleaning should be accomplished in any case up to the limits of the method. With sandblasting or gritblasting all dirt, rust, and scale, including tight mill scale, are removed completely and the surface is roughened to provide keying for the coating, thus producing the best conditions for adhesion. (*See* Chapter 11, Painting Metalwork, the section on Cause of Corrosion.) For metal surfaces exposed to the atmosphere, where excessive condensation or spray does not exist, flame cleaning, wire-brushing, scraping, chipping, and cleaning by a rotary, tooth-edged tool are considered adequate methods and usually are less expensive and troublesome than blast cleaning. Brush-off (light) blasting is highly effective and, for cleaning large quantities of steel subjected to atmospheric exposure, such as structural steel, may also be more economical because the rapid cleaning rate lowers labor costs.

As indicated earlier, the degree of cleaning required varies somewhat for different kinds of paint. Because of adhesion problems, blast cleaning is considered a must for coal–tar enamel and phenolic and vinyl resin paints. Blast cleaning is not essential for alkyd vehicle paints, but a very clean surface is. If wire-brushing or other suitable cleaning is used, the surface should be completely free of rust and loose scale and dirt. Linseed-oil paints are more tolerant of surface impurities and irregularities, allowing more latitude in thoroughness of cleaning, given that a clean surface is still best. The minimum cleaning required will be found in later discussions on the application procedures for various paints.

Regardless of the cleaning method employed, dust and grit from the cleaning process or any other source should be removed before painting proceeds. It is also important to paint as soon as practicable after cleaning. A freshly cleaned surface is very susceptible to rusting, especially a blast cleaned surface in a humid atmosphere. The cleaning and painting schedule should be planned accordingly.

The need for a clean surface does not end with the first coat of paint. Any dust and dirt that collects between coats must also be removed to provide for good adhesion. Also, any grease or oil must be removed both in the initial cleaning and between coats.

WELD TREATMENT

Before preparing the general surface, weld areas may need special attention, to remove grease and resolve and other problems.

Metal spatter is usually poorly bonded. If left in place, later abrasion may knock it off, creating a holiday or blank spot in the coating. Even if it stays in place, the coating is likely to be abraded by such high points. This is true also for high, sharp protrusions on the welds. Chipping and grinding to remove spatter and smooth welds are important contributions to paint durability in these areas.

SOLVENT CLEANING

In general, oil and grease deposits on the surface of metal should be removed before cleaning the surface mechanically. This reduces the danger of leaving a greasy residue on the surface. In the shop, hot alkaline baths and solvent-vapor degreasing units are used extensively for removing oil and grease from relatively small articles. On large pieces of metalwork and in field cleaning operations, oil and grease removal is accomplished by washing with solvents.

Mineral spirits and low-boiling petroleum naphtha are good cleaning solvents as are xylene and low-boiling coal–tar naphtha. Benzenebenzol should not be used because of its excessive toxicity. White gasoline (lead-free) is a good solvent, but it is too dangerous to handle. All of these solvents are flammable and may set up explosive concentrations with air if ventilation is not adequate. Carbon tetrachloride is nonflammable, but it is extremely toxic. It is important that the cleaning solvent be free from high-boiling, such as are found, for example, in kerosene and diesel fuel. Otherwise, a nondrying greasy residue will be left on the surface with detrimental effect on the paint.

Solvent cleaning, unless performed correctly, can actually be detrimental by spreading grease or oil over a larger area than it originally covered. Clean solvent is necessary or more contamination may occur. When grease on the surface has been worked into the solvent, the mixture must be absorbed into clean, dry cloths promptly removed from the surface. Repeated cleanings will often be necessary.

SANDBLASTING AND GRITBLASTING

Blast cleaning is accomplished by forcibly driving hard particles of sand or steel grit under air pressure causing controlled erosion of the surface against which the blast is directed. This treatment not only removes all surface impurities, including tight mill scale, but also imparts an etched texture and a greatly increased bonding area.

The blasting material should be hard, sharp, and free from excessive fines and moisture. Blasting material passing a No. 16 U.S. standard screen, with at least 85 percent retained on a No. 50 U.S. standard screen, is very effective and suitable for a variety of paints. Dry air at a pressure of at least 80 to 100 pounds per square inch is required, and blasting efficiency is greater at higher pressures. Economy of operation can sometimes be improved by reuse of the blasting material, and expensive steel grit is almost always reused. Uncrushed shot should not be used because it peens a surface instead of cutting it.

Steel grit and good hard sand are considered equally effective as blasting media. Although it is very hard and tough, grit breaks down slowly. In repeated use, it also picks up contaminants from the surface being cleaned. Therefore, contaminants must be continuously separated from the smaller sizes. Also the grit must not be allowed to become oily. Similar separation is also required for the reuse of good sand which breaks down more rapidly. Soft sands break down so quickly that reuse is questionable. Local sands may also contain appreciable quantities of clay or dirt, evidenced by distinctive small streaks on the blasted surface where the dirt disintegrates. This indicates unsatisfactory washing of the sand. Large-sized grit or sand tends to be more effective in breaking up and removing thick, hard mill scale from steel, whereas small sizes brighten the surface noticeably by removing smaller contaminant particles more thoroughly. Large sizes also produce a high blast profile, a peak-to-valley distance of perhaps 10 mils for large steel grit. Obviously, this is desirable for thick coatings such as coal–tar enamel but is unsuitable for a 6-mil-thick VR-3 paint system. Thus, for the best and most rapid cleaning, a favorable mixture of sizes can be tailored to the particular paint to be applied and metal being cleaned.

Blast cleaning normally is specified only for severe exposures where maximum durability is sought and where failure will be most costly. Many modern paints exhibit little tolerance for any surface contaminants, which thus must be completely removed. The only apparent exception to obtaining a uniform, gray, well-etched surface involves the slight shadows that occasionally remain when weathered steel, partly covered with mill scale, is thoroughly blasted. Such areas may be considered adequately cleaned when thorough reblasting of a sample area fails to effect a noticeable brightening.

WIRE-BRUSHING

Surface preparation generally specified for atmospheric exposure paint calls for removing everything that poorly adheres to the surface, such as loose rust, dirt, and scale. The method is often termed wire-brushing, although scraping, chipping, blasting, or other effective means are also permitted.

Wire-brush cleaning cannot be expected to remove embedded oxides or tight mill scale, as will blast cleaning. The work is laborious if done by hand, but with power-driven rotary brushes, a good cleaning job can be fairly quickly accomplished. Care should be exerised to avoid burnishing the surface to extreme smoothness which will reduce paint adhesion.

FLAME CLEANING

Flame cleaning is accomplished by passing an oxyacetylene flame over the metal surface. The burner head is designed to provide a series of small, closely spaced, and very hot flames that are projected at high velocity. The effect is to reduce ordinary rust (hydrated ferric oxide) to powdered, black oxide of iron and to pop off loose mill scale through sudden differential expansion caused by the heat. After flame cleaning, the surface is readily wire-brushed to remove any loose material.

Flame cleaning, like direct wire-brushing, does not accomplish as thorough a job as blast cleaning because tight mill scale remains. It has the advantage, if painting proceeds promptly after cleaning, in that the warmed metal will facilitate wetting and bonding of the paint and drying of the paint film. Also, surface moisture, if any, will be removed.

ROTARY ABRADING TOOLS

Various tools facilitate effective surface cleaning, usually for touch-up painting where small areas have developed defects and both corrosion and old coatings are present. One suitable tool is the widely available body sander used in auto body repair. Fitted with the coarsest disks obtainable, the body sander not only exposes bright clean metal but leaves a slightly roughened surface for better coating adhesion.

Cleaning with another abrader tool is accomplished by bundles of toothedged cutter disks mounted on bars protruding about 1⅛ inches from a rotating shaft. The disks themselves are free to rotate on the bar, since the centered holes on the disks are much larger. As the shaft rotates, centrifugal force throws the disks outward. When the cutters strike a surface, the effect is that of a blow, rather than of grinding as would be the case with cutters fixed on the shaft.

Cleaning with these tools should provide faster and better quality metal surface preparation than wire-brushing under almost any circumstances, especially for removing well-bonded coating remnants. For painting purposes, the surface produced is not equal to that obtained from sandblasting, but it is free of loose and poor bonded material and is somewhat roughened. The fine residue from cleaning rust and other matter from the surface must be removed. Also, powered tools often spray oil, necessitating a subsequent solvent wash.

RUST REMOVERS

The use of rust remover is analogous to pickling in that oxide contaminations on the metal surface are removed or converted to innocuous films by application of acid solutions. Rust remover is not regarded to be as effective as sandblasting and normally is not specified for large areas. It also has little effect on thick, hard, tight rust. However, improved adhesion and suppressed blistering have been demonstrated, and the treatment can be highly beneficial. It is also routinely required to obtain coating bond to nonferrous surfaces.

There are a number of effective over-the-counter rust remover preparations. To use any of these you first remove all rust bubbles or debris and other loose materials that are not firmly attached. Then, the surface is treated with a metal conditioner and rust remover (MIL-C-10578, type 1) that can be applied by brushing, dipping, or spraying. The surface is then hosed off after five to ten minutes. Pools of water should be removed promptly and the surface dried. A gray film will remain on the dried surface. Occasionally, reapplication will be necessary for full effectiveness. Painting may proceed directly over this film or it may be delayed for two or three days, if desired, because of the temporary protection against rusting provided by the film.

TREATING GALVANIZED SURFACES

As indicated in the section on Galvanized Metal, best results in painting new galvanized metal will be obtained by using a zinc dust–zinc oxide primer for atmospheric exposures. For other paints, a reasonably good surface for painting is produced if the sheen is first "killed," that is, a dilute (about five percent strength) phosphoric acid solution is applied to wet the surface thoroughly. After the acid dries the surface should be rinsed with clear water and allowed to dry. A good over-the-counter treating agent, applied according to the manufacturer's instructions, is also satisfactory. Galvanized metal that has weathered to a dull, no-gloss appearance may be painted without pretreatment except when certain vinyl or other special paints are to be applied.

Before application of vinyl resin paints (VR-3 and VR-6), both new and aged galvanized surfaces should be treated with a metal conditioner (MIL-C-10578, type 1). (*See* the section on Rust Removers.) Mechanical cleaning is unnecessary, but any grease or oil should be removed, prior to acid treatment, by washing with solvent. However, light sandblasting prior to applying the metal conditioner is advisable when using vinyl paints, since etching of the surface improves the adhesion of these paints.

Sheet galvanized iron may be given a storage or stabilizing treatment to preserve the initial bright spandle of the zinc. The hexavalent chromium deposit is invisible to the eye, and detection requires a chemical colorimetric test performed on the surface. Unfortunately, paints will not bond to chromium, and light sandblasting is essential to remove it and roughen the surface before painting.

PREPARATION OF PAINTS

The discussion in Chapter 10, Painting Woodwork, pertaining to the preparation of wood paints applies to most metal paints as well. General procedures for mixing, thinning, and warming are the same. Special preparatory measures for certain metal paints are covered in later sections dealing with application procedures.

The need for thorough paint mixing prior to use and careful thinning bears repeating here. No paint will give full service unless it is uniformly mixed before use. This applies to pigmented paints, and to other paints that separate on standing or rely on thorough mixing to ensure contact of chemically reactive ingredients. There is no excuse for slighting the mixing operation; the time and effort required are essential to obtaining the full benefit of the specified formulation.

There is no quicker way to ruin paint than by indiscriminate thinning. Most paints used today are supplied ready for use without thinning. Where thinning is required or permissible, as will be indicated later, it is necessary to use correct amounts of the proper thinner.

APPLICATION OF PAINTS

In the following sections, certain general rules for good painting practice are discussed first, followed by procedures applicable to specific paints. For discrepancies between general rules and specific procedures exist, the specific procedures govern.

Atmospheric Conditions

In general, there is little danger of the weather being too warm for satisfactory painting. Nearly all paints will work better, flow better, and dry faster when the metal and surrounding atmosphere are warm. Warmth accelerates the oxidation–polymerization reaction in films of oil and varnish vehicle paints as well as evaporation of the solvent. Adhesion is also improved. All of these factors point to the desirability of painting during warm weather or in warm surroundings.

Some difficulty may ensue with certain paints if the metal surface is very hot, for example, metal exposed directly to the sun in hot weather. With very fast drying paints, such as vinyl resin paint, evaporation of the solvent may be too fast to permit proper flow and leveling. Most multicomponent paints will set very rapidly, possibly too quickly, since their chemical reactions are sharply accelerated by heat. It may be difficult to obtain adequate film thickness without excessive sagging in coatings applied in hot environments. Such cases are exceptions to the general rule; however, painting during the cooler hours of the day may be occasionally necessary. The principal concern with respect to temperature is that it not be too cold.

Unless suitably housed, metalwork should not be painted in rainy weather. High humidity alone frequently introduces complications. It tends to slow the drying of paint, although the effect is not so great as might be thought. The main difficulty with atmospheres of high humidity is the increased chance of condensation on the metal surface. Also, in atmospheres of high humidity, freshly cleaned surfaces rust rapidly, which introduces practical difficulties in scheduling the cleaning and painting sequence. There are no specific restrictions as far as humidity is concerned, but the surface must be dry and free from rust at the time of painting.

Painting cannot always be done in ideal atmospheric conditions and therefore, some limits must be set. Paint should be applied only when the humidity and the temperatures of the air and the metal surfaces to be painted are such that evaporation rather than condensation will result. The lowest temperature of metal and atmosphere at which painting should proceed should be set at 45°F. As temperatures decrease below this value, the chances of obtaining a satisfactory job become increasingly poor. Tolerance may sometimes be accorded the 45°F limit as it applies to atmospheric temperature. For example, coal–tar priming and enameling operations may proceed if necessary at air temperatures less than 45°F, if the metal is warmed to the point where good flow and adhesion are obtained. Also, vinyl resin paints may be applied when steel surfaces or ambient temperatures are as low as 40°F, provided the surfaces are free of moisture or frost. Since the presence of frost or ice crystals may be difficult to ascertain on steel surfaces, extreme caution must be exercised in painting steel that has been recently subjected to freezing temperatures. Before painting it is advisable to warm the steel or allow it to reach a temperature of 45°F to eliminate all frost following subfreezing temperatures.

Thinning beyond that normally specified should not be permitted as an aid to working in cold weather. Warming the paint is permissible when in conformance with the procedure described in Chapter 10, Painting Woodwork, in the section on Warming. Warming is often found to be of little advantage because the improved state of the paint in the container is quickly lost when the paint contacts chilled metal.

If painting cannot be deferred when weather conditions are unfavorable, the best solution is to provide heat with ventilation. Electric heat coupled with positive air change is most desirable. Open flame heating introduces hazards of fire and explosion; it also creates additional moisture to accelerate rusting of cleaned metal surfaces before painting. Heaters which discharge oily fumes can contaminate the surfaces and should not be allowed. Sheet plastic or tarpaulins for enclosing outside work in cold weather is practicable and necessary in many cases.

Dry Surface

A dry surface, as mentioned in the foregoing section, is very important to the successful painting of metalwork. Moisture interferes with intimate contact of the coating and thus impairs the bond. If moisture is worked into the paint, it disrupts the integrity of the film. Moisture also may be responsible for incipient rusting beneath the film, which tends to weaken bond.

Although it is conceivable that an invisible film of moisture could be harmful, such a condition is not considered a practical problem. If condensation of moisture is visible, however, even in minute quantities, painting should not proceed.

Application Methods

Paint materials are applied to metal surfaces by a wide variety of methods. Additional details are covered specifically for each kind of paint later in this chapter.

Brushing. The principal advantage of brush application is the assurance of intimate contact between the paint and the base material. Brushing works the paint into surface pores, cracks, and crevices more effectively than spraying, however, probably the greatest virtue of brushing lies in the ability to work any contaminating dust into the paint rather than allowing it to remain at the surface as a threat to coating adhesion. Thus, with brushing, small amounts of foreign matter can be tolerated. Common practice in most paint systems is to brush on priming coats and spray succeeding coats. Unless performed meticulously, brushing fails to achieve the uniform thickness and good appearance provided by the spray method. Brushes with synthetic fibers such as nylon should not be used with lacquer-type paints because the fibers are likely to dissolve. (*See* Chapter 7, Brush Painting.)

Roller Coating. Many of the advantages attributed to brush application can be obtained with roller application. In addition, smoother films of more uniform thickness can be applied much faster if good techniques are employed. Of course, irregular surfaces will still require brushing. Most paints can be roller applied. Rollering is especially desirable for coat–tar epoxy paint which does not brush out easily on large flat areas. Very satisfactory roller applications have been made to the exterior surfaces of large machinery using high-gloss machinery enamel. Piping, gates, and other metalwork are also suitable for roller coating. Roller coating is particularly suited to painting chain-link fencing. The paint is applied from one side, the nap of the roller wrapping over the wire to the other side and depositing paint which is spread by the roller on that side. Posts and other fence metalwork are generally painted by brush or spray.

In the usual roller process, some paint is placed in a tray with a sloping bottom; paint is picked up by partially immersing the roller. Paint is then evenly distributed by rolling back and forth on the sloped bottom of the tray. The loaded roller is then rolled back and forth over the surface being painted. Variations of this equipment are available, such as pressure-fed rollers or rollers that carry the paint supply in a hollow center core. Except possibly for extremely large areas, the tray and ordinary roller are recommended. This technique is particularly suited, but not restricted to applying architectural finishes to flat wall surfaces.

Rollers with different naps are available, and the proper roller for a particular application should be carefully selected. The naps vary not only in length and texture but also in fiber composition. Each variation has some effect on the appearance of the applied paint film. It is also important that rollers fabricated with naps of synthetic fibers not be used with paints containing high solvency thinners or diluents which might dissolve the nap. Accessory equipment, such as long handles and wire guides, are available to facilitate roller applications. (*See* Chapter 8, Roller Painting.)

Spraying. Spray painting requires special precautions and skilled techniques. Especially when a priming coat is sprayed, exceptionally clean base surfaces are required. If the paint is laid on over any dust film which may be present, adhesion is detrimentally affected. Spray equipment should be kept clean and in good working order, and recommended air caps and needle tips should be used for best results. An agitating pot should be used to maintain the paint in a well-mixed condition, and effective traps should be provided to keep air lines free from moisture and oil. The newly developed synthetic paints, especially, require close adherence to recommended procedures since their working characteristics are often different from those of conventional paints. Spray equipment is available for special materials, including heavy-bodied paints; the widespread use of other equipment, such as that with mixing heads for multicomponent paints, can be expected as these are developed and refined. The success of any painting depends much on skill, but particularly in spray painting, experience, not only with the spray painting operation but with any special paint in use, is necessary for good work.

Paints containing powerful solvents build up hazardous concentrations of noxious fumes if sprayed in confined locations lacking adequate ventilation. Precautions must be taken against inhalation and the possibility of fire or explosion.

Modifications of the familiar spraying operation are now achieving a certain amount of acceptance. One of these is airless spraying, so called because air under pressure is not utilized to atomize the material. Air-operated equipment produces material pressures up to 2,500 pounds per square inch, which, when used with special spray guns, provides atomization. Airless spraying significantly reduces over spray and, since there is no air blast, the paint tends to go where directed. This saves paint and permits spraying in confined areas with appreciably less masking.

Another modification, which may be used in conjunction with either airless or conventional air spray equipment, calls for heating the paint to as much as 150°F or 175°F prior to spraying. This may be done by means of a heat exchanger and hoses through which the material is circulated or by an electrical heater at or near the spray gun. Heating lowers the paint viscosity sufficiently to minimize or eliminate thinning. The solvents evaporate more completely between the gun and the surface than in other processes, and a thicker, dryer, more dense film may be deposited. The thicker coat favors lower application costs. However, solvent bubbles or blistering have been observed with this method. Further, certain paints undergo physical or chemical reactions at high temperatures which render them unsuitable for hot spraying.

An electrostatic feature can be incorporated into airless spray equipment. In this process, the finely atomized paint particles are electrically charged as they leave the gun, and the object to be painted is oppositely charged. The paint is thus attracted to the object. Particles blown by the object tend to draw back or wrap around the sides and back of the object. It thus becomes possible to coat irregularly shaped items by spraying from only one direction.

Electrostatic spraying has been utilized in industrial applications for years, and equipment suitable for field use is available.

Dipping and Flow Coating. Dipping and flow coating are two additional methods of applying protective coatings. Dipping is used for the application of coal–tar pitch to trashracks, and flow coating is utilized in the spinning process of applying coal–tar enamel.

Coverage and Drying

Proper film thickness has much to do with the serviceability metal coatings, especially those subjected to severe moisture conditions. Since preventing moisture and oxygen from reaching the metal surface is the primary basis for protection, a too-thin coating is of little value. This has been proven repeatedly in the laboratory and in service. Proper coverages and film thicknesses are discussed later for each kind of paint. Efforts should be made to assure the proper coverages and thicknesses.

In general, each coat of paint should be thoroughly dry before the next coat is applied. Otherwise, solvent entrapment, softening and lifting of the undercoat, sagging, alligatoring, and other deficiencies in the completed coating commonly result. The proper drying time varies considerably with different paints.

Vinyl Resin Paint

The best quality of sandblast or gritblast cleaning to base metal is essential for the proper adhesion of vinyl resin paint.

VR-6 System. The six coats of the VR-6 system consists of one priming coat, three body coats, and two seal coats. (*See* the section on Underwater Exposure, Cement Mortar.) These materials are distinctly different but are applied to a combined dry-film thickness of 10 to 15 mils. Because the formulations of different manufacturers vary in solids content, the criterion for acceptable coverage is determined by the dry-film thickness required for body and seal coats. Coverage given in the specifications should be viewed only as a general guide.

The prime coat (provided in colors contrasting with blast-cleaned steel) is applied by brushing at a coverage rate of not more than 250 square feet per gallon. Drying time for this coat may vary from one to 12 hours, depending on temperature and air circulation. Four hours is a common drying period. Being a very low solids material, the primer contributes little to coating thickness. It is the only coat in the system that must contain adherent resins for bonding to the metal.

The first overall body coat (iron oxide red) is applied by spraying at not more than 150 square feet per gallon. The second body coat (gray) and third body coat (iron oxide red) are applied in the same manner, allowing 12 hours minimum time between coats.

Vinyl resin mastic VR-M is applied as an edge coat after the first body coat. (*See* the section on VR-M Vinyl Resin Mastic.)

Twelve hours minimum drying time should be allowed between the third body coat and the first seal coat. The seal coat may be any color desired, but aluminum is the best choice for durability unless the coating is to be subjected to acids or alkalies. (*See* the section on Special Conditions, Acids, and Alkalies.) Aluminum seal-coat paint is prepared just before use by incorporating aluminum pigment paste in the clear vehicle at the rate of 1.5 pounds of paste to one gallon of vehicle. (*See* the section on Preparation of Paints.) Seal coats in colors are ready-mixed. The two seal coats are applied by spraying each at a coverage rate of not more than 200 square feet per gallon, at least 12 hours for drying between coats. The finished coating should be allowed to dry hard before the item painted is subjected to service, and this requires about ten days under normal drying conditions.

Because of the low solids content and the extreme volatility of the solvents, the primer must be applied with a full brush or roller and spread rapidly; it should not be spread out to a thin coat. In spraying body and seal coats, air pressures in the paint pot and at the atomizing head must be regulated in relation to the atmospheric temperatures. As a guide, at an air temperature of approximately 70°F, the atomizing pressure should be 60 to

100 pounds per square inch and the paint pot pressure should be 40 to 60 pounds per square inch. For temperatures below 70°F, the pot pressure should be increased, and for temperatures above 70°F, it should be decreased.

Multipass spraying is often used to build the full thickness of the coat without sags. This consists of two or more spray passes over each point on the surface with a short time interval between passes, and the passes should be applied at right angles to each other (cross spraying) to enhance uniform thickness. Because of the high volatility of the solvents in vinyl paints, applying a fully wet coat is most important. The paint loses much of its solvents between the spray gun and the surface. Holding the gun normally, aimed directly and 8 to 10 inches from the surface, will produce a wet coat and virtually eliminate overspray. Overspray, if any, must be removed from any coat by light sanding before more paint will bond well.

Vinyl resin paint should be thinned only as directed by the paint manufacturer and with special thinner provided by the manufacturer. Powerful thinning solvents are required for this paint; ordinary thinners are not suitable since they act as contaminants. Paint brushes, which must be of natural bristles, and spray equipment should be cleaned with the thinning solvent.

VR-3 System. In this system, three or four (or more) similar coats of a single-solution vinyl resin paint are applied to a minimum dry-film thickness of five to six mils, following the same general rules as for the six-coat system. Thickness variations occur because this paint system is put to different uses. For oil reservoirs, three coats and five mils total thickness are specified. For metalwork in contact with water, four coats and six mils thickness are required. Vinyl resin mastic VR-M is applied as an edge coat after the second coat. (*See* the following section on VR-M Vinyl Resin Mastic.) VR-3 vinyl resin paint is formulated to serve both as primer and top coats.

VR-M Vinyl Resin Mastic. The mastic coating mentioned in the preceding sections follows the second coat of the VR-3 and VR-6 systems. This coating is applied to rivets, welds that are not ground flush, bolts, seams, sharp corners and edges, and as a filler between adjacent metal parts in the absence of a weld. The mastic adds protection where the paint is often thin and abrasion is likely to puncture it. Two coats are applied at seven mils per coat, with four hours drying time between coats and 12 hours after the second coat.

As received, the quite viscous mastic is usually hard to apply, and thinning up to a pint per gallon with the manufacturer's special solvent improves its characteristics. Application is usually by a stiff, short-bristled brush. This method meters the mastic accurately and limits it to the desired location. The finished work should be smooth, although not necessarily as smooth as the vinyl resin paints. The top coats which follow conceal the slight roughness, making the mastic hardly noticeable.

Sand-filled Vinyl Paint System

This system is recommended as a repair procedure for inverts of steel pipe previously coated with vinyl resin paint which has been eroded by sand- and gravel-laden water. If the original coating is intact with a remaining dry film thickness of at least four mils in the invert, application of the armor coating can proceed after cleaning the surface and performing touch-up repairs. In the absence of an intact coating, the paint thickness should be brought up to four mils, or the surface should be blast cleaned and given two coats according to standard practice, as necessary.

Following these preparations, a coat of VR-3 is applied at 250 square feet per gallon, adding sand to the wet paint at the rate of about 0.1 pound per square foot. It is necessary to have a helper sprinkling the sand immediately after the paint application to make sure the sand is embedded into wet VR-3. After this coating has dried for at least 12 hours, the loose sand should be blown or brushed away. A third coat of VR-3 is next applied at 250 square feet per gallon to completely embed the sand. The system should be allowed to dry at least 10 days before the pipe is placed in service.

This system should result in a coating 15 to 25 mils thick. The sand used should be natural Ottawa, graded to pass through a No. 20 sieve and be retained in a No. 30 sieve. River sand, properly graded and washed, may also be suitable for embedment, but in view of the small quantities used, Ottawa silica sand is preferable, mainly because the particles are uniform and free of silt and other foreign matter.

Enamels and Aluminum Paints

Normally, wire-brush cleaning is specified for enamels and aluminum paints, both atmospheric paints. Blast cleaning improves paint performance, but for most items the extra cost is not warranted except in a few instances where interrupting service for maintenance painting is very costly, as for certain electrical equipment.

Priming of surfaces to be finished with enamel and aluminum paint is as important, if not more so, than the finish painting because the life of the finish coats will be no better than that of the base to which they are applied. Brush or roller application is generally preferred for the prime coat. (*See* the section on Application Methods.) This is especially true of the quick-drying priming paints. Spray application is satisfactory only if the surface has been vigorously cleaned and roughened and is completely free from dust. Spray application of linseed-oil or linseed-oil alkyd base primers, for instance, is satisfactory if the surface has been cleaned of essentially all mill scale, rust, and other contaminants by sandblasting. Drying time for the primer should be at least 36 hours for linseed-oil base paints, and at least six hours for paints with straight alkyd or phenolic base. It is good practice to follow the overall priming coat with an additional coat of priming paint over rivets, welds, bolts, and sharp corners and edges. In the application of phenolic red lead paints, extended delays between the application of successive coats of the paint should be avoided. Poor cohesion of the phenolic red lead paint coats or between phenolic red lead and a phenolic aluminum top coat may result if the drying time between coats of paint exceeds by 48 hours the time required for the paint films to become "dry through." (A paint film may be considered dry through when it cannot be distorted or removed by exerting moderate pressure with the thumb and turning the thumb 90° in the plane of the paint film.) On the other hand, enamels contain solvents which soften the primer and effect a satisfactory bond between coats.

Epoxy cement to fill irregularities in castings should be applied before priming. It may be applied by brush, troweling, or any convenient method recommended by the manufacturer.

Sufficiently dry cement should be smoothed with several grades of sandpaper or steel wool.

Finish coats of aluminum paint and enamel may be applied by brush, roller, or spray. Spraying is usually preferred because it is much faster and ordinarily provides the most attractive finish. Two coats are desirable for good durability, even though one coat, especially in the case of aluminum paint, may provide adequate hiding and a satisfactory appearance. Aluminum paint should be prepared from the pigment paste and vehicle as needed (not more than a one-day supply) to maintain good leafing of the aluminum pigment. (*See* the section on Preparation of Paints.) Enamels and aluminum paints should be applied at approximately 500 square feet per gallon. Drying time between coats should be at least 16 hours. It is often desirable to add two to three ounces of Prussian blue pigment in oil to one gallon of aluminum paint for the first coat so that it can be readily distinguished from the final coat. The first coat of enamels may likewise be shaded with pigments in oil or by mixing in a small amount of another enamel color.

Metalwork to be finished with aluminum paint or enamel is sometimes supplied by the fabricator with the priming coat already applied. In some cases, an item may be furnished with a complete paint system applied at the factory but a different color than that needed to harmonize with other nearby painting. The obvious remedy is to repaint in the desired color after any necessary repairs to the shop coating are properly made. The shop coat should first be examined to see that it is in good condition and has not been applied over rust or loose scale. Bake-on finishes and high-gloss enamels should be sanded to remove any glaze. If the shop coat is satisfactory, simply clean the surface and touch up abrasions in the coating with priming paint before proceeding with the finish painting. Any rust at abrasions should be removed. If the shop coat is in generally poor condition, it should be completely removed and replaced by a complete paint system, including primer, applied.

Linseed Oil Paints

The section on Outside Atmospheric Exposure, Linseed Oil Finish Paints mentions a rather limited application for these paints in metal painting, except that black graphic paint and black iron oxide paint are sometimes used as finish coats for railroad bridges in relocation work. The general application procedure discussed in the previous section apply. Drying time between coats, however, must be extended to a minimum of 36 hours, and if drying conditions are not favorable, a longer period should elapse. Where two coats of the same color are to be applied, the first coat may be shaded with pigment in oil to assist in distinguishing between coats.

Painting Galvanized Metal

Application procedures for paints to go on galvanized metal are the same as those described for ordinary iron and steel paints. New galvanized surfaces should be pretreated for vinyl resin and other paints not specially intended for galvanized surfaces. (*See* Chapter 9, the section on Special Conditions, Galvanized Metal; and Chapter 10, the section on Treating Galvanized Surfaces.)

Insulating Lacquer

Insulating lacquer may be applied by brushing, spraying, or dipping. It is very fast drying, requiring only one hour. Surfaces should be free from grease, oil, rust, and dirt at the time of painting.

13

Painting Concrete, Masonry, and Miscellaneous Surfaces

In most instances, concrete and masonry is painted primarily for decorative, lighting, or sanitary purposes rather than to protect or preserve the material. An exception is the preservative treatment for concrete that is subject to excessive freezing and thawing. Coatings are also used on concrete for waterproofing and dampproofing. By holding out moisture, they are often valuable in preventing damage to finishes on interior wall surfaces.

Another use for coatings on concrete is for mold and algae control. They prevent growth and thereby keep concrete-lined canals, swimming pools, and basement walls free from offending material. Investigation of such coatings continues because, periodic replacement is required for these coatings to sustain their effectiveness.

A recent development is the application of resin base, paint-like compounds for the curing of concrete. Among other advantages, these compounds prevent rusting and provide a surface which can be top coated with any of several paints or which will retain the normal concrete appearance for long periods.

(*See* Appendix 4, Table 6, Guide for Selecting Paint.)

SELECTION OF PAINTS FOR CONCRETE

Selection of paint for use on *concrete* is influenced by structure, exposure, condition of the surface, and function of the coating. For example, a suitable coating for the exterior exposed surfaces of a concrete building may be entirely unsatisfactory for use on concrete floors or as a waterproofing treatment. One paint may be suitable for use on dense, smoothly finished concrete while another is more appropriate for coating open, porous concrete, even though the functional requirements are the same.

The location of moisture, if any is present in the exposure, vitally affects the choice of coatings for concrete and masonry. In particular, an impermeable, membrane-type coating often performs poorly on concrete if a source of water exists behind the coated surface. Thus, attempts to dry out damp basements by painting interior wall surfaces may be unsuccessful unless inconvenient, costly, and specialized cleaning procedures and materials are employed. The high alkalinity of moisture within concrete deteriorates some paints, such as alkyd base materials, at the paint–concrete interface. Further, few materials adhere well enough an develop sufficient film strength to resist water under appreciable pressure in the concrete. On the other hand, the same membrane-forming paints may do well if the high humidity or liquid water are present only on the coated side of the surface. Thus, if at all possible, a wall generally should be sealed from the water (pressure) side. An alkali-resistant, breathing paint will shed intermittent water from the coated side while permitting the escape of water vapor from within a concrete wall. In general, wherever water is present in the exposure of a concrete and masonry paint, its effect should be carefully considered in selecting the correct paint.

The following sections consider different conditions that influence the selection of suitable coatings.

Walls

This discussion applies to exterior and interior concrete walls exposed to the atmosphere, and also to stucco surfaces, asbestos

Table 6
Coatings (Paints) for Concrete Surfaces

Title	Federal Specification	Finish	Substrate	Remarks
Walls, Exterior, Above Grade				
Portland cement paint	—	Flat, white and colors	Concrete and masonry	Water cure required. Powder.
Portland cement paint	TT-P-0035	Flat, white and colors	Concrete and masonry	No water cure required. Powder.
Vinyl resin	—	Flat or low gloss	Concrete	Impermeable film. Nct for course, rough surfaces.
Oil vehicle	TT-P-24D	White or light tints	Concrete and masonry	Primer required on new surfaces. Alkali vulnerable.
Polyvinyl acetate	TT-P-55B	Flat, white and tints	Concrete and masonry	Grout fill porous surfaces. Self-priming.
Styrene butadiene	TT-P-97D	Flat, white	Concrete, stucco, and masonry	Self-cleaning. Two coats on new work.
Acrylic emulsion	TT-P-19C	Flat, white and colors	Concrete and masonry	Fill porous surfaces. Self-priming.

Walls, Interior

Portland cement paint	TT-P-21	(see exterior walls)		Not easily washed.
Portland cement paint	TT-P-35	(see exterior walls)		Not easily washed.
Polyester epoxy	TT-C-545	A two-component, hard surface paint. For surfaces subject to hard wear and chemical cleaning agents.		
Interior latex	TT-P-29H	Flat, white and tints	Concrete and masonry	No primer or pretreatment.
Oil or varnish base	TT-E-506	Gloss	Only on dry concrete	Require pretreatment with surface sealer.
	TT-E-508	Semigloss		

Floors

Rapid wear from traffic removes paint from surfaces. Better results obtained by incorporating color pigments in the concrete.

Varnish (enamel)	TT-E-487	Gloss	Only on dry, aged concrete	
Rubber base	TT-P-91D		Concrete and masonry	Interior floors subject to dampness.
Polyurethane base	TT-C-542		Concrete	Interior floors subject to dampness.
Floor sealer	TT-S-178B	Clear	Concrete	
Floor sealer	Magnesium fluosilicate and other chemicals are used for surface hardening and to reduce dusting.			
Floor wax	P-W-155	Semigloss	Painted or colored concrete	Easy to apply.
Floor wax	P-W-158	Glossy	Painted or colored concrete	More durable.

cement siding, concrete masonry, and cinder block. Usually, the principal objective of the painting is decoration, but improved lighting for interiors and dampproofing are frequent influences.

For exterior surfaces, several paints are used. These include primarily portland cement base, vinyl resin, oil vehicle, and the three common types of latex paints—polyvinyl acetate, styrene—butadiene, and acrylic. Any of these paints, if properly formulated and applied, will combine very good durability with pleasing appearance in most outside atmospheres. Vinyl resin paint produces an impermeable film that essentially waterproofs the surface. The others have a dampproofing effect, but an oil base film is usually considered most effective in this respect. The exterior latex paints and the portland cement base paints produce films that permit the structure to "breathe"; that is, moisture vapor is transmitted from the inside to the outside of the structure through the walls will also pass through the paint film as a vapor. Blistering caused by severe moisture conditions is thereby eliminated. Portland cement paint produces a flat finish, and vinyl and latex paints generally produce a low gloss or flat finish, whereas various degrees of gloss may be obtained with an oil paint.

Portland cement paint is more suitable for a coarse, rough surface than other paints, although relatively smooth surfaces can be created for the other paints by applying a filler coat. A special treatment to roughen very smooth, dense, or glazed surfaces must precede applications of portland cement paint, or the finish is apt to fail prematurely by flaking. (*See* the section on Roughening.) Portland cement paint is considered especially durable as a coating to be subjected to much moisture. It is not, however, suited for surfaces like concrete floors that are subjected to traffic.

Cement paint, vinyl paint, and the exterior latex paints are inherently immune to alkali in concrete and, for this reason, may be applied while the concrete is relatively new, only a few weeks old. The usual oil paint is vulnerable to attack by alkali, and at least three months and preferably a year should elapse before it is applied. Surface pretreatments are effective in reducing the waiting period before application of oil paint to masonry surfaces, (See the section on Pretreatments.) Also, priming with a surface sealer that is not susceptible to alkali promotes the effectiveness of oil paint. However, with the development of exterior latex paints, the use of exterior oil base masonry paints has gradually declined. There remain but a few instances when an oil base paint is seriously considered for use on masonry. (See Appendix 1, List of Specifications for Paints and Accessory Materials.) Federal Specification TT-P-24 covers an exterior oil-base paint for concrete and masonry in eggshell finish and white or light tints.

For the first coat on surfaces not previously painted, a priming paint prepared by adding two quarts of spar varnish (federal specification TT-V-121) and one pint of mineral spirits (TT-T-291) to one gallon of an exterior oil-base paint for concrete and masonry (TT-P-24) is suggested. This first coat is followed with the same oil paint, applied without modifications, as the finish coat. If a higher gloss is desired, outside wood paint (TT-P-102) or gloss and semigloss enamels (TT-E-489 and TT-E-529) are suggested for the finish coat.

The exterior latex paints (TT-P-19 and TT-P-55) in acrylic emulsion and polyvinyl acetate emulsion (homopolymer or copolymer types) are excellent also. No unusual surface preparation is required on new work with these paints, except that porous surfaces may first be filled with a grout coat. These grout coats will contain a small amount of the base resin. On previously painted surfaces, all loose powdery or flaking material, heavy chalking, and dirt should be removed, preferably by sandblasting. If sandblasting cannot be accomplished, as much loose material as possible should be removed by wire-brushing the surface, then coating with low-solids-content, alkali-resistant varnish that has good penetrating properties. The sealer should be thoroughly dry before application of the paint.

Use vinyl resin paint (VR-3) for sealing interior or exterior concrete and masonry walls exposed to unusually wet conditions, such as walls wet from spray. The coating should go on the water side of the surface, which must be reasonably smooth to enable applying a pinhole-free film. Either surface filler is required, or the vinyl mastic (VR-M) may be applied after the surface has been primed. Three sprayed coats of VR-3 are required; however, the first is thinned with an equal amount of vinyl solvent and applied at about one gallon per 150 square feet to enhance adhesion. The top coats are then applied at normal coverage without thinning.

Interior surfaces subject to hard use may be given a polyester–epoxy coating (federal specification TT-C-545). This two-component hard surface paint may be applied over a variety of surfaces and resists heavy-duty chemical cleaners.

Painting the interior surfaces of outside concrete walls sometimes poses a greater problem than painting the exterior surfaces because a smooth and at least somewhat glossy finish is often desired. Paint that provides such a finish is of the tight-scaling, non-breathing variety—a variety that is apt to blister and peel if moisture penetrates through the wall. If the wall is below grade, the problem is aggravated.

Epoxy paints resist the alkali in concrete, and certain paints are said to develop adhesion and film strength adequate to seal out moisture moving through a concrete wall. Oil or varnish base paint will usually give trouble unless the concrete is completely sealed—with no chance of water moving through it. Where possible, a surface sealer (TT-S-179) followed by one of the interior finish paints, TT-E-508, semi-gloss, TT-E-506, gloss, or a comparable odorless type, is suitable. A very satisfactory paint for interior walls which does not require special priming or pretreatment of the surface is interior latex paint, (TT-P-29). This is usually a flat finish, breathing paint that presents a pleasing appearance. Portland cement paint is satisfactory if a flat finish is not objectionable and easy washability is not required.

Floors

Painting concrete floors for decoration is usually not very satisfactory because of rapid wear from traffic. Better results are obtained by incorporating color pigments in the floor topping, and scaling and waxing to increase gloss and facilitate maintenance.

A varnish vehicle paint, available under federal specification TT-E-487, is intended for use on dry, aged concrete floors, and for wooden floors and decks, as mentioned in the section on Paint for Softwood Floors. A rubber base paint, (federal specification TT-P-91) or a polyurethane base material (TT-C-542) should be used where the concrete is subject to dampness because both these are resistant to alkali attack. They are also considered superior to varnish base paint in wear resistance. They should be used only on interior concrete floors, though, as rapid degradation occurs with outdoor exposure. Floor sealer (TT-S-176) is suggested where a clear treatment is desired. Magnesium fluosilicate and other chemical solutions are sometimes used for surface hardening and reduced dusting. Wax, for finishing painted floors or colored topping, may be of either the solvent type (P-W-158) or the water-emulsion type (P-W-155). The former is considered more durable; the latter is easier to apply and does not require polishing.

Waterproofing and Dampproofing Coatings

Waterproofing concrete walls by applying coatings is not practiced to any great extent in new construction. Reliance is placed on designing and placing concrete of such quality, imperviousness, and thickness that the need for waterproofing is precluded. Cracks and joints usually provide for the ingress of water. A sealing system is often included in the design for the joints. The waterproofing system for the general surface must be able to accommodate small, slow movements at any cracks. Earth placed against a wall to be waterproofed means the application must also resist backfill damage. In the past a buildup membrane system has consisted of coal–tar pitch and coal–tar saturated cotton fabric. Currently, prefabricated composite sheets, composed of asphalt, plastic, and perhaps backfill-shielding materials, appear likely to be favored because of their ease of installation.

A number of waterproofing systems have been applied in recent years to concrete roof decks. Difficulty with the long-specified five-ply coal–tar pitch and felt roofing membrane system prompted investigation of new systems being developed in the industry. Roofing systems consist of (1) sheet neoprene or butyl rubber with liquid-applied chlorosulfonated polyethylene

Table 7
Waterproofing and Dampproofing

Waterproofing of concrete walls is best accomplished by designing and placing concrete of such quality, impermeability, and thickness that the need for waterproofing is precluded.

Walls, Exterior, Below Grade
Built up membrane system of coal–tar pitch and coal–tar saturated fabric. Prefabricated composite sheets.

Bituminous coating	SS-A-674	Asphalt emulsion	Concrete	Satisfactory on damp surfaces.

Walls, Exterior, Above Grade
Any light-colored resin, wax, or drying oil, or a combination of these in an organic solvent.

Linseed oil, two coats				Cover with outside white lead and oil paint.
Oil base paint	TT-P-102D	White and tints	Over linseed oil treatment	To slow rapid deterioration.
Copolymer resins	TT-P-1411A		Concrete and masonry	Waterproofing.
Silicone	SW-W-110		Unpainted concrete and portland cement painted surfaces	Two coats for maximum absorption into surface.

Algae Preventive Paints
To inhibit algae attachment to concrete. Antifouling TT-P-117A used to protect ships' bottoms can be effective. They contain an algicide such as cuprous oxide.

Other Coatings

Paint	TT-P-0033	Latex base	Masonry	Exterior.
Paint	TT-P-95A	Rubber	Concrete and masonry	Swimming pools.
Styrene acrylate	TTP-1181A	Tints and deep tones	Masonry	Exterior.
Coating	TT-C-555	Textured	Masonry	Interior and exterior.

weather-resistant topcoats, (2) liquid-applied neoprene with the weather-resistant top coats, (3) liquid-applied silicone rubber over spray-applied polyurethane foam, and (4) asphalt and felt membrane topped with polystyrene board insulation and gravel.

Depending on the degree of watertightness required and the importance of abrasion resistance, other more economical coatings may be used for waterproofing. For example, vinyl resin paint (VR-3) applied to the interior of a concrete water storage tank would sharply reduce water permeation through the walls. However, achieving a pinhole-free coating over such a surface with this thin film coating requires great care. Coal–tar epoxy paint might give better results. Neither of these coatings tolerate movement at any cracks or joints, which would have to be sealed by other means. Dampproofing, which involves surface treatment to reduce penetration of moisture under no appreciable head, can be accomplished with a number of materials.

For dampproofing exterior concrete below grade, a bituminous coating such as asphalt emulsion can be applied satisfactorily to damp surfaces. Suitable asphalt emulsion is covered by federal specification (SS-A-674, type RS-1 or RS-2K), modified by the added requirement that the emulsion must bond effectively with hydrophilic aggregate in the presence of water.

For dampproofing above grade, as for wall areas subject to a fluctuating water level, a clear material may be desired for the sake of appearance. Basically, such a material may consist of almost any light-colored resin, wax, or drying oil, or a combination of these, dissolved in an organic solvent. This material must be capable of penetrating into the pores of concrete and, after evaporation of the solvent, leaving a nearly colorless residue that is insoluble in water.

Damage to parapet walls, handrailings, and other concrete prominently exposed to freezing and thawing is being noted more frequently as structures age. Deterioration can be retarded by preventing moisture from entering the concrete. A number of paints based on a variety of synthetic resins are in testing in an effort to find a better and more versatile weatherproofing coating.

Silicone dampproofers or water repellents, (federal specification SS-W-110) are used for dampproofing the exterior walls of masonry and concrete buildings. Silicone water repellents are applied in a flood coat, with a rundown of at least 12 inches, so that maximum absorption into the surface occurs. Usually, two such coats are applied within two to four hours of each other. The second application does not increase the water repellency of the treated surface but merely increases the useful life of the treatment. The silicone treatment is moderately effective on smooth, unpainted concrete and masonry and on surfaces painted with portland cement paint. The dampproofing properties of the portland cement paint are enhanced by the subsequent application of silicone water repellent. On the other hand, the water repellent is ineffective in preventing water entering through highly porous masonry blocks or where cracks exist, particularly if the water is wind-driven. Unsatisfactory performance has been experienced where the joint mortar between masonry blocks has been "torn" or distorted by pointing or raking tools, effectively producing a crack in the joint.

PAINTS FOR BRICK AND STONE

Painting brick and stone surfaces is much the same as painting concrete. Although alkaline reactivity is absent from the masonry itself, it occurs at the mortar joints. Selection of paint should be governed by the general considerations given in the section on Selection of Paints for Concrete.

PAINTS FOR WALLBOARD

Under consideration here are wallboard, fiberboard, and hard-pressed board, used commonly for interior walls and ceilings of residences and office buildings.

Interior latex base paints are now in popular use for interior walls. These paints are easy for the novice to apply in a uniform coating, and they do not possess the solvent odor of varnish base paints. The latex base paints are highly regarded for use on interior walls where a flat finish is desired. Specifications requirements for resistance to repeated cleaning are more stringent than for flat varnish base paint, and excellent serviceability can be expected. The paint industry is also developing latexes in a semigloss luster. Latex base paints are easy to apply with either a brush or roller; they do not show lap marks, they dry rapidly; and they may be touched up at a later date without showing spots. Latex base paints often may be applied directly, without a primer, in one or two coats, as necessary to produce the desired appearance. Brushes and other tools may be cleaned by washing with soap and water, provided the paint has not been allowed to dry completely. Latex base paints are available in a variety of colors (TT-P-29). For a textured effect, a latex base texture paint may be used as the first coat, or an inert filler may be added to the regular latex paint to give it sufficient body to achieve a texture.

Where a high-gloss or semigloss finish is desired, varnish base paints are more commonly used than any other paints. The first coat on new surfaces should be a surface sealer (TT-S-179). For a high-gloss finish enamel (TT-E-506) or odorless enamel (TT-E-505) is used; and for a semigloss finish (TT-E-508) enamel or odorless enamel (TT-E-509) may be used. If the surface sealer is tinted to a near match with the finish paint, good hiding will be attained, and only one finish coat may be necessary. Two finish coats, however, are usually recommended to achieve the ultimate in beauty and durability. Two surface sealer coats may be necessary on fiberboard or other porous surfaces so that the finish paints will not be absorbed.

MISCELLANEOUS COATINGS

Many other coatings for concrete and masonry surfaces are on the market. Many are special coatings incorporating such resins as straight vinyl chloride, epoxy, chlorinated rubber, and polyurethane. Some are mastic types, some contain special fillers, and others are designed for one-coat applications.

COATINGS FOR SPECIAL FLOORINGS

Some special flooring materials such as terrazzo, marble, linoleum, and the various tiles do not require painting in the usual sense, but they do need preservative treatment for the best service and appearance. Waxing is a common method of preserving special floorings. Water-emulsion floor wax, (federal specification P-W-155) is usually preferred because it requires no buffing for a medium gloss finish and is not as slippery as a polished solvent-type wax film. In any event, the solvent wax should not be used on asphalt, vinyl, or rubber tile because of the effect of the solvent on these materials. Floor sealer, (TT-S-176, 25 percent nonvolatile class) is satisfactory for terrazzo floors where it is necessary to prevent grease penetration.

PREPARATION OF SURFACES

As in any painting, it is important to have a firm base, free from loose material and contamination, for good service to be obtained from paints applied to concrete, plaster, and similar surfaces. Wax base curing compound acts as a bond breaker or parting compound and must be completely removed. Efflorescence also must be removed and, perhaps, repairs made. Cracks which open and close or move slightly may require sealing with an elastomeric material. Rough surfaces may require filling, and glazed surfaces may need roughening. For some paints, alkalinity may have to be neutralized by a pretreatment. Finally, effective moisture controls must meet the needs of the particular paint being applied.

On occasion, extensive concrete repairs will be required before painting can be accomplished. These compounds, primarily epoxy–polysulfide blends, display outstanding adhesion to portland cement concrete if properly handled and applied. Their use should greatly facilitate repair work on concrete structures.

New plaster surfaces usually require no more than dusting, regardless of the paint used. Concrete, brick, and stone surfaces may require hosing with clean water to remove dirt. Special floorings should be washed with soap and water before waxing. A neutral soap should be used on marble, terrazzo, and ceramic-tile floors. Alkaline cleaning agents, such as washing soda and trisodium phosphate solutions, are harmful to marble and terrazzo and to the mortar joints of ceramic tile. Any soap or other detergent in water solution may be used on linoleum, asphalt-vinyl, or rubber-tile floors.

Removing Efflorescence

Filler coats of paint, whether latex, portland cement, or organic base, should not be applied over efflorescence because of impairment of bond, durability, and appearance. In many cases, most of the deposit can first be removed mechanically by chipping and scraping. Then, use of a 10 percent solution of hydrochloric acid is suggested. The area is wetted first with water. The acid is then applied, and after about five minutes the deposits are scrubbed off with a stiff brush. Thorough rinsing of the treated area with clear water should follow promptly.

Filling and Smoothing

Concrete or masonry may require surface filling for appearance, or for a smooth surface to provide the base for a pinhole-free paint coating. This may be accomplished by applying a cement mortar surface filler, often referred to as a sack-rubbed finish. Before applying the filler, the surface should be hosed down thoroughly and free water drained off. The cement mortar consists of one part portland cement to one part sand, able to pass through a No. 50 screen, and sufficient water to produce a grout having the consistency of thick cream. The preferred method of applying the grout is by scrubbing with a stiff-bristled brush or burlap cloth so as to fill all pits and pores. None of the filler should remain on the surface except in the depressions. When the filler has set, the surface must be kept moist by periodic wetting for at least three days to effect a cure and then moisture conditioned as required for the particular paint.

For vinyl resin paint applied as *moisture proofing*, a pin-hole-free coating requires a good surface. This may be obtained by applying a cement mortar surface filler. Alternatively, the vinyl priming coat may be followed by filling holes and smoothing rough areas with vinyl resin mastic (VR-M) and then applying the remaining paint coats.

Prepared fillers are available for latex paints to be used in atmospheric exposure only. There are fillers to match many latex paints, but there is also a filler suitable for all types. These fillers should all be applied in accordance with the manufacturers' instructions. An important advantage of the prepared fillers is that they are handled and cured as paint materials and require no prolonged water cure.

Pretreatments

The preferred pretreatment for concrete is to age it for as long a time as practicable before painting. This permits the carbonation of lime at the concrete surface, making it inactive with respect to the paint vehicle. It also enables the concrete to dry thoroughly and thus attain a better condition for painting. Next, success in painting the concrete is enhanced if the materials are inherently resistant to the alkali. The popularity of latex, vinyl, and other synthetic paints attests to the validity of this approach.

Oil or varnish base paints are susceptible to alkali attack and, if they must be applied to concrete aged less than a year, a chemical pretreatment should be used. Various treatments have been proposed over the years, but the declining use of oil paints on concrete has precluded obtaining broad experience. It is currently thought that pretreatment with a three percent phosphoric acid solution without a rinse is as simple and yet effective as any method tested. The concrete should be at least three weeks old when treated, and then allowed to dry thoroughly before the subsequent painting.

Roughening

Most paints adhere better to a roughened surface than to a smooth one. This is especially true for portland cement paint.

Adhesion of organic base paints may be affected adversely when applied to a glazed surface. Hard-burned brick and concrete that has been cast against steel or plywood forms or finished by steel troweling are apt to give trouble in this respect.

There are a number of methods of roughening such surfaces. Light sandblasting has been found very effective; dry rubbing with coarse-grit abrasive stone is another suitable method. A common method of roughening concrete floors is etching with five to ten percent hydrochloric acid, followed by rinsing with clear water.

Moisture Conditioning

Concrete and masonry can absorb moisture and retain it for long periods, affecting the initial paint adhesion and later performance. Since paints vary widely in tolerating or needing moisture when applied, care should be devoted to attaining the necessary moisture levels at the concrete surface.

Concrete and masonry surfaces must be dry when painting with any organic solvent paint, including silicone water repellents. Preferably, all painting requiring a dry surface should be delayed to at least three weeks after the curing procedures for new concrete, thus facilitating fairly thorough drying for some depth into the concrete. For portland cement paint, the surface should be thoroughly wetted to prevent excessive water absorption in the fresh paint and to assist in the curing of the coating. The latex emulsion paints may be applied to damp surfaces; however, no free water should be present. If a surface is moderately porous and extremely dry conditions prevail, a prewetting of the surface before applying emulsion or portland cement paint is advised. This reduces absorption of the water from the paint vehicle and promotes better, more uniform drying.

PREPARATION OF PAINTS

Procedures for preparation of oil and varnish base paints are discussed in Chapter 1, Paints and Paint Materials.

Preparation for latex emulsion paints is similar to that for oil and varnish base paints, except mechanical impeller stirrers or shaking is not recommended because these paints tend to foam upon vigorous agitation. Hand mixing of latex paints generally is easily accomplished, liquid and dry components rarely separate seriously. The materials are furnished ready-mixed and of proper consistency for use without ordinarily having to be thinned with water.

Details on adding water and otherwise preparing portland cement paint are given in excerpts quoted from the ACI standard in the section on Portland Cement Paint in this chapter. This standard also gives information for mixing basic ingredients to make a job-mixed white paint, which is quoted in the following. Although job-mixed paints have given satisfactory results with some savings in material cost, a well-formulated factory product is generally superior because of greater uniformity and the fact that finer grinding improves suspension and brushing qualities.

". . . Following is a typical mix which will be found effective under normal conditions where the coating has the primary functions of decoration and water repellency:

	Percent
White portland cement	75
Hydrated lime	17
Opaque pigment (zinc sulfide or titanium dioxide)	3
Calcium chloride	4
Calcium or aluminum stearate	1

Where sand is to be incorporated with the paint, it should be held to not more than 50 percent of the total. The sand should be dry mixed with the paint powder before the gaging water is added.

The minimum mixing considered essential to satisfactory results consists of thoroughly stirring the dry ingredients together in a suitable container, and then sifting this mixture through a No. 14 mesh fly screen. Batches of 100 pounds or more may be mixed in a small stucco or mortar mixer.

Paste water repellents and calcium chloride or sodium chloride, if used, should be mixed with the gaging water."

APPLICATION OF PAINTS

General rules of good practice for painting concrete and plaster surfaces are the same as discussed in the painting of woodwork. (*See* Chapter 10, Painting Woodwork, section on Selection of Paints.) The value of favorable weather conditions is greater in the painting of concrete and masonry surfaces than in the painting of woodwork. The temperature of the surface is lower, there is more likelihood of condensation on the surface, and the adhesion problem is greater.

Portland Cement Paint

Correct surface moisture conditions prevent too rapid absorption of water from portland cement paint, facilitating both application and curing. At the same time, some suction should remain. Saturating the surface is most easily accomplished with fine water spray, repeated several times or until no more water is absorbed. The prewetting should precede painting by less than an hour, but the thoroughness and timing should be geared to the porosity of the surface and the atmospheric conditions. No free water should remain when painting begins.

The paint should be mixed and applied as instructed by the manufacturer. It must be well scrubbed into the surface to fill voids, and stiff, short fibered brushes usually do the best job. Two coats should be applied about 24 hours apart.

Some portland cement paints require moisture to hydrate the portland cement and develop a bond with the surface. Thorough prewetting of the surface contributes to curing as the stored moisture is released, but additional curing water is needed between coats and for at least two days after the application is completed. Beginning as soon as the paint is dry, fog spraying a minimum of two or three times a day will usually suffice.

Exterior Oil Paints

For application of exterior oil paints, the surface should be completely dry and clean, and weather conditions should be favorable. Air temperature should be above 50°F. If a phosphoric acid pretreatment is to be used, the solution should be applied liberally to ensure thorough wetting of the surface. (*See* the section on Pretreatments.) The treated surface should be allowed to dry completely before painting.

The prime coat should be thinned as follows: four parts paint, two parts nonreactive spar varnish, and one part mineral spirits, by volume. Application of priming paint and finish paint may be by brush or spray, although brushing is usually preferred to be sure the paint is worked into surface irregularities well. Coverages will vary widely, depending on the roughness of the surface. As little as 100 square feet of very rough surface or as much as 400 square feet of smooth surface may be covered with one gallon in a single coat; the second coat will go farther than the first because some smoothing results from the first. In some cases, two finish coats may be required to obtain the desired effect, but one coat in addition to the primer is usually adequate.

Each coat of paint should dry thoroughly before the next coat is applied. Twenty-four hours is considered a minimum for the prime coat even though varnish has been added; at least 48 hours should be allowed for drying between coats of straight linseed oil base paints.

Interior Varnish Paints

General rules for applying a surface sealer and finish coats of flat, semigloss, and full gloss varnish base paints to plaster and concrete surfaces are the same as for painting interior woodwork. (*See* Chapter 10, the section on Painting Interior Woodwork.)

Difficulty frequently arises in painting unbroken expanses, such as ceilings, without lap marks in the finish coat. Work should be planned so that a wet edge is maintained as much as possible. A heavy grade of mineral spirits (TT-T-291) added to the paint may advantageously slow the drying and thus provide more time before the paint reaches a tacky condition. A very satisfactory method of applying paint to smooth walls is by roller coating, described in Chapter 12, Preparation of Metal Surfaces and Paints and Application of Paints, in the section on Roller Coating.

One gallon of varnish base interior paint will cover about 500 square feet of smooth wall. Drying times between coats should be at least 24 hours.

Emulsion Paints

Surfaces receiving emulsion paints may be dry or damp, but no free water should be present. Results will usually be enhanced if very porous, absorptive surfaces are dampened prior to painting. Application of either interior or exterior latex emulsion paint types, does not differ much from the application of varnish base paints. Brush, spray, or roller coating may be used. The last method is especially suitable for interior latex-base paints.

The drying of emulsion paint is considerably faster than that of most varnish base paints. Some varieties may dry within 30 minutes although one to three hours is usual. A second coat may be applied after drying overnight. One of the advantages of latex base water paint is that lap marks are practically unnoticeable, making it unnecessary to work to a wet edge.

The equipment for emulsion painting should be cleaned before the paint has hardened by washing thoroughly with warm water and mild soap, followed by rinsing in clear water, not in a organic solvent.

Vinyl Resin Paint

The three-coat system of vinyl resin paint is used for concrete surfaces. (*See* Chapter 12, the section on Vinyl Resin Paint.) Proper surface preparation is very important to the success of vinyl resin paint. Etching of smooth concrete surfaces with a 20 percent solution of hydrochloric acid, followed by thorough rinsing with clear water is recommended. The surfaces must be dry.

The first coat of paint should be thinned by adding one part vinyl resin thinner to one part paint, by volume. The manufacturer's directions for application should be followed. Application may be by brush or spray, although the latter is preferred for better coverage of the prime coat and the greater uniformity and more pleasing appearance of all costs. Coverage should not exceed 150 square feet per gallon for the prime coat and 225 square feet per gallon for the top coats. Drying time between coats should be four hours minimum.

Concrete Floor Paints

Thick paint coatings on concrete floors are not usually desirable. Wearing capacity is not much greater than for a relatively thin coating, and when a thick film is worn through in traffic lanes, repainting the smoothed surface is more difficult. The objective should be a coating which, through good penetration, will adhere firmly to the floor surface. (*See* the preceding section on Selection of Paints for Concrete, Floors, for limitations on the use of concrete floor paints.)

Paint for the first coat of varnish or rubber base paint on a concrete floor should be well thinned. For varnish base enamel (TT-E-487), one quart of a mixture of two parts spar varnish (TT-V-121) and one part gum-spirits turpentine (TT-T-801), should be mixed with one gallon of paint. A straight mineral spirits thinner will curdle some brands of rubber base paint. The first coat of either paint should be applied at 300 to 400 square feet per gallon, working the paint in thoroughly. Etching prior to painting with 10 to 15 percent solution of hydrochloric acid will aid in opening the surface for good penetration and will provide keying for improved adhesion; it is especially recommended for rubber base paint.

Paint for the finish coat, whether varnish base or rubber base, should not be thinned. It should be brushed out to cover about 600 square feet per gallon. Drying time between coats should be at least 12 hours.

A polyurethane floor coating requires a surface conditioner recommended by the manufacturer; thereafter, two top coats are applied without thinning at 300 to 400 square feet per gallon.

Waxing Floors

Application of wax to floors, whether painted concrete, terrazzo, ceramic tile, linoleum, asphalt tile, vinyl tile, or rubber tile, should follow the general procedures set forth for waxing finishing wood surfaces. (*See* Chapters 10, 11, and 12; and the section on Coatings for Special Floors in this chapter.)

Neoprene Waterproofing

Concrete surfaces to which neoprene waterproofing is to be applied must be sound, completely dry, and free from loose and foreign material. For aged concrete surfaces, light sandblasting is usually the most efficient method of proper surface preparation. The keying provided by blasting is desirable for obtaining best adhesion even though the surface is sound and clean without the sandblasting.

Application of neoprene for waterproofing concrete is essentially the same as for waterproofing metal, which is discussed in Chapter 12, the section on Neoprene (liquid). Cracks and joints that need filling should be treated with neoprene troweling cement after priming. One or two prime coats, perhaps a "tie" coat, and sufficient body coats to build up adequate thickness are required. Both ready-mixed and multicomponent neoprene paints are available. These paints vary widely in build per coat and application procedures, but particularly in the time allowed between coats and the special techniques necessary to obtain coat cohesion. Therefore, each must be applied in rigid accordance with the manufacturer's instructions. Ordinarily, a minimum of 25 mils is needed for most severe service exposures and to bridge tiny cracks in the surface that may tend to work slightly. The manufacturer's required curing temperature, as well as the required time to ensure solvent release and, for multicomponent paints, completion of the chemical curing reaction, must be met fully.

Dampproofing

Surfaces to which asphalt emulsion dampproofing is to be applied should be free of foreign material; they need not be dry but should not be dripping wet. For clear organic solvent dampproofing compounds, including the silicones, the surface must be completely dry as well as clean.

Asphalt emulsion is applied by spraying in two coats, the first coat at a coverage of 65 square feet per gallon, the second at 100 square feet per gallon. The second coat may be applied as soon as all free water has disappeared from the first coat. The coating should be protected from direct sunlight for three days after application; heat from the sun could raise the coating temperature above the softening point of the asphalt and cause sagging. Backfilling should not proceed until three days after application. Care must be taken not to puncture or otherwise damage the coating in the interim and during backfilling operations. Asphalt emulsion materials, like other emulsions, must not be subjected to freezing temperatures during storage.

The effectiveness of clear dampproofing materials other than the silicone depends largely on their ability to penetrate and fill voids below the surface. The material should be thin and the surface should be dry, warm if possible, to facilitate penetration. The first coat should be applied at approximately 200 square feet per gallon. For a porous surface that continues to take the compound, a coverage of about 100 square feet per gallon is suggested. The second and third coats should each be applied at a rate of approximately 400 square feet per gallon. Excessive material overlying the surface is not usually desirable. If not colorless, such coatings will discolor the surface, and in any event they will probably separate in a short time. Application may be by spraying or brushing, with 24 hours between coats.

The weatherproofing treatment consisting of linseed oil and oil-base paint is used for *concrete parapets* and *railings*. *Other prospective treatments* using synthetic resin-base coatings, such as the proprietary epoxy paint, will require cleaning, exposing sound concrete, and roughening the surface, possibly by sandblasting. The first coat of paint may be clear and thinned with an equal volume of appropriate solvent to achieve the maximum penetration, adhesion, and sealing within the concrete. The first coat should be applied by brush or roller. On porous surfaces, the material can be applied until retention of a surface film indicates that no more will be absorbed. Since the clear material often resists weathering poorly, the priming coat is then top coated with the same paint, unthinned and pigmented to a color generally matching the concrete. The timing between coats and other manufacturer's instructions for mixing and applying the synthetic resin paints should be followed carefully. In service, epoxy paint exhibits typical chalking and slow erosion of the surface but retains its sealing properties for long periods.

Clear silicones impart dampproofing properties to surfaces to which they are applied because of a unique hydrophobic (or water "hating") characteristic. A clear silicone solution will contain only two to five percent of silicone resin in thinner. When applied, the silicone solution is absorbed into the capillary pores of the masonry with deep penetration. The pores and voids are not bridged or filled by the treatment but are lined with the water repellent. Preferred application is by low-temperature, low-pressure spray, using a pressure not exceeding ten pounds per square inch at the gun and the lowest possible fluid pressure that will maintain a continuous flow. The solution should be flooded onto the wall surface to the point of maximum absorption, indicated by a rundown of at least 12 inches. Application should be made from the top down to grade at a rate of 75 to 100 square feet per gallon on masonry of normal porosity. On dense masonry, which will not accept and absorb the solution at that rate, the coverage may be extended to a maximum of 150 square feet per gallon. The ambient temperature at the time of application should be between 30°F and 100°F. Two coats generally are applied with only two to four hours drying time between coats, although more time may be allowed if needed. A distinct advantage of silicone water repellents is that no noticeable discoloration and no surface films are produced.

MAINTENANCE PAINTING

The discussion in Chapter 10, Painting Metalwork, in the section on Maintenance Painting, covers the general approach to maintenance painting. In evaluating the coating condition and defects of concrete and masonry, some special causes for paint deterioration will have to be considered, notably alkalinity and moisture in the surface under the paint. Paint durability on these surfaces, with the exception of floors, is generally excellent if appropriate materials of good quality have been selected and proper surface preparation and application procedures have been employed. A service period of eight to ten years or more before repainting is not uncommon. For normal service, where no special problems have arisen, repainting with the same materials may be in order.

The principal enemy of paint on concrete and masonry is moisture. Excessive moisture causes the rapid deterioration of many coatings, especially if the moisture is available from the underside of the film. Thus, in repainting where a coating has failed prematurely, investigation should be made to determine whether excessive moisture has been a contributing factor. Blistering and peeling of the paint or discoloration and water-making, often accompanied by efflorescence, are symptoms of failure. If moisture has been the chief cause, little will be accomplished by repainting unless steps are taken to eliminate the source, or a resistant material is found and applied. This trouble most commonly occurs on the interior surfaces of walls below grade, where moisture is available from the ground adjacent to the exterior of the wall. Proper waterproofing applied on the exterior side, or improved drainage, should rectify the trouble. (*See* Chapter 14, Paint Failures.)

This costly and laborious procedure usually prompts recourse to second-best remedies suitable for the interior surface. If slight dampness has disrupted alkali-susceptible, impermeable films such as oil base paint, it may suffice to remove the old paint and apply an alkali-resistant, breathing film. Portland cement paint is least vulnerable to moisture damage and, unless efflorescence disfigures and disrupts the coating, it will not usually be damaged. This paint provides a dampproofing effect, even when applied to the side of the wall away from the moisture contact. The exterior latex paints also exhibit a dampproofing effect under mild moisture conditions, but they are not as satisfactory as cement paint under more severe conditions.

More often, dampness on the interior is objectionable, and appreciable quantities of water must be sealed off. It should be recognized immediately that a coating on the nonpressure side of a wall ordinarily will not long contain a hydrostatic head of more than a few feet. However, impermeable synthetic resin coatings that develop unusually strong bond and are alkali resistant may solve many problems. Commercial products designed for this purpose are available. Epoxy paints generally bond well to concrete and masonry and form hard, tight, moisture retaining films. Providing a tight seal on such surfaces may not be inexpensive; old coatings may have to be completely removed to expose sound concrete; unusual drying and application measures might be needed; and relatively expensive materials may have to be applied so as to produce a fairly thick, pinhole-free coating.

Surface Preparation

The discussion of desirable surface conditions and methods of preparation, given in the sections on Preparation of Surfaces, Removing Efflorescence, Filling and Smoothing, and Pretreatments, should be consulted before maintenance painting of concrete or masonry surfaces is undertaken. When a different paint is contemplated or the old coating is in such poor condition that complete removal is indicated, methods of surface preparation are similar to those employed in new work. There are a few additional considerations.

Before repainting, cracks should be filled and defective mortar joints pointed up. Neat cement paste is suggested for filling fine cracks in concrete, and cement mortar for filling large cracks in concrete and for pointing mortar joints. A firm base is essential for proper bonding of cement mortar and for successful plaster patching. Remember that cement mortar patches require adequate curing and will react to oil and varnish base paints for several months after they are placed.

Although oil or varnish base paints and exterior latex paints can be applied satisfactorily over a sound, properly aged portland cement paint film, portland cement paint should *not* be applied over organic base or emulsion coatings because of poor adhesion. To repaint such surfaces with portland cement paint, the original paints must be removed completely. Usually, sandblasting is most effective for this purpose. The performance of latex emulsion paints over oil or varnish base paints depends on the condition of the old paint film. In the event of excessive chalking, a coat of special sealer should be applied before the latex paint in order to attain satisfactory adhesion.

To remove an old organic base paint film from a concrete floor, the surface may be soaked with a solution of about two pounds of caustic soda in a gallon of water. After standing for a time, the film softens so that it can be scraped off. Scraping should be followed by a thorough rinsing with clear water. Caustic soda solution at this concentration is severely corrosive. Workers should wear goggles, rubber gloves, and shoes (or disposable gloves and shoe covers) and should avoid spilling the solution on clothing. If the solution does contact the skin, the area should be flushed immediately with water and bathed with vinegar.

Wax films should be removed before repainting, otherwise the drying and adhesion of the paint will be affected. Commercial preparations are effective in removing wax. It can also be removed by wetting with mineral spirits and scouring with a stiff brush or steel wool, followed by wiping with cloths. Two applications are recommended.

Repainting

Application procedures in repainting concrete, brick, or masonry surfaces are the same, in general, as for new work. (*See* the sections on Application of Paints, in this chapter.) The number of coats needed depends on the condition of the old coating. Usually, one is sufficient on an old coating in good condition.

Patched areas should be treated like new work. In some cases, especially if the old surface is generally porous, it is desirable to use primer-sealer over the entire area before applying finish paint.

Painting of silicone-treated surfaces presents a special problem. If a combination silicone-paint treatment is planned, the order of application depends on the paint. With portland cement paint, the paint is first applied and cured normally; the surface then treated with the silicone solution. Repainting with portland cement paint, however, cannot be accomplished until the silicone water repellent has degraded to the extent, possibly for several years, that the surface can be wetted. On the other hand, oil or varnish paints can be applied over silicone-treated surfaces without difficulty. A paint in which water acts only as the carrier (or volatile portion) can be applied over silicone-treated surfaces. If, however, water acts as a reactive chemical essential to the curing of the coat, as in portland cement paint, the paint is not recommended for use over silicone-treated surfaces. Silicone treatment over oil, varnish, or latex based paints is not recommended.

Retreatment of silicone-treated surfaces presents no problem as the solvent in the new solution readily penetrates the treated surface, carrying the silicone resin with it. This happens because the resin used in the specifications material is soluble in the organic solvent used in the solution. The resin already present in the surface merely redissolves in the new solution when it is applied.

SECTION 5

PAINT FAILURES, WHITEWASHING, AND PAINTING SAFETY

Paint, like all other products, may occasionally provide unsatisfactory service, but usually, neither the paint nor the wood, metal, concrete, and masonry surface directly cause the trouble. Generally, the source of difficulty is one or more of the following factors:

—Galvanized steel surfaces painted too soon.

—Plaster, drywall, or masonry surfaces painted without having been cleaned.

—New concrete painted too soon.

—Masonry surfaces painted without dirt, loose particles, or efflorescence being removed.

14

Paint Failures

The most practical method of keeping the home perpetually clean and attractive is to establish a definite program of paint maintenance. Such a program should provide for a periodic cleaning of gutters and inspection of downspouts, flashing, and calking. Condition of the paint should also be checked annually.

Given the application of a quality paint and primer according to the manufacturer's instructions and normal weathering of the paint film, four to six years usually elapse before repainting is necessary. In the North, where sunlight is less intense, paint may last longer.

Throughout the South, where yearly exposure to the sun and chalking is more severe, slightly more frequent repainting may be necessary. An annual inspection, will enable the homeowner to determine when the paint film is sufficiently thin, as the wood grain shows prominently through the weathered coating, to warrant repainting.

Repainting too frequently should be avoided. Painting before the old paint film has chalked sufficiently only builds up an excessively thick coat of paint. Frequently, washing is enough to restore the appearance of such a surface. By allowing the old paint to weather sufficiently, the home can be attractively repainted again and again with no worry of excessive paint thickness.

An annual inspection of the home and proper intervals between repainting allow the homeowner to expect improved paint performance and spares the expense of applying paint unnecessarily.

CONTROL OF MOISTURE

If an excessive moisture reaches the paint film from the underside, paint blistering and peeling may occur. Moisture arising from laundering, use of the shower, cooking, and the like, if not vented and confined by suitably placed vapor barriers, can penetrate into wall cavities and condense on the sheathing or siding. Rainwater entering the walls at siding laps through capillary action may also add moisture to the wood beneath the paint film.

Occasionally, excess moisture in the wood siding results in a loss of paint adhesion and the formation of water-filled blisters under the paint film. For this reason, adequate protection should be provided against moisture from within the home as well as rainwater entering the walls from the outside.

The Vapor Barrier

A properly installed vapor barrier will protect exterior walls and paint from moisture arising within the home. The purpose of the vapor barrier is to restrict the movement of moisture through the wall. Vapor-resistant paper, plastic, metal foil, or paint are used for this purpose. It is desirable for the barrier to meet the minimum requirements of the Federal Housing Administration.

To prevent accidental puncturing, the vapor barrier should be installed after heat ducts, plumbing, and wiring are in place. The barrier is stapled over the edges of the studs immediately beneath the interior wall facing and sealed around electrical outlets, pipes, and ducts.

Properly installed, interior wall facing materials or insulation bats including a vapor barrier eliminate the need for a separate barrier. Be sure that the vapor barrier side of the insulation bat is placed toward the inside of the room and covers the entire stud space from ceiling to floor.

Many older homes and some new ones have been constructed without vapor barriers. For such homes, good vapor protection can be achieved with a quality wall paint recommended for this purpose by the manufacturer. Inside walls and ceilings should be given two coats.

Houses with damp crawl spaces need a vapor barrier over the ground to seal out moisture. For this purpose, a layer of 55-pound coated roll roofing has been found to be very effective.

Ventilators

Additional protection from interior moisture is provided by crawl space, soffit and roof ventilators which replace moisture-laden air with dry air from the outside. Crawl space vents should provide two square feet of opening for every 25 linear feet of exterior wall. Vents should be located to allow cross-ventilation. Adequately sized roof vents provide one square foot of opening for every 300 square feet of attic floor. The following increases in the size of the total vent opening are recommended by the Housing and House Finance Agency when ventilators are protected by louvers and/or screen.

Vent Protection	Increase in Total Area of Vent Opening (Percent)
No. 8 mesh	25
No. 16 mesh	100
Louvers—No. 8 mesh	225
Louvers—No. 16 mesh	300

Protection From Outside Water

A house constructed in accordance with good building practice offers the best protection against the entrance of rainwater. Flashing around dormers, chimneys, roof valleys, and over doors and windows should extend at least six inches under roof shingles and siding. Over doors and windows, flashing should extend under the siding and over the top edge of frames.

Outside water may enter when ice and snow in gutters cause water to back up under the roofing along the eaves. In areas where this condition prevails, builders usually prevent entrance of water by laying heavy asphalt felt over the eaves and up under the shingles for the width of the roll.

Defective exterior putty and calking should be inspected and replaced. Even a liberal application of paint will not seal open, uncalked or poorly calked joints at corner boards and around windows and doors.

Wide roof overhangs at eaves and gables offer added assurance against rainwater penetration of walls. Siding boards may be given additional protection by a ten-second dip or brush coat of a paint-like water-repellent preservative before they are applied. *Note:* Water repellent preservatives vary in composition, but should leave no residue which may affect the color, drying, and adhesion of the subsequently applied paint.

For houses where the entrance of rainwater is suspected, a liberal brush application of a paint-like water-repellent preservative is recommended along the butt edge of siding boards before repainting. Improved paint performance will usually result.

Finally, the lowest course of siding boards and sheathing should begin at least six inches from the ground. If grading is above this point, it should be lowered to allow a six-inch space between the siding and the grade around the entire house. Trees and shrubs should also be trimmed to provide good drying conditions after rainfall.

How to Correct Paint Problems

The source of paint problems is usually found in one or more of the following factors:

1. Poor painting techniques or failure to follow label instructions for mixing, priming, and application.

2. Lack of proper protection of exterior walls against moisture.

3. Use of the wrong paint for the given service conditions.

4. Use of inferior quality paints.

5. Excessive intervals between repaintings.

6. Too frequent repaintings.

PAINTING DEFECTS AND HOW TO CORRECT THEM

The life of any paint job largely depends on correct surface preparation and proper application of a good quality paint. However, several defects will sometimes appear in a finished job even though preliminary precautions have been taken. Some defects are unavoidable. Varying atmospheric conditions or moisture will cause other defects that cannot be blamed directly on either the method of application or the material used.

Blistering and Peeling

Excessive moisture in walls, either from the interior or from outside water may cause blistering (Fig. 1) and peeling. Unsatisfactory exterior house paint performance can usually be traced to water behind the paint film. To correct, proceed as follows:

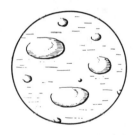

Fig. 1. Blistering.

1. Check basement or crawl space for dampness or condensation. Paint basement walls with moistureproof paint. Cover crawl spaces with 55-pound roll-roofing, if required. Open crawl space vents to aid in removing moisture from the ground.

2. Use kitchen and attic exhaust fans if the house is so equipped.

3. Vent automatic clothes dryers to the outside.

4. On houses constructed without a vapor barrier, two coats of a quality wall paint on the inside walls and ceilings will provide additional protection from excess moisture.

5. Wall cavities and roof overhang at eaves can be ventilated by installing small screened vents sold for this purpose.

6. Check flashing and all outside calking, especially if peeling occurs around windows, doors, or corner boards. If rainwater enters around windows and doors, apply a generous bead of calking compound about ⅜-inch deep.

7. Lower grade line, if earth is closer than six inches to bottom course siding, and trim shrubs growing against siding.

8. Consider the use of blister-resistant paint.

9. Before repainting, generously apply a paintable water-repellent under the edges and at the end joints of siding boards.

Excessive Chalking

Quality paints wear away so that, normally, painting is required in four to six years. Should the paint film become so thin that repainting is necessary appreciably earlier, 1. the previous paint job was scanty in thickness, 2. the paint was thinned excessively, or 3. an inferior product was used. *To correct:* Brush, to remove chalk, and apply two coats of quality paint. Permit the first coat to dry thoroughly (about three days of fair weather) before applying the top coat. (*See* Fig. 2.)

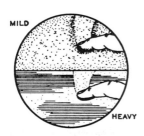

Fig. 2. Chalking.

Wrinkling

Wrinkling (Fig. 3) may occur when paint is applied too generously, especially in the hot sun, or if too much oil has been added in mixing. Painting at low temperatures also tends to produce this condition. To correct: Sand the wrinkled surface. Paint when the temperature is above 40°F, and brush out the paint well.

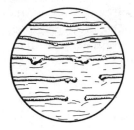

Fig. 3.   Wrinkling.

Cross-grain Cracking

Paint which is applied too frequently can build up an excessively thick, brittle coat and fail by cracking (Fig. 4) and peeling across the grain of the wood. *To correct:* Remove all paint down to the bare wood. Complete removal of paint will never be required if the coating is permitted to weather for a normal length of time before repainting.

Fig. 4.   Cracking.

Mildew

In certain areas where continuous warm and damp conditions prevail, discoloration by mildew (Fig. 5) may be prevented by paint containing a mildew inhibitor. In these areas, many paints offered by manufacturers incorporate mildewcides or fungicides which minimize the mildew problem. Other paints can be made mildew-resistant by adding of proprietary compounds available from the paint dealer. *To correct:* On old paint where mildew has collected, wash with strong soap and water or a solution of two ounces of trisodium phosphate in a gallon of water; rinse with clear water. Where mildew is heavy, use two ounces of trisodium phosphate plus two ounces of a mildew preventive in a gallon of water to "kill" the mildew that cannot be removed easily by washing. *Caution:* Rubber gloves should be used when handling trisodium phosphate and mildew preventive.

Fig. 5.   Mildew.

Alligatoring

Alligatoring (or reticulation) is a condition where the breaks are rather large and have the appearance of an alligator hide (Fig. 6). This defect is usually caused by applying a hard finish coat over a soft primer. It will also occur if the finish coat has been applied before the primer has had sufficient time to dry thoroughly. To avoid this condition, the priming coat should always be as hard as or harder than the outer or finish coats.

Fig. 6.   Alligatoring.

Gas Discolorations

Gas fumes emanating from neighboring industrial plants, sewage, and other sources tend to darken some paints to a metallic gray that closely resembles graphite. This cannot be entirely avoided unless the cause is removed. The discoloration can be removed from the painted surface by sponging it with a weak solution of muriatic acid, hydrogen peroxide, or similar bleaches. When using muriatic acid, be sure to wear rubber gloves and goggles.

Metal Stains

Metal stains are caused by corrosion from screens, gutters, flashings, and other hardware. Painting or varnishing these metal surfaces will materially reduce the amount of stain from them.

Premature Paint Weathering, According to Location

With some exceptions, it is natural for the paint on your home to weather away faster on the southern and western exposures. Likewise, it is natural for paint to weather slightly faster on horizontal surfaces such as steps, and window sills, than on vertical surfaces. The time to repaint is determined by the part of the old paint film on your home which has weathered away the most.

The magic of color is seen everywhere in the United States today. Its superior appeal is now taken for granted in advertising, printing, movies, television, and thousands of consumer products, including automobiles.

In the home, color is now used as a fourth dimension of design to work subtle changes which give special and attractive effects. Wood siding and shingles lead this trend since homes feature this facing more than any other kind. In addition, wood has a history of satisfactory performance as a base for paint and other protective coatings.

The instructions and recommendation in this chapter will help every house paint user to achieve the fine results possible with the proper methods and materials.

Precautionary Measures to Prevent Painting Defects

Select the proper paint and use quality products only.

Be sure that the surface is dry before painting and that appropriate steps have been taken to prevent moisture entering from beneath the film.

Be sure to remove part or all of the old coatings that have become too thick. Do not apply new coats that are too thick or dense.

Allow each coat to dry thoroughly before another is applied.

Remove all rust and corrosion from surrounding and adjacent metal surfaces.

Be sure that adjoining metal is also painted.

Keep brushes clean and pliable.

If paint has been allowed to stand overnight or longer, strain through cheesecloth before using.

15

Whitewashing

Whitewashing is a relatively simple and inexpensive way to brighten the interior of livestock and other service buildings. Whitewash may be applied with either a brush or a spray gun.

SURFACE PREPARATION

Remove all dirt, scale, and loose materials by scraping or brushing with a wire brush. Many whitewashing jobs have been quite satisfactory without further surface preparation. However, for the best job, wash off as much of the old coat of whitewash as possible with hot water and vinegar or a *weak* hydrochloric acid solution.

Dampen the walls before applying whitewash. Unlike most paints, the application and adherence of whitewash are improved when the surface is slightly damp.

MIXING

Lime paste is the basis of whitewash. *Protect your eyes and skin during mixing.* It may be prepared by either of the following procedures:

1. Soak 50 pounds of hydrated lime in six gallons of water. Refined limes, such as chemical hydrate, agricultural spray hydrate, finishing lime, and pressure hydrated lime have few lumps and will make a smoother paste.

2. Slake 25 pounds of quick lime in ten gallons of boiling water. Cover and allow to slake for at least four days.

Each of the preceding preparations makes about eight gallons of paste.

Different whitewash mixes are suggested for different surfaces. Smaller batches of whitewash may be prepared by reducing the ingredients by an equal proportion in the formulas given in the following sections.

General Woodwork

Dissolve 15 pounds of salt in five gallons of water. Add this solution to eight gallons of paste, stirring constantly. Thin the preparation to the desired consistency with fresh water.

To reduce chalking, use five pounds of dry calcium chloride instead of the salt.

Brick, Concrete, or Stone

Add 25 pounds of white portland cement and 25 pounds of hydrated lime to eight gallons of water. Mix thoroughly to a thick slurry. Thin to the consistency of thick cream. Mix only enough for a few hours use.

To reduce chalking, add one to two pounds of dry calcium chloride, dissolved in a small amount of water, to the mix just before using.

Plaster Walls

Any one of these three formulas is recommended:

1. Soak five pounds of casein in two gallons of water until thoroughly softened—about two hours. Dissolve three pounds of trisodium phosphate in one gallon of water, add this solution to the lime, and allow the mixture to dissolve. When the lime paste and the casein are thoroughly cool, slowly add the casein solution to the lime, stirring constantly.

Just before use, dissolve three pints of formaldehyde in three gallons of water, and add this solution to the whitewash batch, stirring constantly and vigorously. *Do not add the formaldehyde too rapidly.* If the solution is added too fast, the casein may form a jelly-like mass, thus spoiling the batch.

2. Dissolve three pounds of animal glue in two gallons of water. Add this solution to the lime paste, stirring constantly. Thin the mixture to the desired consistency.

The first formula, or mix, given in the preceding for use on plaster walls, is a time-tested, long-life mix also suitable for general use. The following is also: Dissolve six pounds of salt in three gallons of boiling water. Allow the solution to cool, and then add it to the lime paste. Stir three pounds of white portland cement into the mix.

COLORING

Pigments may be added to whitewash to provide color. The following have proven satisfactory:

Black: Magnetic black oxide of iron
Blue: Ultramarine or cobalt blue
Brown: Pure precipitated brown oxide of iron with turkey or Indian red
Green: Chromium oxide, opaque, or chromium oxide, hydrated
Red: Indian red made from pure ferric oxide
Violet: Cobalt violet and mixtures of reds, whites, and blues
White: Lime itself
Yellow: Precipitated hydrated iron oxides

APPLICATION

Some surfaces may require two coats of whitewash. Two coats are better than one coat that is too thick.

Strain the mix through three layers of cheesecloth before using a spray gun.

16

Painting Safety

Painting conditions and situations present actual or potential danger to workers and others in the vicinity. The frequently necessary toxic and flammable materials, pressurized equipment, ladders, and scaffolding always present a potential hazard. Hazards may also be inherent in the very nature of the environment, or caused by the ignorance or carelessness of the worker. It is, therefore, extremely important to be aware of all potential hazards, since continuous and automatic precautionary measures will minimize the risks and improve efficiency.

PAINTING ACCIDENT HAZARDS

The three major kinds of painting accident hazards are as follows:

    1. Hazards involving the use of ladders and scaffolds.

    2. Fire hazards from flammable materials in paints.

    3. Health hazards from toxic (poisonous) materials in paints.

Equipment Hazards

Accidents during painting operations are caused by unsafe working equipment, unsafe working conditions, and careless workers.

LADDER HAZARDS

1. Store wood ladders in a warm, dry area protected from both weather and the ground.

2. Protect wood ladders with clear coatings only, so that cracks, splinters, or other defects will be readily visible.

3. Inspect all ladders frequently for loose or bent parts, cracks, breaks, or splinters.

4. All straight and extension ladders must have safety

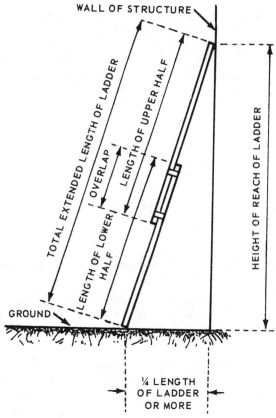

Fig. 1.   Ladder stability.

shoes. For metal ladders, these should be made of insulating material.

5. Do not use portable ladders greater in length than can be readily carried and placed by two workers. Never splice ladders to form a longer ladder.

6. Pretest all ladders and scaffolding before use. To do so, place the ladder or scaffold horizontally, with blocks under each end. "Bounce" in the center or walk along the ladder or scaffold.

7. Extension ladders should have a minimum overlap of 15 percent for each section. (*See* Fig. 1.)

8. Do not use stepladders over 12 feet high. Never use one as a straight ladder. Never stand on the top platform.

9. Place ladders so that the horizontal distance from the top support to foot is at least one-fourth of the working length. Be sure that the ladder is securely in place. Rope off all doorways in front of the ladder and post warning signs.

10. Use hand lines to raise or lower tools and materials. Do not overreach when working on ladders; move the ladder instead.

11. Never use metal ladders in areas where contact with electric power lines is possible.

SCAFFOLDING SAFETY

1. Inspect all parts before use. Reject metal parts damaged by corrosion and wood parts with defects such as checks, splits, unsound knots, and decay.

2. Provide adequate sills or underpinnings when erecting on filled or soft ground. Be sure that scaffolds are plumb and level. Compensate for uneven ground by blocking or using adjusting screws.

3. Anchor scaffolds to the wall about every 28 feet of length and 18 feet of height. Do not force braces to fit. Use horizontal diagonal bracing at the bottom and at every 30 feet of height.

4. Lumber should be straight grained. All nails should be driven full length and not subject to direct pull.

5. Provide guard railings, regardless of height, on the full length of the scaffold and also on the ends.

6. Erect scaffolding so that ladders are lined up from top to bottom. Always use ladders when climbing scaffolding.

7. Tubular pole scaffolds should be made of two-inch outer diameter galvanized steel tubing or other corrosion-resistant metal of equal strength.

8. Planking with at least a two-foot overlap should be well-secured to wood scaffolding. Platforms should be made of uniform thickness planking, laid close together. They must overlap and be fastened at supports and must not extend over the edge without being properly supported. An unsupported plank is a deadly trap. Do not use planking for other purposes; paint them only at the ends for identification. Nominal sizes of planking should be determined from Table 8. Values are given in pounds for loads at the center and allow for the weight of the planking.

Table 8
Safe Center Loads for Scaffold Plank

Span feet	2 x 8*	2 x 10*	2 x 12*	3 x 8*	3 x 10*	3 x 12*
6	200	255	310	525	665	805
8	150	190	230	390	500	605
10	120	155	185	315	400	485
12	100	130	155	265	335	405
14	—	110	135	225	285	346
16	—	—	115	195	250	305

The preceding values are for planks supported at the ends, wide side of plank face up, and with loads concentrated at the center of the span. For loads uniformly distributed on the wide surface throughout the length, the safe loads may be twice those given in the table. Loads given are net and do not include the weight of the plank. If select structural coast region Douglas fir, merchantable structural longleaf southern pine, or dense structural square edge sound southern pine are used, above loads may be increased 25 percent.

*Dressed sizes of planks, reading left to right, are: 1⅝ x 7½, 1⅝ x 9½, 1⅝ x 11½, 2⅝ x 7½, 2⅝ x 9½, 2⅝ x 11½, respectively.

9. Test scaffolds and extensive planking (extended to working length) by raising them one foot off the ground and loading them with weights at least four times the anticipated working load.

PRESSURIZED EQUIPMENT RULES

These rules apply to all equipment used for both spraying and blasting.

1. Use only approved equipment. Use remove control deadman valves on high-pressure equipment (60 pounds or higher). These should be activated by the same air used for blasting or spraying.

2. Conduct a hydrostatic test at least once, but preferably twice a year. Test safety relief valves daily.

3. Use conductive hose. Ground all nozzles, tanks, and pressure equipment when in use, as well as the object being sprayed.

4. Store hose in dry areas. When in use, avoid sharp bends, especially when curved around an object. Secure high-pressure hose no more than ten feet from the worker.

5. Never point gun or nozzle at anyone or any part of the body. When handling or carrying, hold by the grip and remove the fingers from the trigger.

6. Release all pressure before disconnecting any part of the equipment.

FIRE HAZARDS

Certain general rules regarding fire and explosion hazards apply to all situations. All paint materials should have complete label instructions which stipulate the potential fire hazards and precautions to be taken. Painters must be continuously advised and reminded of the particular fire hazard conditions of each job, to insure their awareness of the dangers involved. Advice and warnings also assure that the necessary precautions are taken and maintained. Proper firefighting equipment must always be readily available in the paint shop, work areas, and spray room, where potential fire hazards exist. Electric wiring and equipment installed or used in the paint shop, including the storage room and the spray room, must conform to the applicable requirements of the National Electrical Code for Hazardous

Areas. The following precautions against fire must be carefully observed by all:

1. Prohibit smoking near where paint is stored, prepared for use, or applied.

2. Provide for adequate ventilation in all storage, preparation, and application areas.

3. Perform recurrent spray operations on portable items, such as signs, in an approved spray booth equipped with adequate ventilation, a waterwash system of fume removal, and explosion-proof electrical equipment.

4. Wet down all spray booth surfaces before cleaning them.

5. Use rubber feet on metal ladders, and be certain that the personnel working in hazardous areas wear rubber-soled shoes.

6. Use nonsparking scrapers and brushes to clean metal surfaces near fire hazards.

7. Wet down paint sweepings, rags, and waste with water, and store in closed metal containers until disposed of in an approved manner. Do not burn in heaters or furnaces.

8. Extinguish all pilot lights on water heaters, furnaces, and other open flame equipment on all floors of the structure being painted. Be sure to turn the gas valve off.

9. When painting in confined areas near machinery or electrical equipment, open and tag all switches to prevent them from being turned on inadvertently.

10. Be sure that all mixers, pumps, motors, and lights used in the paint shop, spray room, or on-the-job are explosion-proof and electrically grounded.

11. Use pails of sand (never sawdust) near dispensing pumps and spigots to absorb any spillage or overflow.

12. During painting operations, keep fire extinguishers nearby. Be sure that they are the proper type. (*See* Table 9.)

13. Check ventilation and temperature regularly when working in confined areas.

14. Before painting, check where high-voltage lines and equipment are located.

15. Keep all work areas clear of obstructions.

16. Clean up before, during, and after painting operations. Dispose of sweepings and waste daily.

Table 9
Use the Proper Fire Extinguisher

	Three Classes of Fires		
Choose from these 5 basic types of extinguishers	*Class A Fires* Paper, wood, cloth, excelsior, rubbish, etc., where quenching and cooling effect of water is required.	*Class B Fires* Burning liquids (gasoline, oil, paints, cooking fats, etc.) where smothering action is required.	*Class C Fires* Fires in live electrical equipment (motors, switches, appliances, etc.) where a nonconducting extinguishing agent is required.
Carbon Dioxide	Small surface fires only.	*YES* *Excellent* Carbon dioxide leaves no residue, does not affect equipment or foodstuffs.	*YES* *Excellent* Carbon dioxide is a nonconductor, leaves no residue, will not damage equipment.
Dry Chemical	Small surface fires only.	*YES* *Excellent* Chemical absorbs heat and releases smothering gas on fire; chemical shields operator from heat.	*YES* *Excellent* Chemical is a nonconductor; fog of dry chemical shields operator from heat.

Water	YES *Excellent* Water saturates material and prevents rekindling.	NO Water will spread fire, not put it out.	NO Water, a conductor, should not be used on live electrical equipment.
Foam	YES *Excellent* Foam has both smothering and wetting action.	YES *Excellent* Smothering blanket does not dissipate, floats on top of most spilled liquids.	NO Foam is a conductor and should never be used on live electrical equipment.
Vaporizing Liquid	Small surface fires only.	YES Releases heavy smothering gas on fire.	YES Liquid is a nonconductor and will not damage equipment.

HEALTH HAZARDS

Many ingredients used in manufacturing paint materials are injurious to the human body in varying degrees. Although the body can withstand nominal quantities of most of these poisons for relatively short periods of time, continuous exposure or overexposure may be harmful. Furthermore, prolonged exposure to some may cause the body to become sensitized so that subsequent contact, even in small amounts, causes an aggravated reaction. To this extent, these materials are a very definite threat to the normally healthy individual and a serious danger to persons with chronic illnesses or disorders. These materials are divided into two major groups, such as, toxic materials and skin irritating materials.

Nevertheless, health hazards can easily be avoided by the common sense approach of avoiding unnecessary contact with hazardous materials and strictly adhering to established safety measures.

The following rules should always be strictly observed.

1. Toxic or dermatitic materials must be properly identified and kept tightly sealed when not in use.

2. Designate a competent person to check the operation of paint spray booths. Check at regular intervals to ensure that the equipment is in safe and proper operating condition.

3. Be sure that ventilation is adequate in all painting areas. Provide artificial ventilation when natural ventilation is inadequate. Use supplied air respirators, if necessary.

4. Spray all portable items inside exhaust ventilated booths especially designed for that purpose.

5. Wear goggles and the proper respirator when spraying, blast cleaning, or performing any operation that entails the formation of abnormal amounts of vapor, mist, or dust.

6. When handling dermatitic materials, use protective creams or preferably gloves, and wear appropriate clothing. Change and clean work clothing regularly.

7. Avoid touching any part of the body, especially the face, when handling dermatitic materials. Wash hands and face thoroughly before eating and at the end of the day.

SELECTING A LADDER

Today, the range of ladder designs, types, sizes, and materials is broad enough to fit your particular needs—if you know what you want.

Before you buy a ladder, think about your needs. Will the ladder be used indoors or outdoors? How high will you want to climb? Who will be using it? Where will it be stored?

If you live in an apartment, a stepladder can probably meet all your needs easily. Its size should depend on the highest point you want to reach, bearing in mind that you should stand no higher than the step below the ladder top. *Never* stand on the top of a stepladder.

If you live in a house, you may need two ladders—a stepladder for indoor work and a straight ladder or extension ladder for outdoor use. The outdoor ladder should be long enough to extend a minimum of three feet higher than the highest area you want to reach. See the recommended lengths indicated in Table 10.

Table 10

Height You Want to Reach	Recommended Length of Sections
9½ feet	16 feet
13½ feet	20 feet
17½ feet	24 feet
21½ feet	28 feet
24½ feet	32 feet
29 feet	36 feet

Do not let price alone guide you. Let your needs be your guide.

Do not let the sales person hurry you into making a quick purchase. Check the ladder for weak steps, loose rungs, or other weaknesses before you take it from the store.

Do not buy an unidentified ladder. Be sure that the name of the manufacturer or distributor is on the label. This information may be important in case of a quality deficiency or accident.

Look for a seal (probably a decal) affixed to the ladder, indicating that the ladder conforms to the standards of the American National Standards Institute (ANSI) or the Underwriters' Laboratories, Inc. (UL). The absence of a seal, however, does not necessarily imply poor quality.

MATERIALS

Wood, aluminum, magnesium, and fiber glass are the principal materials used in the construction of modern ladders. Each has its advantages and disadvantages.

Wood

Wood ladders are sturdy and bend little under the loads for which they are designed. They are heavier than metal ladders, and the large sizes are harder to handle. When dry, wood ladders are safe to use around electrical circuits or when you are working with power tools.

If wood ladders are used indoors, or are adequately protected from moisture and sunlight, they will last a long time. Unprotected in the open, however, they may be attacked by wood-destroying insects, weakened by rot, or cracked and split by the action of sun and rain. Once weakened, wood may break easily and suddenly.

Metal

Metal ladders are generally a little more expensive than wood ladders of the same quality, but they last longer because they do not deteriorate from moisture and sunlight and are not attacked by insects. Aluminum and magnesium ladders are comparatively light, weighing only about two-thirds as much as those made of wood. Although roughly the same in weight, magnesium ladders are somewhat more costly. (Magnesium is actually a lighter metal than aluminum, but not as strong; therefore, the siderails and legs of magnesium ladders are constructed with thicker cross-sections to provide comparable strength.) Magnesium corrodes (turns black) more than aluminum and is less resistant to impact. Aluminum and magnesium ladders are not recommended for use around electrical circuits.

Fiber Glass

Fiber glass is the newest material to appear on the ladder market. It is used to make the siderails of high-grade metal stepladders and straight and extension ladders. The result is a nonconductive ladder that is light, corrosion-resistant, serviceable, and practically maintenance-free. These ladders do not dry, rot, or absorb moisture, and the fiber glass siderails have greater impact resistance than wood, aluminum, or magnesium. Ladders of this kind are still so expensive that their use is generally restricted to industry.

TYPES OF LADDERS

The stepladder and the extension ladder are the two most commonly used around the home. They come in many materials and designs, but the following discussion will help you choose a ladder to fit your particular needs. The straight ladder lacks the versatility and popularity of the adjustable extension ladder, and has therefore been excluded from detailed discussion in this chapter.

Ladder Codes

Codes have been established by the American National Standards Institute (ANSI) that cover wood and metal stepladders and extension ladders. Any stepladder or extension ladder you buy with an ANSI seal conforms to the code for wood ladders or the code for metal ladders.

The code for wood ladders is dimensional. It covers, for example, the depth and thickness of steps.

The code for metal ladders is based on performance. It

prescribes the methods for testing the strength of ladders with emphasis on siderails, steps, fastening hardware, and the back legs of stepladders.

Stepladder

A stepladder is a self-supporting portable ladder. It is nonadjustable in length with flat steps and a hinged back. Size is determined by the length of the ladder measured along the front edge of the siderails. Stepladders are useful for many indoor and outdoor jobs where the height to be reached is low and the ladder can be rested on a firm surface.

Both wood and metal stepladders are available in three categories. They are: Type I, heavy-duty (250 pounds load-carrying capacity); Type II, medium-duty (225 pounds); and Type III, light-duty (200 pounds). These categories are accepted and widely used by the ladder industry. Look for the duty rating when you purchase a ladder.

WOOD STEPLADDER CONSTRUCTION FEATURES

Steps

Steps should be flat, parallel, and level when the ladder is open with no more than 12 inches between steps. (*See* Fig. 2.)

They should be at least ¾ inch thick and at least 3½ inches deep.

Each step should be braced either with a metal reinforcing rod or a metal angle brace (Figs. 3 and 4). If reinforcing rods are used, the bottom step should always be braced with metal angle braces. The ends of the reinforcing rod should pass through metal washers of sufficient thickness to prevent pressure and damage to the siderails.

A wood or metal truss block should be fitted to the bottom of each step when metal reinforcing rods are used and

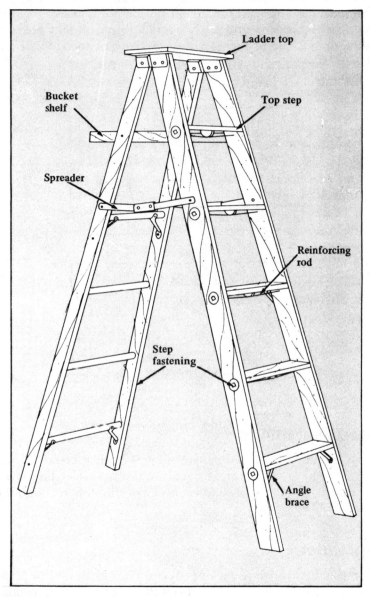

Fig. 2. Wood stepladder.

positioned at the center between the rod and the step. The bottom step should be reinforced with metal angle braces securely attached to the step and each siderail. (Steps should not protrude more than ¾ inch beyond the front of the siderail and should have no splits, cracks, chips, or knots.)

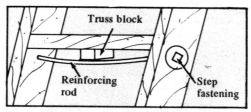

Fig. 3.   Wood or metal truss block.

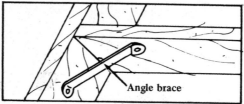

Fig. 4.   Metal angle brace.

Step Fastenings

Steps should be fastened to the siderails with a metal bracket (Fig. 5) or by grooving (Fig. 6). At least two 6-penny nails (or the equivalent) should be used at each end of the step, through the side rail.

Spreader

The metal spreader or locking device (Fig. 2) should be large and strong enough to securely hold the front and back sections in the open position. It should be resistant to rust and corrosion.

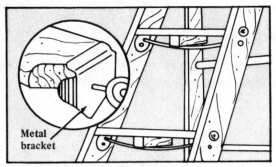

Fig. 5. Metal bracket.

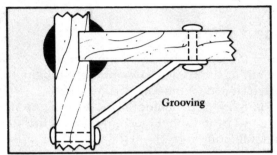

Fig. 6. Grooving.

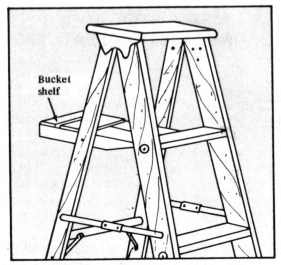

Fig. 7. Bucket shelf.

Bucket Shelf

The bucket shelf (Fig. 7) should be capable of holding 25 pounds and folding completely within the ladder.

Feet

The feet of the ladder should be level in an open position. They can be equipped with safety shoes. (*See* the section on Ladder Accessories.)

Slope and Width

The slope of the ladder should be a minimum of 3½ inches per foot of length of the front section and a minimum of 2 inches per foot of the length of the back section—in the open position.

The width between the siderails at the top step should be no less than 12 inches and should increase toward the bottom of the ladder at a minimum rate of one inch per foot of length.

METAL STEPLADDER CONSTRUCTION FEATURES

Steps

Steps should be flat, parallel, and level when the ladder is open. Also, the steps should have raised patterns, or be corrugated, dimpled, coated with skid-resistant materials, or otherwise treated to minimize the possibility of slipping. There should be no more than 12 inches between steps. (*See* Fig. 8.)

The depth of the step or tread should be not less than 3 inches for 225- or 250-pound capacity ladders; 2½ inches for 200-pound capacity ladders.

Steps should have no sharp edges, and should not be bent or dented. The bottom step should always be reinforced with metal angle braces (Fig. 9).

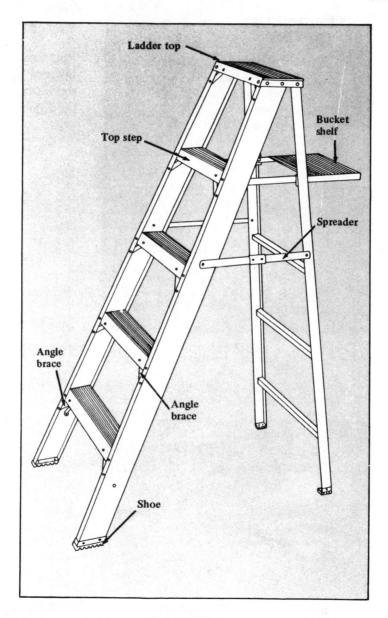

Fig. 8. Metal stepladder.

Step Fastenings

Each step should be fastened with at least one fastener through the back and the front of the siderail.

Look at the front of the siderails on a metal ladder. If steps have only one fastening on each side, they should also have diagonal metal braces under both the top and bottom steps. If the steps have two fastenings on each side, the ladder should have diagonal metal braces under the bottom step (Fig. 10).

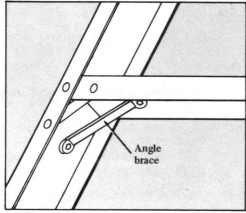

Fig. 9.   Metal angle brace.

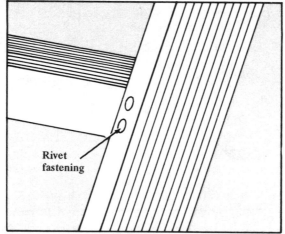

Fig. 10.   Step fastener.

Spreader

The characteristics of the spreader or locking device of metal stepladders should be the same as of wood stepladders. (*See* Fig. 11.)

Bucket Shelf

The bucket shelf should be capable of holding 50 pounds and folding completely within the ladder.

Feet

The bottom of the four rails should be covered for safety with insulating material, such as rubber or plastic nonslip shoes (Fig. 12).

Slope and Width

Slope and width of metal stepladders should be the same as for wood stepladders.

STEPLADDER STABILITY

Before purchasing a stepladder, test its stability by climbing to the second step from the bottom and shaking the ladder moderately back and forth while you hold onto the siderails. If the ladder feels loose, consider purchasing a heavier ladder or one made by another manufacturer.

OTHER STEPLADDERS

There are three other kinds of ladders that are closely related to the stepladder: the platform ladder (Fig. 13), the trestle ladder (Fig. 14), and the extension trestle ladder (Fig. 15). Although

Fig. 11.   Spreader.

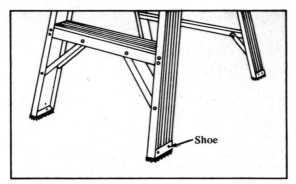

Fig. 12.   Nonslip shoe.

Fig. 13.   Platform ladder.

Fig. 14.   Trestle ladder.

these ladders are primarily for commercial use, the platform ladder does have value for use around the home.

At least one kind of platform ladder, with a low platform, has a guardrail that lessens the danger of falling. It should have widely spaced legs to provide good balance. Two of these ladders, used in tandem, provide a good scaffold base. A platform ladder is also easy to store.

Extension Ladder

An extension is a straight ladder of adjustable length. It consists of two or more straight sections traveling in guides or brackets, so arranged as to permit length adjustment. Its size is designated by the sum of the lengths of the sections, measured along the siderails.

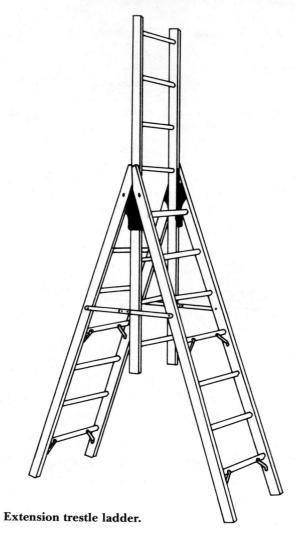

Fig. 15.   Extension trestle ladder.

Each section of an extension ladder should overlap the adjacent section by a minimum number of feet, depending on the overall length. If an extension ladder is up to 36 feet long, the overlap should be 3 feet; if total length is between 36 and 48 feet, overlap should be 4 feet; if the two sections add up to between 48 and 60 feet, overlap should be 5 feet.

Also, a ladder should be equipped with positive stops to ensure that it cannot be opened too far.

The Federal Trade Commission requires that the total length and working length of extension ladders be clearly marked to eliminate confusion in measuring caused by overlap. For example:

Maximum working length 17 feet
Total length of sections 20 feet

Choose the right size extension ladder for your needs, according to the recommended relation between working height for a ladder and total length of the sections. The recommended total length of the sections allows for the proper overlap plus three feet more than the greatest working height. The extra three feet is the minimum required for safe use.

WOOD EXTENSION LADDER CONSTRUCTION FEATURES

Feet

The feet of a wood extension ladder should be equipped with safety boots or shoes, which can be ordered as an accessory. (*See* Fig. 16; also the section on Ladder Accessories.)

Rope and Pulley

The pulley should not be less than 1¼-inch outside diameter. The rope should not be less than ⁵/₁₆ inch in diameter, with a minimum breaking strength of 560 pounds. (*See* Fig. 17.)

Rungs

The rungs should be round and made of hard wood. They must be free from crossgrain, splits, cracks, chips, or knots. Rungs should not be less than 1⅛ inches in diameter and spaced not more than 12 inches apart.

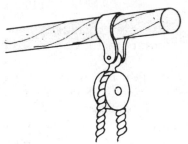

Fig. 17.   Rope and pulley for wood extension ladder.

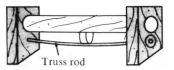

Fig. 18.   Truss rod for wood extension ladder.

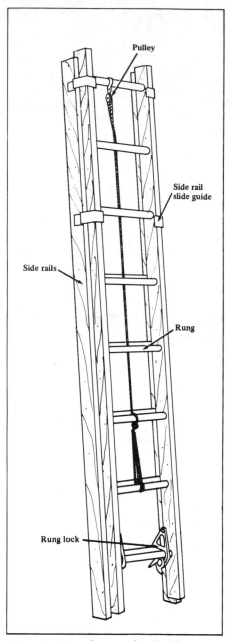

Pulley

Side rail slide guide

Side rails

Rung

Rung lock

Fig. 16.   Wood extension ladder.

Spring lock

Fig. 19.   Spring rung lock for wood extension ladder.

Truss Rod

The truss rod (Fig. 18) is not required by the standards of the American National Standards Institute or Underwriters' Laboratories, Inc., but it is highly desirable that at least the bottom rung be reinforced with a truss rod.

Safety Rung Locks

The safety rung locks (Fig. 19) should be resistant or protected against rust and corrosion. Either spring or gravity locks are appropriate.

Siderail Slide Guides

The siderail slide guides (Fig. 20) should be securely attached and placed so as to prevent the upper section from tipping or falling out while the ladder is being raised or lowered.

Width

The width of the ladder should not be less than 12 inches between the rails of the upper section. The bottom section should be a minimum of 14½ inches for ladders of up to and including 28 feet.

METAL EXTENSION LADDER CONSTRUCTION FEATURES

Feet

The feet of a metal extension ladder should have rubber, plastic or other slip-resistant safety tread or shoe secured to a foot bracket. (*See* Figs. 21 and 22.) The bracket should pivot freely, allowing the tread to rest squarely when ladder is inclined for use.

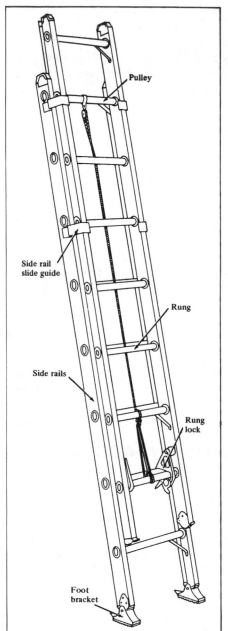

Pulley

Side rail
slide guide

Rung

Side rails

Rung
lock

Foot
bracket

Fig. 21.   Metal extension ladder.

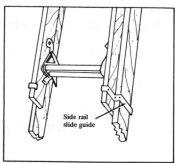

Side rail
slide guide

Fig. 20.   Siderail slide guides
for wood extension ladder.

Safety shoe

Fig. 22.   Safety tread or shoe
for metal extension ladder.

Rope and Pulley

Rope and pulley features on metal extension ladders should be the same as for wood extension ladders.

Rungs

The rungs should be round or round with a flat step surface (Fig. 23), with a slip-resistant tread. The flat surface should be horizontal when the ladder is placed at a 75° angle. Top and bottom rungs should be not more than 12 inches from the ends of the siderails to provide for extra strength and stability.

Rung Brace

The rung brace is not required by the standards of the American National Standards Institute or Underwriters' Laboratories, Inc., but is highly desirable. At least the bottom rung should be reinforced with a metal rung brace (Fig. 24).

Safety Rung Locks

Safety rung locks on metal extension ladders should be the same as for wood extension ladders (Fig. 25).

Siderail Slide Guides

The siderail slide guides are the same for fiber glass extension ladders as for wood ladders. These not required, however, on aluminum extension ladders where the siderails interlock (Fig. 26).

Width

The width for the upper section should not be less than 12 inches; the bottom section should be not less than 12½ inches for ladders up to 16 feet, 14 inches for ladders up to 28 feet, and 15 inches for ladders up to 40 feet.

Fig. 23.   Rung for metal extension ladder.

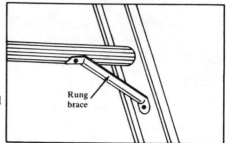

Fig. 24.   Rung brace for metal extension ladder.

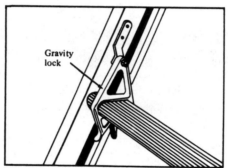

Fig. 25.   Safety rung lock for metal extension ladder.

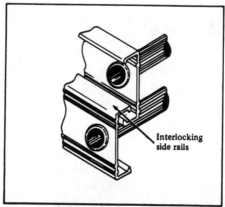

Fig. 26.   Interlocking siderails for metal extension ladder.

LADDER ACCESSORIES

A number of useful ladder accessories can add substantially to your safety and convenience.

Hangers

Hangers are used for storing long ladders horizontally to prevent sag and permanent set. Use at least three for each ladder (Fig. 27).

Trays

Trays are attached to extension ladders to hold paint, tools, or work materials (Fig. 28).

Safety Shoes

Safety shoes should be attached to all metal ladders and to all wood ladders used in slippery or wet places. Although metal ladders are usually sold equipped with safety shoes, wear may make replacement necessary. Shoes for wood ladders are usually bought as accessory items (Fig. 29).

Safety Wall Grip

Rubber or plastic strips can be attached to the top of extension ladder siderails. These strips keep the top of a ladder from slipping on the surface it leans against (Fig. 30).

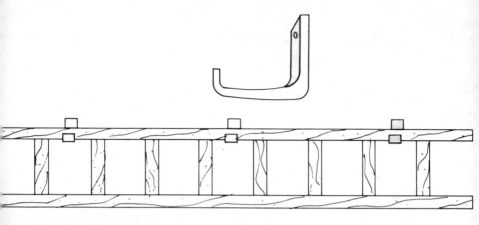

Fig. 27. Hangers for storing long ladders horizontally.

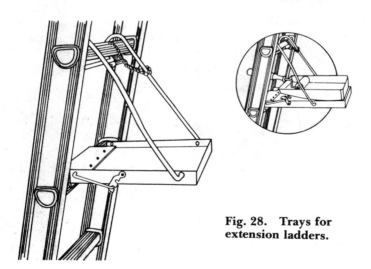

Fig. 28. Trays for extension ladders.

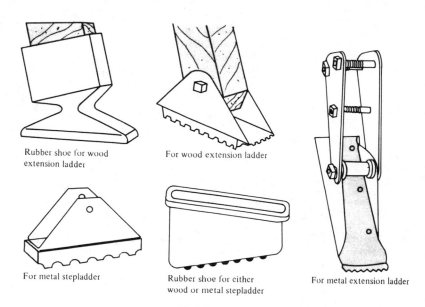

Rubber shoe for wood
extension ladder

For wood extension ladder

For metal stepladder

Rubber shoe for either
wood or metal stepladder

For metal extension ladder

Fig. 29.   Kinds of safety shoes.

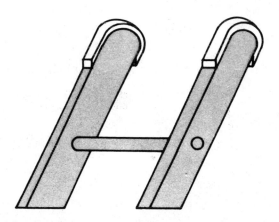

Fig. 30.   Safety rubber or plastic strips.

APPENDIX 1

List of Specifications for Paints and Accessory Materials

Specifications are listed by basic numbers. The latest revision in effect at the time of use of the specification should be used to ensure that materials meet the latest requirements.

Federal Specifications

P-W-155	Wax, floor, water-emulsion
P-W-158	Wax, general purpose, solvent type
	Type I. Liquid
	Type II. Paste
R-P-381	Pitch, coal–tar (for) aggregate-surfaced built up roofing, waterproofing, and dampproofing
	Type II. Coal–tar pitch (for) waterproofing and dampproofing
SS-A-281	Aggregate, (for) portland-cement-concrete
SS-A-674	Asphalt, paving, emulsion
SS-C-192	Cement, portland
SS-P-385	Pipe, steel, (cement-mortar lining and reinforced cement-mortar coating)
SS-W-110	Water-repellent, colorless, silicone resin base
TT-C-542	Coating, polyurethane, oil free, mositure curing
TT-C-545	Coating: polyester-epoxy (two component) high-build, gloss and semigloss, white and tints (for interior use)
TT-C-598	Calking compound, oil and resin base type
TT-C-650	Creosote coal–tar solution
TT-C-655	Creosote, technical, wood preservative, (for) brush, spray or open-tank treatment
TT-D-651	Drier, paint, liquid
	Type I. Lead and manganese
	Type II. Cobalt (lead-free)
TT-E-487	Enamel: floor and deck
TT-E-489	Enamel, alkyd, gloss (for exterior and interior surfaces)[1]
	Class A. Air-drying

TT-E-490	Enamel, silicone alkyd copolymer, semigloss, exterior
TT-E-505	Enamel, odorless, alkyd, interior, high gloss, white and light tints
TT-E-506	Enamel, alkyd, gloss, tints and white (for interior use)
TT-E-508	Enamel: interior semigloss, tints and white
TT-E-509	Enamel, odorless, alkyd, interior, semigloss, white and tints
TT-E-527	Enamel, alkyd, lustreless
TT-E-529	Enamel, alkyd, semigloss
TT-E-543	Enamel, interior, undercoat, tints and white
TT-E-545	Enamel, odorless, alkyd, interior-undercoat, tints and white
TT-F-336	Filler, wood, paste
TT-F-1098	Filler, solvent thinned, for porous surfaces (concrete, concrete block, stucco, etc.) for interior and exterior use)
TT-G-410	Glazing compound, sash (metal) for back bedding and face glazing (not for channel or stop glazing)
TT-L-26	Lacquer, cellulose nitrate, brushing, gloss
TT-L-190	Linseed oil, boiled (for use in organic coatings)
TT-L-215	Linseed oil, raw (for use in organic coatings)
TT-P-21	Paint; cement-water, powder, white and tints (for interior and exterior use)
TT-P-24	Paint, oil, concrete and masonry, exterior eggshell finish, ready-mixed
TT-P-25	Primer coating, exterior (undercoat for wood, ready-mixed)
TT-P-29	Paint, latex base, interior, flat, white and tints
TT-P-31	Paint, oil: iron-oxide, ready mixed, red and brown
TT-P-35	Paint, cementitious, powder, white and colors (for interior and exterior use)
TT-P-37	Paint, alkyd resin; exterior trim, deep colors
TT-P-47	Paint, oil, nonpenetrating-flat, ready-mixed tints and white (for interior use)
TT-P-52	Paint, oil (alkyd and oil) wood shakes and rough siding

TT-P-53	Paint, ready mixed, outside, medium yellow
TT-P-55	Paint, polyvinyl acetate emulsion, exterior
TT-P-59	Paint, ready-mixed, international orange
TT-P-71	Paint, exterior, green, ready-mixed
TT-P-86	Paint; red lead base, ready-mixed

Type I. Red lead, linseed oil paint
Type II. Red lead, mixed-pigment, alkyd varnish, linseed oil paint
Type III. Red lead, alkyd varnish paint
Type IV. Red lead, mixed-pigment, phenolic-varnish paint

TT-P-91	Paint, rubber base, for interior use (concrete and masonry floors)
TT-P-96	Paint, latex base, for exterior surfaces (white and tints)
TT-P-102	Paint, oil alkyd (modified), exterior, fume resistant, ready-mixed, white and tints
TT-P-103	Paint (titanium-zinc and oil, exterior, fume-resistant, ready-mixed, white)
TT-P-320	Pigment, aluminum; powder and paste for paint
TT-P-381	Pigments in oil, tinting color
TT-P-390	Pigment, iron oxide; black, synthetic, dry
TT-P-636	Primer coating, alkyd, wood and ferrous metal
TT-P-641	Primer coating; zinc dust–zinc oxide (for galvanized surfaces)
TT-P-791	Putty: linseed oil type (for wood-sash-glazing)
TT-P-1046	Primer coating; zinc dust, chlorinated rubber: (for steel and galvanized surfaces)
TT-R-251	Remover; paint (organic solvent type)
TT-S-171	Sealer, floor: lacquer
TT-S-176	Sealer, surface, varnish, floor, wood or cork
TT-S-179	Sealer, surface: pigmented oil, plaster and wallboard
TT-S-190	Sealer, sanding, lacquer (for wood furniture)
TT-S-227	Sealing compound elastomeric type, multi-component (for calking, sealing, and glazing in buildings and other structures)
TT-S-300	Shellac, cut
TT-S-708	Stain, oil; semitransparent, wood exterior
TT-S-711	Stain, oil type, wood, interior

TT-S-720	Stain: wood, nongrain raising, solvent-dye type
TT-T-291	Thinner-paint, volatile spirits, petroleum spirits
TT-T-295	Thinner paint, mineral spirits, volatile, 'odorless'
TT-T-306	Thinner: synthetic resin, enamels
TT-T-390	Tinting medium, concentrate general-purpose
TT-T-801	Turpentine; gum spirits, steam distilled, sulfate wood and destructively distilled
TT-V-71	Varnish, interior, floor and trim
TT-V-81	Varnish mixing, for aluminum paint
TT-V-86	Varnish, oil, rubbing (for metal and wood furniture)
TT-V-119	Varnish, spar, phenolic-resin
TT-V-121	Varnish, spar, water-resisting
TT-W-568	Wood preservative; creosote-petroleum solution
TT-W-570	Wood preservative: pentachlorophenol, solid
TT-W-571	Wood preservation: treating practices
TT-W-572	Wood preservative: water repellent

Federal Standard No. 595 Colors

---

[1] Interim specification at the time of writing

American Water Works Association (AWWA) Standard Specifications

C203	Coal–tar protective coatings and linings for steel water pipelines—enamel and tape—hot-applied
C602	Cement-mortar lining of water pipelines in place

Bureau of Reclamation Specifications

Clear dampproofing compound
Coal–tar dampproofing compound
CA-50 cold-applied coal–tar paint
CRC-101 clear resin base curing compound
CTP-1 cold-applied coal–tar paint
CTP-3 cold-applied coal–tar paint
Paste-type asphalt emulsion
Phenolic-resin varnish for sanded aluminum paint
    system

Vinyl resin mastic coating, VR-M
Vinyl-resin paint, VR-3
Vinyl-resin paint, VR-6
Zinc chromate aluminum mixing paint

Maritime Administration Specifications

52-MA-602   Compounds; rust preventive
                 Grade B. Medium

Military Specifications

MIL-C-10578   Corrosion removing and metal conditioning
                compound (phosphoric acid base)
MIL-C-15203   Coating compound, bituminous, emulsion
                type, coal–tar base
MIL-C-16173   Corrosion preventive compound, solvent cut-
                back, cold application
MIL-C-24176   Cement, epoxy, metal repair and hull smooth-
                ing
MIL-E-46141   Enamel, silicone-alkyd copolymer, gloss (for
                exterior surfaces)
MIL-I-17384   Insulating compound, electrical, quick-drying
                Type G. General use
MIL-P-15931   Paint, antifouling, vinyl-red
MIL-P-23236   Paint coating systems, steel ship tank, fuel and
                salt water ballast

Western Pine Association Specifications

WP-578   Western Pine Association Formula No. WP-578, for
           priming and sealing knots

American Wood Preservers' Association

Manual of Recommended Practice
AWPA Specification P-8

Steel Structures Painting Council

SSPC-SP 10-63T   Near white blast cleaning
SSPC-SP 7-63   Brushoff blast cleaning
SP-6-63   Commercial blast cleaning

APPENDIX 2

Code *Acoustical surfaces often require only a thin coating that will lend decorative properties but that will not affect the surface's soundproof characteristics.

Almost every new or bare surface will require the use of a primer or prime coat before application of the top coat. Often this primer is a product specially formulated to protect the surface, as well as provide a coating to which the top coat can tightly adhere. In some situations, the top coat material can be applied as a prime coat, according to manufacturer's directions, after which a second, and possible third, top coat would be applied.

The following is a list of primers used with top coats applied to surfaces found in a home's interior. Each primer has a key number which appears on the chart. Remember these primer–top coat combinations are *general* recommendations. For *specific* priming instructions, consult the container label.

1. Alkyd Metal Primer
2. Alkyd Primer
3. Enamel Undercoater
4. Exterior Masonry Paint
5. Latex Metal Primer
6. Latex Primer
7. Masonry Block Filler
8. Masonry Surface Conditioner
9. Oil-Base Primer
10. Portland Cement Metal Primer
11. Topcoat Material Used as Primer
12. Wood Filler
13. Wood Sealer
14. Zinc-Rich Metal Primer

Table 1

Interior Paint Selection Chart[1]

Paint Choice / Surface	Alkali resistant enamel	Alkyd exterior masonry paint	Alkyd flat enamel	Alkyd floor enamel	Alkyd glossy enamel	Alkyd semigloss enamel	Epoxy enamel (opaque)	Epoxy finish (clear)	Lacquer	Latex exterior masonry paint	Latex flat wall paint	Latex floor enamel	Latex glossy enamel	Latex semigloss enamel	Pigmented wiping stain	Portland cement masonry paint	Portland cement metal paint	Shellac	Urethane enamel (opaque)	Urethane finish (clear)	Varnish
Masonry Brick	X 11	X 11	X 8, 11		X 8, 11	X 8, 11	X 11, 7			X 11	X 8, 11		X 8, 11	X 8, 11		X 11			X 11, 7		
Cement block	X 11		X 4, 7		X 11	X 4, 7	X 4, 7				X 4, 7	X 11	X 4, 7	X 4, 7					X 11, 7		
Ceramic tile flooring				X 11			X 11					X 11							X 11		
Concrete	X 11		X 4, 11	X 11	X 4, 11	X 4, 11	X 11				X 4, 11	X 11	X 4, 11	X 4, 11		X 11			X 11		

Table 1 (cont.)

Concrete flooring	X/11															X/11
Drywall	X/6	X/11	X/6	X/6,11		X/6	X/6,11	X/11	X/6	X/6	X/1		X/14	X/14	X/6,11	X/13
Plaster	X/6,2	X/11	X/6,2	X/6,2 6,11		X/6,2	X/6,11		X/6,11	X/6	X/1		X/14	X/14	X/6,11	X/11,12
Metal																
Aluminum	X/1		X/1	X/1		X/1	X/1		X/1	X/1	X/1				X/1	
Galvanized steel	X/14		X/14	X/14		X/14	X/14		X/14	X/14	X/14	X/10	X/10		X/14	
Iron and steel	X/1,5		X/1,5	X/1,11 1,5		X/1,5	X/1,5		1,5	X/1,5	X/1,5	X/10	X/10		X/14	
Steel flooring		X/11		X/11			X/11					X/10	X/10		X/11	
Wood																
Flooring		X/11		X/11	X/11		X/11	X/11	X/11	X/11	X/13,12		X/13,12		X/11	X/13
Trim and paneling	X/3		X/3	X/3,11	X/11		X/3		X/3	X/3	X/3		X/3		X/11	X/11,12
Miscellaneous																
Accoustical Tile*	X/2								X/11							

Table 1 (cont.)

Vinyl wallcovering, smooth, with design		X 11	X 11			X 11		X 11	X 11		
Vinyl wallcovering, smooth, without design			X 11			X 11					
Vinyl wallcovering, textured		X 9, 11	X 9, 9, 11			X 11					
Wallpaper		X 6,2	X 6,2 6,2			X 6,2		X 6,2	X 6,2		

¹X = Paint choice and Numbers = Primer choice; see Code.

Table 2

Exterior Paint Selection Chart[1]

Surface	Aluminum paint	Asphalt emulsion	Awning paint	Cement base paint	House paint (oil)	House paint (latex)	Metal primer	Porch and deck enamel	Primer or undercoater	Roof cement or coating	Spar varnish	Transparent sealer	Trim and trellis paint	Water repellent preservative	Penetrating wood stain (latex or oil)
Masonry															
Asbestor cement	×			×	×●	×			×			×			
Brick					×●	×			×						
Cement and cinder block	×			×	×●	×			×			×			
Cement porch floor						×		×							
Stucco	×			×	×●	×			×			×			
Metal															
Aluminum windows	×				×●	×●	×						×●		
Galvanized surfaces	×●				×●	×●	×						×●		
Iron surfaces	×●				×●	×●	×		×				×●		

Table 2 (cont.)

Siding (metal)	X•					X•	X•	X•				X•
Steel windows and doors	X•					X•	X•	X			X•	X
Wood												
Frame windows	X			X•	X•	X•		X	X•		X•	X
Natural siding and Trim									X	X		X
Porch floor							X					X
Shingle roof										X		X
Shutters and other trim			X• X•	X• X•		X• X•	X X		X X		X•	X X
Siding												X X
Miscellaneous												
Canvas awnings		X										
Coal–tar felt roof			X						X			

¹X = Paint choice and • = Primer or sealer may be required; check container label.

APPENDIX 3

Glossary

Abrasive. A material used for wearing away a surface by rubbing. Some abrasives are used for smoothing rough surfaces before painting.

Acetone. A fast-evaporating, highly flammable solvent.

Acid stain. A water-soluble stain made with an organic acid.

Acoustic paint. Paint that absorbs or deadens sound.

Acrylic resin. A clear resin derived from polymerized esters of acrylic acid and methacrylic acid.

Adhesion. Bonding strength; the attraction of a coating to the surface to which it is applied.

Air-dry. To dry a coating under ordinary room conditions (60°–80°F. with 40–60% relative humidity).

Air entrapment. Inclusion of air bubbles in paint film.

Airless spraying. Spraying that involves the use of hydraulic pressure to atomize the paint.

Alcohol. A flammable solvent; alcohols commonly used in painting are ethyl alcohol (ethanol) and methyl alcohol (methanol, wood alcohol).

Alkali. A caustic, such as sodium hydroxide or lye.

Alkyd. A synthetic resin, made usually with phthalic anhydride, glycerol, and fatty acids from vegetable oils.

Alkyd resins. Resins prepared from polyhydric alcohols and polybasic acids.

Alligatoring. Cracking of a painted surface, thus resembling the hide of an alligator. A common cause of alligatoring is the application of thick films which prevent the under-surface of a coating from becoming thoroughly dry and hard.

Aluminum paint. A mixture of finely divided aluminum particles, in flake form, combined with a vehicle.

Ambient temperature. Room temperature or the temperature of one's surroundings.

American gallon. 23 cubic inches.

Amide. A curing agent combined with epoxy resins.

Aniline colors. A term loosely used to indicate coal-tar dyes or derivatives.

Anti-corrosive paint. A metal paint designed to inhibit corrosion; it is applied directly to metal.

Antimony oxide. A finish applied to furniture to give it the appearance of age.

Arcing. Swinging a spray gun away from the object being painted.

Asbestine. Trade name of the natural fibrous magnesium silica, which is pure white in color. Used as an extender pigment in paints.

Asphalt. Residue from petroleum refining; also a natural complex hydrocarbon.

Atomize. To break a stream of paint into small particles.

Baking finishes. A method used to improve certain types of coatings used on metal articles such as automobiles and refrigerators. Baking may be done in an oven, under infrared lamps, or by induction heating, according to the demands of shape, space, and other requirements. The article that is coated must be able to withstand the temperature required for proper baking.

Banding. Identifying an item with strips of tape.

Barytes. Natural barium sulfate; this is used extensively as an extender pigment in paint and as a base for diluted colors.

Benzene. Sometimes called *benzol;* benzene is often confused with *benzine* because of similarity in pronunciation. It is a very powerful solvent for many materials. Benzene's use is restricted, however, by its toxicity; it is also a fire hazard.

Benzine. A highly volatile petroleum product often used as a lacquer diluent. Benzine is highly flammable and a fire hazard in shipping and storage, or when used by an inexperienced person.

Binder. The non-volatile portion of a paint which serves to bind or cement the pigment particles together. Oils, varnishes, and proteins are examples of binders. (*See* Vehicle.)

Bitumen. Originally asphalt; now any mineral hydrocarbon, but usually black pitchy material.

Bituminous coating. A coal tar- or asphalt-based coating.

Blanc fixe. Artificially prepared barium sulfate.

Bleaching. Removing color.

Bleeding. The seepage of a dye or stain from stained wood or an undercoat into subsequent coats. Bleeding usually occurs as the result of solubility in the vehicle portion of the top coat. It can often be prevented or reduced by the application of an intermediate coat of shellac, aluminum paint, or emulsion paint.

Blistering. A condition caused usually by applying paint to a surface containing excessive moisture. Blistering can also occur when moisture enters painted wood through some indirect source, such as poor joints or careless carpentry work.

Bloom. A deposit or cloudiness on a surface. This is sometimes caused by a thin film of foreign material such as smoke, dust, or oil.

Blow torch. A gasoline torch used in burning off paint film.

Blue lead. A basic sulfate of lead containing small amounts of lead sulfide and carbon, which impart a bluish-gray color. Blue lead is used primarily for its rust-preventive value.

Blushing. Whitening and loss of gloss due to moisture or improper solvent balance.

Body. (1) Viscosity or thickening; (2) the middle or under coat of a substance.

Boiled oil.   A fatty oil treated with driers to shorten the drying time.

Bronzing liquid.   A vehicle specially formulated as a binder for aluminum or gold bronze powder.

Brushability.   The ease with which a paint can be brushed onto a surface under practical conditions.

Bubbling.   A term used to describe the appearance of blisters on a surface while a coating is being applied.

Burnt sienna.   Sienna that has been roasted; it is reddish brown in color.

Burnt umber.   Umber that has been roasted; it is dark brown in color.

Caking.   Hard settling of pigment from paint.

Calcimine.   A paint composed essentially of calcium carbonate (or clay) and glue; it is sometimes written *kalsomine*.

Calking compound.   A semi-drying or slow-drying plastic material used to seal joints or fill crevices around windows and chimneys. It is usually made in two grades: the gun type (for application by a special gun) and the knife type (for use with a putty knife).

Carbon black.   A black pigment made by burning natural gas.

Casein.   The protein of milk and the principal constituent of cheese. Casein is used extensively in the manufacture of water paints.

Castor oil.   Non-drying oil obtained from the castor bean. It may be converted to a drying oil by chemical treatment.

Catalyst.   An accelerator, curing agent, or promoter.

Cat-eye.   A hole or holiday shaped like a cat's eye; cratering.

Cellulose acetate.   A binder formed by the chemical reaction of acetic acid on cellulose (cotton linters).

Cellulose nitrate.   A binder formed by the chemical reaction of nitric acid on cellulose (cotton linters); also known as nitrocellulose and pyroxylin.

Chalking.   Powdering of a surface.

Checking.   The formation of slight breaks in a film that do not penetrate to the underlying surface.

China clay.   A mineral used as extender pigment.

Chinese red.   A vivid red to reddish orange; vermilion.

Chroma.   Intensity; the quality of a color with regard to its strength.

Chrome green.   A green pigment composed of iron blue and chrome yellow.

Chrome orange.   An orange pigment composed principally of basic lead chromate.

Chrome yellow.   A yellow pigment composed primarily of lead chromate.

Chromium oxide.   (*See* Chromium oxide green.)

Chromium oxide green.   A dark green pigment. This should not be confused with *chrome green.*

Cleaner.   A detergent, alkali, acid or other material or solvent used for cleaning paint equipment.

Coal tar-epoxy paint.   Paint in which the binder or vehicle is a combination of coal tar and epoxy resins.

Coal tar pitch.   The black residue remaining after coal tar is distilled.

Coal tar solvent.   A derivative from the distillation of coal tar. Four main products for the paint industry are benzene, toluene, xylene, and solvent naphtha.

Coatings.   Surface coverings; paints; barriers.

Coat of paint.   A layer of dry paint resulting from a single wet application.

Cobalt blue.   A blue pigment composed of the oxides of aluminum and cobalt.

Cohesion. The property of holding or bonding together.

Cold-checking. Checking caused by low temperatures.

Cold-cracking. Cracking occurring at low temperatures.

Cold-water paint. Paint in which the binder or vehicle portion is composed of casein, glue, or a similar material dissolved in water. It is usually employed on concrete, masonry, or plaster surfaces.

Color-fast. Non-fading.

Color-in-japan. A paste formed by mixing a color pigment with japan; it is used principally for tinting.

Color-in-oil. A paste formed by mixing a color pigment with linseed or another vegetable oil. It is used principally for tinting.

Color retention. The ability of a substance to retain its original color.

Copal. A type of natural resin widely distributed throughout the world.

Cracking. Splitting; disintegration of paint by breaks through film to the substrate.

Crawling. Shrinking of paint, forming an uneven surface, shortly after application.

Cross-spray. Spraying first in one direction and then at a right angle to that direction.

Curing. Setting up, hardening.

Curtains. Sags having the appearance of drapes.

Dead flat. Having no gloss at all.

Decalcomania. Paint films that come in the form of pictures or other decorations. They can be transferred from a temporary paper mounting to other surfaces.

Decorative painting. Painting done primarily as ornament.

Dehydrated castor oil. A drying oil prepared from castor oil.

Delamination. Separation of layers of paint films.

Density.   Weight per unit volume.

Dew point.   The temperature at which moisture condenses.

Doctor blade.   A knife applicator of fixed film thickness.

Driers.   Compounds of certain metals that hasten the drying action of oils when added to paints or varnishes. Some driers are in dry form, others in paste form. Most of them are solutions of metallic soaps in oils and volatile solvents. They are known as driers, oil driers, japan driers, liquid driers, and japans. The metallic soaps most commonly used are those of lead, manganese, and cobalt.

Drop black.   (*See* Bone black.)

Drop cloth.   A large piece of fabric used while painting a room to protect furniture, rugs, and other articles from damage.

Drop (scaffold).   One vertical descent of the scaffold.

Drying oils.   Oils that are converted to solids when exposed to the oxygen in air. Linseed oil, tung oil, and perilla oil are the three principal vegetable drying oils. Menhaden, or fish oil, is the only animal drying oil suited for use by the paint industry. (*See* Semi-drying oils.)

Drying time.   The time interval between paint application and a specified condition of dryness.

Dry to handle.   A film of paint is "dry to handle" when it has hardened sufficiently to be handled without becoming marred.

Dry to recoat.   The time interval between paint application and the ability to receive the next coat satisfactorily.

Dry to touch.   The condition when a film of paint has hardened sufficiently to be touched lightly without any paint adhering to the fingers.

Dull finish.   Almost a dead flat.

Dull rubbing.   Rubbing a dried film of finishing material to a dull finish, usually with abrasive paper, pumice stone, steel wool, and oil or water.

Dust-free. The condition when dust no longer adheres to a film of paint.

Dye. A substance used for dyeing or staining.

Earth pigments. Pigments found in the earth. Ochre, umber, sienna, Vandyke brown, chalk, barytes, and graphite are some of the most important of these substances.

East India gum. A resin in two grades: pale and black.

Edging. Stripping.

Efflorescence. A deposit of water-soluble salts on the surface of masonry or plaster. It is caused by the dissolving of salts present in the masonry, migration of the solution to the surface, and deposition of the salts when the water evaporates.

Eggshell luster. Luster or sheen closely resembling that of eggshell.

Elasticity. The degree of recovery from stretching.

Emulsion. A preparation in which minute particles of one liquid (such as oil) are suspended in another (such as water).

Emulsion paint. A paint made by emulsifying the film-forming portion in a volatile liquid, usually water.

Enamel. A special type of paint made with lacquer or varnish as the vehicle. The line of distinction between enamels and oil paints is very indefinite.

Epoxy ester. Epoxy-modified oil; single package epoxy.

Epoxy resins. Film formers usually made from bisphenol A and epichlorohydrin.

Etch. Surface preparation of metal by chemical means.

Extender. A colorless pigment of low hiding power. When used properly, extenders contribute desirable properties to paint products.

Fading. Reduction in brightness of color.

Fanning. (Spray gun technique). Arcing; moving the spray gun away from the surface being painted.

Feather edge. Tapered edge.

Feathering. Triggering a gun at the end of each stroke; tapering an edge.

Ferrous. Containing iron.

Field painting. Painting at the job site.

Filler. A composition used to fill the pores of wood before a paint or varnish is applied.

Film build. Dry thickness characteristics per coat.

Film former. A substance that forms a skin or membrane when dried from a liquid state.

Film integrity. The degree of continuity of a paint film.

Film thickness. The depth of an applied coating, expressed in millimeters.

Filter. Strainer, purifier.

Fingers (airless spray). A broken, airless spray pattern.

Fire-retardant paint. A paint that will delay flaming or overheating of a surface.

Fish oil. Oil from marine animals, such as menhaden, sardines, and whales.

Flaking. Detachment of small pieces of paint film.

Flammability. The measure of ease with which a material catches fire; ability to burn.

Flash point. The lowest temperature at which a given material will flash if a flame or spark is present.

Flatting agent. An ingredient—usually a metallic soap such as calcium, aluminum, or zinc stearate—used in lacquers and varnishes to reduce the gloss or to give a "rubbed" appearance.

Flatting oil. A varnish-like composition made of thickened oil dissolved in a thinner, used to reduce paste paint to a flat paint.

Flat wall paint. A type of interior paint designed to produce a lusterless finish.

Floor varnish. A varnish made specifically for application to floors.

Flowing varnish. A varnish designed to produce a smooth, lustrous surface without rubbing or polishing.

Forced drying. Speeding the drying process by increasing the temperature above the ambient temperature with an oven, infrared lamp, or other heat source.

Furane resins. Dark, chemical-resistant resins made from furfural alcohol, furfural, and phenol.

Gel. A jelly-like substance.

Glazing. A process of applying transparent or translucent coatings over a painted surface to produce blended effects.

Gloss. Shininess; the ability to reflect.

Gloss oil. A varnish composed primarily of limed rosin and petroleum thinner.

Grain. Surface appearance, mainly of wood.

Graininess. Roughness of a protective film resembling grains of sand.

Graining. Simulating the grain of wood with paint.

Grain raising. Swelling of the fibers of wood by water.

Ground coat. The coating material applied before graining colors or the glazing coat.

Guide coat. A coat similar to the finish coat, but of a different color to help obtain complete coverage.

Gum. A natural mucilaginous material derived from certain trees, sometimes erroneously applied to resins.

Gum arabic. The dry, gummy exudation of *Acacia senegal*. This white-powdered resin is sometimes used in cold-water paint and in show-card colors.

Gypsum. An extending pigment.

Hardener. A curing agent or promoter.

Hairlines. Very narrow cracks in a paint or varnish film.

Hard oil finish. A varnish giving the effect of a rubbed-in-oil finish but producing a hard surface. The term has gradually been extended to cover all sorts of interior architectural varnishes with a moderate luster.

Hazing. Clouding.

Heavy-bodied oil. A high-viscosity oil.

Hiding power. The capacity of a paint to obliterate colors that lie beneath it.

Holiday. A pinhole, skip, or void.

Hot spray. Spraying material heated to reduce viscosity.

House paint, outside. Paint designed for use on the exteriors of buildings, fences, and other surfaces exposed to the weather.

Hue. The name of a color, such as red, green, or blue.

Humidity. The measure of moisture content in air.

Hydraulic spraying. Spraying by hydraulic pressure.

Inert. (*See* Extender.)

Insulating varnish. A varnish specially designed for the electrical insulation of wires, coils, and electrical appliances.

Internal mix. A spray gun in which the fluid and air are combined before they leave the gun.

Iron blue. A blue pigment, essentially ferric ferrocyanide; Prussian blue.

Iron oxide. A substance available in three forms: red, brown, and yellow. It is sold under a variety of names such as red oxide, Indian red, red ochre, mineral rouge, Spanish oxide, and Turkey red.

Iron phosphate coating. Conversion coating; a chemical deposit.

Isocyanate resins. Urethane resins.

Ivory black. A high-grade bone-black pigment. Its name is accounted for by the fact that it was formerly made by charring or burning ivory.

Ketones. Flammable organic solvents such as acetone.

Lacquer. A material that dries by evaporation of the thinner or solvent. There are many different types of lacquers, the most important being that based on cellulose nitrate. Besides the cellulosic compound, lacquers contain resins, plasticizers, solvents, and dilutents.

Laitance. The milky-white deposit on new concrete.

Lake. A colored pigment produced by precipitating a dye on a base such as aluminum hydrate or calciums carbonate.

Lampblack. A black pigment that consists of finely divided carbon obtained by burning oil in an insufficient supply of air.

Latex. Rubber-like; a common binder for emulson paints.

Lead carbonate, basic. A type of white lead.

Lead drier. A compound of lead and an organic acid used for hastening the drying of paint. Examples include lead linoleate and lead naphthenate.

Leaded zinc. A mixture of zinc oxide and basic sulfate white lead.

Lead oxide. Several combinations of lead and oxygen; examples include litharge and red lead.

Leafing. Orientation of pigment flakes in horizontal planes.

Leveling. The formation of a smooth film on either a horizontal or vertical surface, independent of the method of application. A film that has good leveling characteristics is usually free of brush marks or orange-peel effects.

Linoleum and oilcloth varnishes. Special highly flexible and elastic varnishes.

Linseed oil. Oil obtained from flaxseed (linseed), used in paints, varnishes, lacquers, and rubber substitutes. Linseed oil is also used in the linoleum, leather, and oilcloth industries.

Liquid driers.   Solutions of driers in paint thinners.

Liquid wood filler.   Varnish of low viscosity, usually containing extending pigment, for use as a first coating on open-grain woods. Its purpose is to provide a non-absorbent surface for succeeding coats of varnish. It is frequently colored so as to stain and fill in one operation.

Litharge.   Lead monoxide in flake or powdered form; it is used in vitreous enamels.

Lithopone.   A mixture of zinc sulfide and blanc fixed, white in color. It is used as a pigment.

Livering.   A thickening in the consistency of a paint or enamel, which results in a liver-like mass.

Long-oil varnish.   Varnish made with a relatively high proportion of oil to resin. It is generally slower-drying, tougher, and more elastic than a short-oil varnish.

Maintenance painting.   Repair painting; painting after the initial paint job.

Mandrel test.   A physical bending test for adhesion and flexibility.

Manila resin.   A copal resin found in Indonesia and used in varnish manufacture.

Marine varnishes.   Varnishes specially designed to resist long immersion in salt or fresh water or exposure to a marine atmosphere.

Masking.   Covering areas not to be painted.

Mildew.   Fungus or mold.

Mill white.   White paint used to augment illumination on interior wall surfaces. The vehicle is usually of the varnish type.

Milori blue.   An iron-blue pigment; Prussian blue.

Mineral black.   A natural black pigment based on graphite.

Mineral spirits. An aliphatic hydrocarbon solvent.

Miscible. Capable of mixing or blending uniformly.

Misses. Skips or voids in a paint job.

Mist-coat. A thin coat.

Mobility. The degree to which a material flows.

Mottling. Speckling.

Mud-cracking. Irregular cracking of dried film.

Naphtha. Hydrocarbon suitable for use as a paint thinner.

Natural resins. Essentially the exudate of trees. They are divided into two large classes—damars and copals. Resins are usually named after the locality in which they are found or their port of shipment.

Neoprent. A rubber-like film former based on the polymerization of chloroprene.

Nitrocellulose. (*See* Cellulose nitrate.)

Non-volatile. The solid, non-evaporating portion of paint left after the solvent evaporates.

Ochre. Yellow iron-oxide earth pigment.

Oil color. (*See* Color-in-oil.)

Oil stains. Dye solutions in blends of oil or varnish and aromatic solvents, such as toluene.

Oleoresinous. Describing a varnish made of oil and resin.

Opacity. Hiding power.

Orange mineral. Red lead prepared by roasting basic carbonate white lead. It is used mainly in printing ink for its characteristic color.

Orange peel. A surface resembling an orange peel.

Organic colors. Pigments of animal, vegetable, or dyestuff origin. Examples include alizarin crimson and carmine.

Orifice. An opening or hole.

Overcoat. Top coat.

Overlap. The width of fresh paint covered by the next layer.

Overspray. Sprayed paint that does not reach the target.

Oxidize. To unite with oxygen.

Paint. A mechanical mixture or dispersion of pigments or powders in a liquid or vehicle. The finished product is suitable for application to surfaces by means of brushing, spraying, roller coating, or dipping; it solidifies or dries to form an adherent, protective, sanitary, or decorative coating.

Pass. The motion of a spray gun in one direction.

Pattern length. The length of a spray pattern.

Pattern width. The width of a spray pattern.

Peeling. Detachment of a paint film in relatively large pieces. Paint applied to a damp or greasy surface usually "peels." Sometimes it is due to moisture in back of the painted surface.

Pickling. A dipping process for cleaning steel and other metals.

Pigments. Fine powders substantially insoluble in oils, varnishes, lacquers, thinners, and the like. They are used to impart color, opacity, certain consistency characteristics, and other effects.

Pitting. Small, shallow depressions or cavities.

Pinholing. The formation of small holes through the entire thickness of a coating.

Pock marks. Pits or craters.

Pole gun. A spray gun equipped with an extension.

Polyvinyl acetate. Synthetic resins used extensively in water paints.

Pot life. The time interval after mixing reactive components during which liquid material is easily usable.

Prime coat. First coat.

Primer. Material used for the first coat.

Protective life. The interval of time during which a paint system protects a surface from deterioration.

Prussian blue. Iron blue.

Putty. A dough-like mixture of pigment and oil (usually whiting and linseed oil—sometimes mixed with white lead). It is used to set glass in window frames and fill nail holes and cracks.

Pyroxylin. (*See* Cellulose nitrate.)

Quick-drying. Having a relatively short drying time.

Raw oil. Oil that is received from the press or separated from the solvent in the solvent-extraction process.

Recoat time. Time between coats.

Red label. Flammable or explosive materials with flash points below 80°F.

Red lead. An oxide of lead, red in color, used as a rust-inhibiting pigment and as a source of lead in driers.

Refined shellac. A grade of orange or white shellac from which the wax has been removed.

Removers. Compositions designed to soften old varnish or paint coats so that they may be easily removed by scraping or washing.

Resin. A solid or semi-solid organic material, of vegetable origin or synthetic derivation. It is usually yellow or amber to dark brown, and transparent or translucent. Examples of natural resins are Congo, rosin, and damar. Synthetic resins are alkyds and phenolics.

Respirator. A safety breathing mask.

Rosin. A resin obtained from pine trees containing principally isomers of abietic acid. Wood rosin is obtained from stumps or dead wood, using steam distillation. Gum rosin is obtained from the living tree.

Rottenstone. A brown, siliceous stone used as an abrasive. It is similar in nature to pumice stone but softer in texture.

Rubbing varnish. A hard-drying varnish varnish that may be rubbed with an abrasive and water or oil to a uniform leveled surface.

Runs. (Also known as "sags.") Irregularities of a surface due to uneven flow of paint.

Rust. Corroded iron.

Sags. (*See* Runs.)

Sandblast. Blast cleaning using sand as an abrasive.

Scale. Rust occurring in thin layers.

Scaler. A hand-held cleaning chisel.

Seal coating. A coating applied to prevent absorption of the first coat.

Sealer. A coat of paint (or other substance) intended to close or seal the pores in a surface.

Semi-drying oils. Oils that possess the drying properties of drying oils to a lesser extent. The principal semi-drying oil used in the paint industry is soybean oil.

Settling. Caking or sediment.

Shade. The degree of color in a tint.

Shelf life. The maximum time a material can be stored and still be usable.

Shellac. Lac in the form of flakes. (*See* Lac.)

Shop coat. A coating applied in a fabricating shop.

Short-oil varnish. Oil made with a relatively low proportion of oil to resin. (*See* Long-oil varnish.)

Sienna. An earth pigment that is brownish yellow when raw, orange red or reddish brown when burnt. The color comes from the oxides of iron and manganese.

Silica. Ground quartz, which is used as an extender pigment.

Silicate paints. Paints including silicates as binders.

Size. A sealer.

Skin. A tough layer formed on the surface of a paint or varnish in the container, caused by exposure to air.

Skips. Misses or uncoated areas.

Slow-drying. Requiring 24 hours or longer before recoating.

Soybean oil. A semi-drying oil obtained from soybeans.

Spalling. The cracking or splintering of materials.

Spar varnish. A very durable varnish designed for severe service on exterior surfaces. Such a varnish must be resistant to rain, sunlight, and heat. It is named for its suitability on the spars of ships.

Specular gloss. Mirror-like reflection.

Spirit stain. A stain made by dissolving dye in an alcohol.

Spirit varnish. A varnish made by dissolving a resin in a solvent. It dries primarily by evaporation rather than by oxidation.

Stand oil. Heat-thickened vegetable oil (or a combination of vegetable oils, such as linseed and tung).

Stroke. A single pass with a spray gun in one direction.

Substrate. A basic surface.

Surface conditioner. A preparatory coating applied to a chalked, painted masonry surface for bonding chalk to an undersurface.

Surface preparation. All operations necessary to prepare a surface for a coat of paint.

Surfacer. A paint used to smooth the surface before finishing coats are applied.

Sweating. Condensing moisture on a surface.

Tack. The degree of stickiness of paint or another substance.

Tails (airless spray). A finger-like spray pattern.

Talc. A hydrous magnesium aluminum silicate used as an extender in paints. It is also known as talcum powder and soapstone.

Tank white. A self-cleaning white paint with good opacity used for exterior metal surfaces.

Tar. A thick brown or black liquid with a characteristic color. It is a residue from the distillation of wood, peat, coal, shale, or other vegetable or mineral material.

Tempera. A water-thinned or water-emulsion paint.

Texture paint. Paint that can be manipulated by brush, trowel, or other tool to form various patterns.

Thinners. Volatile liquids used to lower or otherwise regulate the consistency of paint and varnish.

Tie coat. An intermediate coat used to bond different types of paint coats.

Tint. A color thinned or diluted with white. Tints are made by blending a full-strength color with a white paint.

Titanium dioxide. A compound of titanium, white in color, which is used as a pigment in paints and enamels.

Tooth. A profile; surface roughness.

Top coating. Final coat.

Touch-up painting. Spot repair painting, usually done after initial painting.

Toxic. Poisonous.

Tung oil. A drying oil obtained from the nut of the tung tree.

Turpentine. A colorless, volatile liquid with a characteristic odor and taste. It is obtained by distillation of the oleoresinous secretions found in living and dead pine trees.

Tuscan red. A red pigment consisting of a combination of iron oxides and a lake.

Ultramarine.   Artificial lapis lazuli used as a blue pigment.

Umber.   A hydrated iron-manganese ore running from olive shades in its raw state to dark; rich brown shades when burnt. It is used exclusively as a pigment.

Undercoater.   In a multicoat system, any intermediate coat.

Undertone.   The color of a paint observed through transmitted light.

Unit cost.   Cost per given area.

Urethane resins.   A particular group of film formers such as isocyanate resins.

Useful life.   The length of time a coating is expected to last.

Value.   The lightness or darkness of a color.

Vandyke brown.   A brown pigment consisting of decomposed vegetable matter that has almost approached the coal state.

Varnish.   A liquid composition that is converted to a translucent or transparent solid film after application in a thin layer.

Varnish stain.   A varnish containing a stain.

Vegetable oils.   Oils obtained from the seeds or nuts of vegetable growth. Examples are linseed, soybean, perilla, hempseed, tung, and castor oil.

Vehicle.   A liquid carrier or binder.

Venetian red.   A pigment usually consisting of calcium sulfate and red iron oxide.

Vermilion.   A sulfide of mercury used as a pigment.

Vinyl coating.   A coating in which the major portion of the binder is a vinyl resin.

Vinyl resins.   Synthetic resins made from vinyl compounds such as vinyl acetate.

Viscosity.   A measure of fluidity.

Volatiles.   Fluids that evaporate rapidly.

Water blasting.   Blast cleaning done with high-velocity water.

Wash primer.   A thin rust-inhibiting paint which provides improved adhesion to subsequent coats.

Washing.   Erosion of a paint film after rapid chalking.

Water spotting.   Spotty changes in the color or gloss of a paint film. It may be caused by various factors, including emulsification or the solution of water-soluble components.

Water-thinned paint.   A paint whose thinner is mainly water. The binder may be a material that requires water for setting (e.g., portland cement), that is soluble in water (e.g., casein), that is emulsifiable in water (e.g., flat wall paint binders).

Wet edge.   Fluid boundary.

Wet film thickness.   Thickness of liquid film immediately after application.

White lead.   Compounds of lead used as white pigments in many types of paint. There are two types: basic lead carbonate and basic lead sulfate.

Whiting.   Calcium carbonate, limestone, or chalk in pigment form. Used extensively for making putty and as an extender in paints.

Wire brush.   A hand-cleaning tool comprised of bundles of wires.

Wrinkle finish.   A varnish or enamel film that exhibits fine wrinkles or ridges. It is used extensively as a novelty finish.

Yellowing.   Development of yellow color in white paints as they age.

Zinc chromate.   (*See* Zinc yellow.)

Zinc dust.   Finely divided zinc metal, gray in color. It is used primarily in metal primers.

Zinc oxide.   A compound of zinc used as a white pigment in many types of paint, including American (direct) and French (indirect).

Zinc sulfide. A compound of zinc used as a white pigment in many types of paint. (*See* Lithopone.)

Zinc yellow. A yellow pigment, primarily zinc chromate, used in metal primers for its rust-inhibiting property.

APPENDIX 4

Table 3

Treatment of Various Substrates

	Wood	Steel	Metal Other	Concrete Masonry	Plaster Wallboard
Mechanical					
Hand Cleaning	S	S	S	S	S
Power Tool Cleaning	S*	S		S	
Flame Cleaning		S			
Blast Cleaning:					
Brush-Off		S	S	S	
All Other		S			
Chemical and Solvent					
Solvent Cleaning	S	S	S	S	
Alkali Cleaning		S		S	
Steam Cleaning		S		S	
Acid Cleaning		S			
Pickling		S			
Pretreatments					
Hot Phosphate		S			
Cold Phosphate		S			
Wash Primers		S	S		
Conditioners, Sealers, and Fillers					
Conditioners	S			S	
Sealers	S			S	
Fillers					

S—Satisfactory for use as indicated
*—Sanding only

Table 4

Characteristics of Wood

Name of Wood	Soft Closed	Hard Open	Hard Closed	Notes on Finishing
Ash		X		Requires filler.
Alder	X			Stains well.
Aspen				Paints well.
Basswood			X	Paints well.
Beech			X	Paints poorly; varnishes well.
Birch			X	Paints and varnishes well.
Cedar	X			Paints and varnishes well.
Cherry			X	Varnishes well.
Chestnut		X		Requires filler; paints poorly.
Cottonwood			X	Paints well.
Cypress			X	Paints and varnishes well.
Elm		X		Requires filler; paints poorly.
Fir	X			Paints poorly.
Gum			X	Varnishes well.
Hemlock	X			Paints fairly well.
Hickory		X		Requires filler.
Mahogany		X		Requires filler.
Maple			X	Varnishes well.
Oak		X		Requires filler.
Pine	X			Variable depending on grain.
Redwood	X			Paints well.
Teak		X		Requires filler.
Walnut		X		Requires filler.

Note: Any finish may be applied unless otherwise specified.

Table 5

Guide for Selecting Paint

	Aluminum paint	Casein	Cement base paint	Emulsion paint (including latex)	Enamel	Flat paint	Floor paint or enamel	Floor varnish	Interior varnish	Metal primer	Rubber base paint (not latex)	Sealer or undercoater	Semigloss paint	Shellac	Stain	Wax (emulsion)	Wax (liquid or paste)	Wood sealer
Floors:																		
Asphalt tile																X•	X•	
Concrete							X									X	X•	
Linoleum																X	X	
Vinyl and rubber							X	X									X	
Wood							X•	X•						X			X	
Masonry:																		
Old	X	X	X	X	X•	X•					X	X	X•					
New			X	X	X•	X•					X	X	X•					
Metal:																		
Heating ducts	X				X•	X•				X	X		X•					
Radiators	X				X•	X•				X	X		X•					

Table 5 (cont.)

Stairs:													
Treads				X●	X●	X	X				X●	X X	X X	
Risers					X●		X				X	X X	X X	X
Walls and ceilings:													
Kitchen and bathroom		X X		X	X●				X X X	X X X	● ● ●			
Plaster				X	X● X●				X X X	X X X	● ● ●			
Wallboard				X	X● X●				X X X	X X X	● ● ●			
Wood paneling				X●	X● X●		X X		X	X	X●	X	X	
Wood trim				X●	X● X●		X X		X	X	X●	X	X	X
Windows:													
Aluminum		X X		X●	X● X●			X X	X X	X X	X● X●	X X		
Steel		X		X●	X● X●									
Wood sill				X●	X●		X		X	X			X	X

Black dot (X●) indicates that a primer or sealer may be necessary before the finishing coat (unless the surface has been previously fin shed).

APPENDIX 5
USEFUL DATA—
PAINTING INTERIOR SURFACES

Interior painting and exterior painting are similar in some ways but different in others. Because of the differences, the two types of painting will be treated in separate sections. Some repetition will be unavoidable, but it will be kept to a minimum.

Priming

Previously painted surfaces usually do not require primer coats except where the old paint is worn through or the surface has been damaged.

Wood Surfaces

Unpainted wood to be finished with enamel or oil base paint should be primed with enamel undercoat to seal the wood and provide a better surface. If the unpainted wood is not primed, the enamel coat may be uneven.

Unpainted wood to be finished with top coat latex should first be undercoated. Water-thinned paint could raise the grain of the bare wood and leave a rough surface.

If clear finishes are used:

—*soft woods* such as pine, poplar, and gum usually require a sealer to control the penetration of the finish coats. In using stain, a sealer is sometimes applied first in order to obtain a lighter, more uniform color.

—*open grain hard woods* such as oak, walnut and mahogany require a paste wood filler, followed by a clear wood sealer.

—*close grain hard woods* such as maple and birch do not require a filler. The first coat may be a thinned version of the finishing varnish, shellac, or lacquer.

Masonry Surfaces

Smooth, unpainted masonry surfaces such as plaster, plaster-board, and various drywall surfaces can be primed with latex paint or latex primer sealer. The color of the first coat should be similar to the finish coat.

Coarse, rough, or porous masonry surfaces, such as cement block, cinder block, and concrete block cannot be filled and covered satisfactorily with regular paints. Block filler should be used as a first coat to obtain a smooth sealed surface over which almost any paint can be used.

Unpainted brick, while porous, is not as rough as cinder block and similar surfaces and can be primed with latex primer sealer or with an exterior latex paint.

Enamel undercoat should be applied over the primer where the finish coat is to be a gloss or semigloss enamel.

Carefully follow the manufacturer's label instructions for painting masonry surfaces.

Metal Surfaces

Unpainted surfaces should be primed for protection against corrosion and to provide a base for the finish paint. Interior paints do not usually adhere well to bare metal surfaces, and provide little corrosion resistance by themselves.

Primer paints for bare metal surfaces must be selected according to the metal to be painted. Some primers are made especially for iron or steel; others for galvanized steel, aluminum, or copper.

An enamel undercoat should be used as a second primer if the metal surface is to be finished with enamel; that is, apply the primer first, then the undercoat, and finally the enamel finish. Most enamel undercoats need a light sanding before the top coat is applied.

Paints and Finishes

Unless you are an experienced painter, shop for a salesman or a paint store owner before you shop for paint. Find one who is willing and able to help you match the paint to the job. Read labels and company leaflets carefully. They are usually well-written, accurate, and helpful.

Paints for Light Wear Areas

Latex interior paints are generally used for areas where there is little need for periodic washing and scrubbing; for example, living rooms, dining rooms, bedrooms and closets.

Interior flat latex paints are used for interior walls and ceilings since they cover well, are easy to apply, dry quickly, are almost odorless, and can be quickly and easily removed from applicators.

Latex paints may be applied directly over semigloss and gloss enamel if the surface is first roughened with sandpaper or liquid sandpaper. If the latter is used, carefully follow the instructions on the container label.

Flat alkyd paints are often preferred for wood, wallboard, and metal surfaces since they are more resistant to damage; also, they can be applied in thicker films to produce a more uniform appearance. They wash better than interior latex paints and are nearly odorless.

Paints for Heavy Wear Areas

Enamels, including latex enamels, are usually preferred for kitchen, bathroom, laundry room, and similar work areas because they withstand intensive cleaning and wear. They form especially hard films, ranging from flat to a full gloss finish.

Fast-drying polyurethane enamels and clear varnishes provide excellent hard, flexible finishes for wood floors. Other enamels and clear finishes can also be used, but unless specifically recommended for floors they may be too soft and slow drying, or too hard and brittle.

Polyurethane and epoxy enamels are also excellent for concrete floors. For a smooth finish, rough concrete should be properly primed with an alkali resistant primer to fill the pores. When using these enamels, adequate ventilation is essential for protection from flammable vapors.

Clear Finishes for Wood

Varnishes form durable and attractive finishes for interior wood surfaces such as wood paneling, trim, floors, and unpainted furniture. They seal the wood, forming tough, transparent films that will withstand frequent scrubbing and hard use, and are available in flat, semigloss or satin, and gloss finishes.

Most varnishes are easily scratched, and the marks are difficult to conceal without redoing the entire surface. A good paste wax applied over the finished varnish—especially on wood furniture—will provide some protection against scratches.

Polyurethane and epoxy varnishes are notable for durability and high resistance to stains, abrasions, acids and alkalis, solvents, strong cleaners, fuels, alcohol, and chemicals. Adequate ventilation should be provided as protection from flammable vapors when these varnishes are being applied.

Shellac and lacquer have uses similar to most varnishes, and these finishes are easy to repair or recoat. They apply easily, dry fast, and are also useful as a sealer and clear finish under varnish for wood surfaces. The first coat should be thinned as recommended on the container, then sanded very lightly and finished with one or more undiluted coats. Two coats will give a fair sheen, and three a high gloss.

Wax Finishes

Liquid and paste waxes are used on interior surfaces. They provide a soft, lustrous finish to wood and are particularly effective on furniture and floors. Waxes containing solvents should not be used on asphalt tile; wax emulsions are recommended.

Waxes should be applied to smooth surfaces with a soft cloth. Rub with the grain. Brushes should be used to apply liquid waxes to raw-textured wood.

Wax finishes can be washed with a mild household detergent, followed by rinsing with a clean, damp cloth.

A wax finish is not desirable if a different finish may be used later, for wax is difficult to remove.

Paint Types, Properties, and Uses

Types	Properties	Typical Uses
Latex primer sealer (water thinned)	Simple to apply. Dries quickly and can be recoated in about two hours. Not flammable, almost odorless. One coat usually sufficient. Thinning unnecessary unless recommended by manufacturer.	Unpainted interior walls and ceilings of wallboard, plaster, masonry and all drywall.
Enamel undercoater (alkyd base—low odor)	Hard, tight films. Provides good base for enamel. Easy brushing, smooth leveling. Dries in about 12 hours.	Undercoater for interior enamels.
Latex wall paint (water thinned)	The most popular of the interior paints. Durable, excellent coverage, good washability, quick-drying, and easy to touch up. Safe to use and store; nontoxic, practically no odor.	Primer sealer and also finish coat for interior walls and ceilings of wallboard, wallpaper, plaster, and other porous, absorptive materials. Use on primed wood but not on bare wood.
Flat alkyd enamel	Made with alkyd resins. Has flat finish practically free of sheen. Used same as latex wall paint but has slightly better washability and abrasion resistance. Dries in about four hours. Practically no odor.	Primer sealer and also finish coat on interior walls and ceilings of plaster, wallboard, masonry, and similar surfaces.

Semigloss and full gloss enamel (alkyd base)	Made with alkyd resins. Has good gloss retention, grease and oil resistance, and better washability and resistance to abrasion than flat alkyd enamel.	On primed plaster and wall-board, and on suitably pre-pared wood trim and metal. Very useful for kitchens and bathrooms, and for decorative use on properly primed woodwork.
Semigloss and full gloss latex enamel (water thinned)	Has most properties of alkyd enamels plus usual advantages of latex paints: easy application and cleanup, rapid drying, low odor, and nonflamma-ble. Good leveling but lapping does not compare favorably with alkyd enamels.	Walls and ceilings of wall-board, wallpaper, wood, and plaster. Very useful for kitch-ens, bathrooms, and for de-corative use on properly primed woodwork.
Epoxy enamel	Hard film, wide gloss range, low odor, ideal where vigorous and frequent cleaning is done. Has ex-cellent adhesion and resistance to abrasion, water, solvents, greases, and dirt. Packaged in two containers—enamel in one and curing agent in the other. Contents of both containers mixed together prior to use. Cost comparatively high but durability is excellent.	Highly effective in heavy wear areas such as hallways, kitch-ens, bathrooms, and for dec-orative use on properly
Dripless enamel (special alkyd base)	Does not drip from brush or roller. Made with spe-cial alkyd resins to form a soft gel which liquefies with agitation but gels again on standing. Soft, buttery, easy brushing, low odor, self-sealing. Has excellent color retention; solvent and water re-sistant.	Decorative enamel for properly primed walls and ceilings of plaster, wallboard, and similar surfaces; also, for wood trim and primed metal.

Paint Types, Properties, and Uses (cont.)

Types	Properties	Typical Uses
Interior floor and deck enamel	Alkyd and latex used successfully but polyurethane types provide harder, more flexible, and more abrasion-resistant surfaces. Polyurethane enamels are packaged in one- and two-container forms. The latter has paint in one can and curing agent in the other. Contents of both are mixed together prior to use. When applying polyurethane enamel, follow manufacturer's instructions explicitly and also keep room well ventilated.	General application to properly primed floors and covered decks.
Clear varnish finishes for wood	Provide durable and attractive finish; seal wood better than lacquer; and form tough, transparent coat that will withstand frequent scrubbings and hard use. Tend to darken the wood surface and give impression of visual depth. Readily show scratch marks which are difficult to conceal without redoing entire surface. Some varnishes turn yellow with age. Extra coat recommended on new work. Can be flat, satin, semigloss, or glossy finish.	For all interior smooth wood. Recommended for washrooms, kitchens, or other areas exposed to dirt, grease, and moisture and subject to frequent scrubbing. A rubbed-in coat of paste wax will provide some protection against scratches.
Shellac	Available in clear and "orange" finishes. Fast drying. Thinned first coat provides excellent seal for new wood. Can be overcoated in about 30 minutes. Should be lightly sanded between coats. Paste wax, as final coat, provides lustre and some protection against scratches.	For wood walls, trim, furniture, or any wood surface requiring only occasional dusting. Unsuitable for kitchens, washrooms, or other areas exposed to dirt, grease, and moisture.

Lacquer	Fast drying; can be overcoated in about 30 minutes. Provides gloss or sheen when two or more coats are applied. Paste wax, as final coat, provides attractive lustre and some protection against scratches. Available in clear and a variety of color finishes.	For wood walls, trim, furniture, or any wood surface requiring only occasional dusting. Unsuitable for kitchens, washrooms, or other areas exposed to dirt, grease, and moisture.
Stains	Available in natural finish and in a variety of colors which provide attractive, natural appearance. Several coats are required for bare wood, with light sanding between coats. Final coat of paste wax provides lustre and some protection against scratches, particularly on furniture. "Thick" stains can be thinned with turpentine or mineral spirits.	For interior wood surfaces such as walls, trim, and furniture.
Aluminum paints	Resistant to water. Can be brushed or sprayed on new metal and wood surfaces. When brush is used, apply in one direction only for best results.	As a sealer for wood surfaces (especially knots) and as a primer for metal surfaces. Can be used as a finish coat if color is not objectionable. Particularly useful for aluminum and steel windows, heating ducts, radiators, and heating pipes.
Oil base primers	Good adhesion and sealing; resistant to cracking and flaking when applied to unprimed wood; good brushing and leveling; controlled penetration; and low sheen. Unsuitable as a top coat and should be covered with finish paint within a week or two after application.	As primer on unpainted woodwork or surfaces previously coated with house paint.

Paint Types, Properties, and Uses (cont.)

Types	Properties	Typical Uses
Antirust primers	Prevent corrosion on iron and steel surfaces. Slow-drying type provides protection through good penetration into cracks and crevices. Fast-drying types are used only on smooth, clean surfaces, and those which are water resistant are effective where surfaces are subject to severe humidity conditions or fresh water immersion.	Priming of steel and other ferrous metal surfaces when good resistance to corrosion is required.
Galvanizing primers	High percentage of zinc dust provides good anti rust protection and adhesion. Galvanizing and zinc dust primers give excellent coverage, one coat usually being sufficient on new surfaces. Two coats are ample for surfaces exposed to high humidity.	Priming of new or old galvanized metal and steel surfaces. Satisfactory as finish coat if color (metallic gray) is not objectionable.
House paints (oil or oil alkyd base)	Made with drying oils or drying oil combined with alkyd resin. Excellent brushing and penetrating properties. Provides a good adhesion, elasticity, durability, and resistance to blistering on wood and other porous surfaces. Often modified with alkyd resins to speed drying time. Apply with brush to obtain strong bond, especially on old painted surfaces.	General exterior use on properly primed or previously painted wood or metal surfaces.

House paints (latex)	Exterior latex paints have durability comparable to oil base paints. Resistant to weathering and yellowing, and so quick-drying that they can be re-coated in one hour. Can be applied in damp weather over a damp surface. Easy to apply and brush or roller can be cleaned quickly with water. Free from fire hazard.	Covers properly primed or previously painted concrete, stucco, and other masonry and wood surfaces.
	White latex paints usually offer better color retention than oil or oil and alkyd exterior paints.	
Trim paint	Usually made with oil modified alkyds. Slow drying (over night). Made in high sheen, bright colors; have good retention of gloss and color. More expensive silicone-alkyd enamels are also available for trim painting. They are substantially more durable than conventional oil and alkyd enamels.	Applied over primed wood and metal surfaces such as aluminum and steel windows, metal siding, shutters and other trim, and wood frame windows.
Porch and deck paints (for concrete and other masonry surfaces)	Many made with natural rubber base (chlorinated rubber resin). Good flow and leveling; good resistance to rain, moisture, and detergents. Coverage about 300 square feet per gallon. New concrete should age at least two months before painting. Three coats recommended, including thinned first coat. Good ventilation required if used indoors.	For both interior and exterior concrete and masonry porches and decks. Effective for swimming pools, shower rooms, and laundries. Manufacturer's instructions must be followed carefully.
Porch and deck paints (for wood surfaces)	A variety of alkyd base and other types available. Tough, flexible, and abrasion resistant. Good drying properties. Thin coats promote thorough drying. Allow ample drying time between coats.	Interior and exterior decks and porches.

Paint Types, Properties, and Uses (cont.)

Types	Properties	Typical Uses
Aluminum paints	Resistant to water and weather and provide excellent durability in marine environments. Can be applied on new metal or wood surfaces—in one direction for best results. Creosote-treated wood must age for about six months prior to application of aluminum paint.	Particularly useful in marine environments; as a sealer for wood knots; and as a combination sealer and finish coat for wood surfaces treated with creosote or other preservatives. Can also be used as a finish coat for metal and wood if aluminum color is not objectionable.
Cement powder paint	Made from white portland cement, pigments, and (usually) small amounts of water repellent. They are mixed with water just before application. Painted surfaces should be kept damp by sprinkling with water until paint film is well cured. This paint does not provide a good base for other finishes. Apply with a fiber brush.	Useful, low cost finish for rough masonry surfaces, both interior and exterior, including brick, cement and cinder block, and stucco.
Wood stains	Semitransparent type available for exterior wood but not as durable as house paints. Improves appearance of wood by highlighting the grain and texture of the surface. Available in many colors, the most popular being cedar, light redwood, and dark redwood.	For smooth and rough wood surfaces. Can be used for staining house siding and wood fencing, but should not be used on surfaces that may soon be painted or on previously painted surfaces. Not recommended for frames, windows, and doors which need a high degree of protection against the weather.

Clear finishes (for wood)	Not as durable as pigmented paint. Alkyd varnishes have good color and color retention but may crack and peel. Some synthetics such as polyurethane varnishes have good durability but may darken on exposure. Spar varnish (marine varnish) is quite durable but will also darken and yellow. Use thin penetrating coats on the bare wood, followed by the unreduced varnish.	For clear finish on wood surfaces where natural appearance is desired.
Roof coatings	Bituminous roof coatings are made of asphalt (chosen for good weather resistance), dissolved in a suitable solvent. Asbestos and other fillers are added to prevent sagging on sloping roofs and to permit application of relatively thick coatings. Basically made in gray and black; however, addition of aluminum powders provides for other colors. Asphalt emulsion roof coatings can be applied over damp surfaces. Special application techniques are usually required and manufacturer's instructions must be followed carefully.	Used primarily for coal tar felt roofs.
Water repellent preservative (silicone)	Silicone water repellents are transparent liquids that help repel water without changing the surface appearance. Must be applied strictly in accordance with instructions to ensure adequacy of film and water repellency. Should not be top-coated with paint until surface has weathered for at least two years.	For wood shingle roofs, brick walls, and other surfaces where some degree of water repellency is desired.

Index